Cato the Censor and the Beginnings of Latin Prose

Cato the Censor and the Beginnings of Latin Prose

FROM POETIC TRANSLATION TO ELITE TRANSCRIPTION

Enrica Sciarrino

 THE OHIO STATE UNIVERSITY PRESS · COLUMBUS

Copyright © 2011 by The Ohio State University.
All rights reserved.

Library of Congress Cataloging-in-Publication Data
Sciarrino, Enrica, 1968–
  Cato the Censor and the beginnings of Latin prose : from poetic translation to elite transcription / Enrica Sciarrino.
     p. cm.
  Includes bibliographical references and index.
  ISBN-13: 978-0-8142-1165-6 (cloth : alk. paper)
  ISBN-10: 0-8142-1165-8 (cloth : alk. paper)
  ISBN-13: 978-0-8142-9266-2 (cd-rom)
  1. Latin prose literature—History and criticism. 2. Cato, Marcus Porcius, 234–149 B.C.—Criticism and interpretation. I. Title.
  PA6081.S35 2011
  878'.01—dc22
                    2011006020

This book is available in the following editions:
Cloth (ISBN 978-0-8142-1165-6)
CD-ROM (ISBN 978-0-8142-9266-2)

Cover design by Mia Risberg.
Text design by Jennifer Shoffey Forsythe.
Typeset in Times New Roman.
Printed by Thomson-Shore, Inc.

♾ The paper used in this publication meets the minimum requirements of the American National Standard for Information Sciences—Permanence of Paper for Printed Library Materials. ANSI 39.48-1992.

9 8 7 6 5 4 3 2 1

Contents

Preface and Acknowledgments — vii
List of Abbreviations — xi

Chapter 1	Situating the Beginnings of Latin Prose	1
Chapter 2	Under the Roman Sun: Poets, Rulers, Translations, and Power	38
Chapter 3	Conflicting Scenarios: Traffic in Others and Others' Things	78
Chapter 4	Inventing Latin Prose: Cato the Censor and the Formation of a New Aristocracy	117
Chapter 5	Power Differentials in Writing: Texts and Authority	161
Conclusion		203

Bibliography — 209
Index Locorum — 229
General Index — 231

Preface and Acknowledgments

This book treats a moment in Roman cultural history that in the last decade or so has become one of the most contentious areas of discussion in classical scholarship. To put it rather simply, on the one side are those who insist on the primacy of literature as a category for understanding the earliest textual remains in Latin. For them the pivotal question is why the Romans developed a literary tradition in Latin at all when, to cite the most notable example, Fabius Pictor, a member of the Roman aristocracy, had, during the third century B.C.E., found little problem in writing his account of Rome's history in Greek. On the other side are those who focus on the sociohistorical transformations that led the Romans to give away their performance practices in favor of alien forms of cultural production. While the first view draws force from the Hellenistic precedents and its focus on the establishment of a poetic tradition in Latin built upon them, the second relies on a cluster of Latin terms as indicators of the sociohistorical dynamics that governed Rome's cultural history and sees Latin literature as one expression of them.

My aim in this study is to bridge the current divide and open up new areas of inquiry. I examine how the establishment of Latin poetry in the late third and early second centuries B.C.E. intersected with formal choices, social subjectivities, and historical contingencies. At the same time, I expand our purview on the period in question by focusing on the largely neglected but near contemporary formation of Latin prose writing associated with Cato the Censor. This would be well and good were it not that in the last few years the divide between the two camps has grown exponentially. For this reason, the challenges that this book now has to meet have grown too. As recently put, the situation is such that to try to account for what authors aimed to do when they wrote what they did means to face up to the powerful "epistemological dogma" whereby such an effort is "always already" compromised, if not doomed to outright failure.[1] If this were not enough, the materials I am seeking to rescue from the margins are also some of the least Greek-saturated texts in the available literary archive; as a result, my approach risks being perceived as a suspicious attempt to decouple Latinity from Hellenism.

I believe that the present situation calls us to reengage with the body of evidence that we have; if this book should not fully succeed in promoting this engagement, at least it will have shown that concepts like authorship, text, literature, and genre are the product of uneven processes that are culturally, historically, and geographically specific.

I consider this book a homage to the multicultural and multilingual make-up of classics today; however, the way I went about composing it inevitably reflects my own background. This ranges geographically, culturally, and linguistically from Siracusa to Bologna in Italy to Berkeley in the U.S. (via a brief period at Utrecht in the Netherlands) to Christchurch in New Zealand. I wrote this book in English with a readership familiar with the Anglo-(North)American scene of scholarly inquiry in mind. It could not have been otherwise. For better or worse, my academic work and professional life participate in that scene and my Italian has devolved to the status of *lessico famigliare*.[2] I believe that each and all of these factors explain, reduce, and empower the argumentative thrust of this book in ways with which I am still coming to terms. One of the thoughtful readers for The Ohio State University Press commented that my writing style betrays an Italian penchant for having an argument emerge at the level of the paragraph and pointed out to me that English prefers the punch of one point per sentence. This same reader applied the label *écriture féminine* to the former and *écriture masculine* to the latter. In the process of revising the manuscript I have tried to make the presentation of my arguments more 'masculine.' I regard any remaining traces of *écriture féminine* as a

---

1. Gildenhard 2007b: 73.

2. *Lessico famigliare* is the title of a book written by Natalia Ginzburg in the early sixties in which she recounts her childhood, adolescence, and early adulthood through the words and phrases of the various members of her family.

tribute to Giulia, my daughter, who has gracefully lived through the ups and downs of this project from the very first day of her life. It is to her that I dedicate this book.

I am happy to finally express my gratitude for the help I have received at every step of writing this book. Some of the ideas unfolded here are scattered in my Berkeley dissertation. I should like to thank Trevor Murphy, Kathleen McCarthy, and the late Ruggiero Stefanini for embracing my project and for letting me get away with an output that bears the imprint of the rough waters I was navigating at the time. If I did not drown then, it is because of the support I received from my family in Italy and the many people I had the fortune to meet in California. These include Julie Shirar, Jed Parsons, Liz Harris, Musashi Lethridge, Melissa Mueller, Dylan Sailor, Yelena Baraz, James Ker, Sarah Stroup, Pat Larash, Mark Griffith, and Donald Mastronarde.

In 2002 my colleagues in the classics department at the University of Canterbury made my move 'down-under' both smooth and enjoyable. I would like to thank each and all of them: Tim Parkin for introducing me to the All Blacks, Alison Griffith for sharing her thoughts about juggling motherhood and academia, Alison Holcroft for being always enthusiastic about our Classics Days, Graham Zanker for offering me his wise advice whenever I needed it, Robin Bond for keeping my mood up at all times, Gary Morrison for enduring my daily moaning, Patrick O'Sullivan for his sophistic arguing, and Victor Parker for reminding me about the traditional historical method. Although some of them have moved on, they are all responsible for making classics in Christchurch a very successful enterprise in spite of a long chain of restructures and downsizings. In Christchurch I have also met people whose friendship I can no longer do without: Nabila Jaber, Terry Austrin, Marco Reale, Brunella Olivieri, Ester Vallero, Lisa Fazi, and Nicola Di Cosmo.

Over the years I have presented my work piecemeal in a variety of conferences and settings in North America, Italy, New Zealand, and the UK. I would like to single out Alessandro Barchiesi, who invited me to speak in Arezzo on more than one occasion; Gualtiero Calboli, who made me think in new ways about Roman law; Jon Hall and Bill Dominik, who gave me the chance to participate in their 'companion' enterprise; and Francesca Martelli, who organized a most challenging and rewarding conference in Oxford in September 2009 in order to discuss the kind of theoretical issues I have been struggling with for a number of years. Above all, however, I must thank Tom Habinek. Without his vision and commitment, classics would doubtless be a less interesting discipline. Although I was never one of his students, I believe that this project would not have been possible without his support and feedback.

This book has gone through more revisions than I would want to remember. I would like to acknowledge here the help I received from James Ker, Jon Hall, Robin Bond, and Patrick O'Sullivan who took the time to read through entire chapters and offered me practical advice and support. I have also benefited from constructive conversations with Siobhan McElduff, David Konstan, Matthew Roller, Andrew Riggsby, Clifford Ando, Mary Jaeger, Eric Gruen, Sander Goldberg, William Fitzgerald, Hector Reyes, Claudia Moatti, and Nicola Terrenato. I owe special thanks to Ann Kuttner who has generously allowed me to use her drawings of censorial scenes. These are now inserted in chapter 5. I would also like to acknowledge here the professional and warm support I have received from Eugene O'Connor at The Ohio State University Press at every stage of the publication process.

The cover and internal art is by Julia Shirar. Thanks go, finally, to Jeff Carnes for his work on the indices.

The University of Canterbury and the various schools under which the Department of Classics has been subsumed in the last few years have been incredibly generous with me. During my study leave in 2006 I was able to write the first draft of chapters 4 and 5. Thanks to a Humanities grant in 2008 I was able to speed my writing by hiring Anna Milne and Elizabeth Lochhead as research assistants. I hope that they obtained from our conversations about single points of my argument as much as I did. In the last phase of this project I relied on a Canterbury Fellowship at Oxford and the support of Alan Bowman and Nicholas Purcell. In Oxford I have also benefited from a Plumer Research Fellowship at St Anne's College for which I have to thank Matthew Leigh and Tim Whitmarsh. During this time my parents, my brothers, my sister Alessandra, and Federico, her son, taught me yet another spectacular lesson in love and resilience. On February 22, 2011 while I was working on copyediting this book, a 6.3 earthquake shook Christchurch, taking numerous lives and destroying many homes. I must here thank Chris Jones for helping me get the work done despite the chaos of the weeks following. The publication of this book is a small token of recognition of the admirable resolve and tenacity of the people of Christchurch. As Salvatore Quasimodo says in the last line of his *Al Padre, oscuramente forte è la vita.*

All translations are my own, unless otherwise specified.

List of Abbreviations

Baehrens	Baehrens, E. 1874. *XII Panegyrici Latini.* Leipzig: Teubner.
CIL	*Corpus Inscriptionum Latinarum.* Berlin: Brandenburg Academy of Sciences and Humanities.
C&Sbl	Cugusi, P. and Sblendorio Cugusi, M.T. 2001. *Marco Porcio Catone Censore. Opere.* 2 vols. Torino: UTET.
FPL	Blänsford, J. 1995. *Fragmenta Poetarum Latinorum Epicorum et Lyricorum praeter Ennium et Lucilium.* Third edition. Leipzig: Teubner.
GL	Keil, H. 1855. *Grammatici Latini.* Leipzig: Teubner.
Helm	Helm, R. 1956. *Eusebius Werke 7: Die Chronik des Hieronymus.* Second Edition. Griechischen Christlichen Schriftsteller 47.
Lightfoot	Lightfoot, J. L. 1999. *Parthenius of Nicaea. The Poetical Fragments and the Ἐρωτικὰ παθήματα.* Oxford: Clarendon Press.
Malcovati[4]	Malcovati, E. 1976. *Oratorum Romanorum fragmenta liberae rei publicae.* Fourth edition. Torino: Paravia.
Morel	Morel, W. 1927. *Fragmenta Poetarum Latinorum Epicorum et Lyricorum praeter Ennium et Lucilium.* Leipzig: Teubner.
P2	Peter, H. [1906] 1914. *Historicorum Romanorum Fragmenta.* Second Edition. Leipzig: Teubner.

Ribbeck	Ribbeck, O. 1897. *Scaenicae Romanorum Poesis Fragmenta.* Third Edition. Leipzig: Teubner.
Sbl	Sblendorio Cugusi, M. T. 1982. *Marci Porci Catoni Orationum Reliquiae.* Torino: Paravia.
Sk	Skutsch, O. 1985. *The Annals of Q. Ennius.* Oxford: Clarendon Press.
Stangl	Stangl, T. 1912. *Ciceronis orationum scholiastae Asconius, scholia bobiensia, scholia pseudasconii sangallensia, scholia cluniacensia et recentiora ambrosiana ac vaticana, scholia lugdunensia sive gronoviana et eorum excerpta lugdunensia.* Hildesheim: Olms.
Sudhaus	Sudhaus, S.1892. *Philodemi Volumina Rhetorica.* Leipzig: Teubner.

Chapter 1

Situating the Beginnings of Latin Prose

In this study I take as a point of departure the fundamental claim of cultural studies that the production and consumption of culture are human practices characterized by relations of dominance and subjection. Far from aiming to disavow or sublate philological and literary analyses, I take this claim as a driving force for expanding current notions of text, form, literature, and genre. By regarding texts as integral to practice, I envision them as the result of a series of judgments and perceptions of the ordering of the world and their authors as social agents constrained by practical schemes strictly associated with their perception of reality. In this instance reality is not simply a context to which texts are to be linked; rather, it consists of a web of restrictions and possibilities experienced by each agent in relation to other agents. Accordingly, I understand generic inclinations, formal choices, thematic preferences, and modes of textual construction as practical manifestations of a shared sense of reality and as clear indicators of the authors' different experiences of limitations and options.

My first basic argument is that in early second century B.C.E. Rome, the author's positioning in the larger scheme of social relations was connected with his choice to produce either poetry or prose in Latin. It is significant that Latin poetry was a practice initiated by professional immigrants, whereas the beginnings of Latin prose were interlaced with the career of Cato the Censor, a man from Tusculum who lacked a history of family achievements and yet managed to enter Rome's political scene and remain at its center for about half a century. To elaborate this proposition, I will be employing the useful notion of subjectivity.

The centrality of this notion in a variety of disciplines has produced a wide range of definitions.[1] In philosophy subjectivity is generally defined as the opposite of objectivity understood as an ontological realm that is independent of any arbitrary influence of a thinking being. Nonoppositional definitions of subjectivity in other fields share a concern with how agents are constituted by cultural and social determinations and how, more or less consciously, these determinations shape the cognitive and affective frameworks through which agents perceive themselves in relation to others and decide about a course of action. I cannot claim, of course, that my description of a plurality of late-third- and early-second-centuries B.C.E. subjectivities is neutral. In fact, I see no escape from the fact that as soon as we set out to describe we immediately participate and cease to be observers on the sidelines. If this were not enough, our access to the subjectivities in question is mediated by texts that are also, for the most part, fragmentary. By declaring the death of the author, deconstruction has been teaching us that texts have no fixed meaning and that words act as unstable signifiers and purveyors of multiple significations whose meaning is supplied or completed by the reader. In this book I take in the claim of deconstruction but resist the preeminence that it grants to the reader in order to map a number of complex historical dynamics, cultural representations, and individual positionings.

My second argument is that the specific forms and themes that distinguish early Latin poetry from Cato's prose bear the imprint of the distinct subjectivities of their producers. Everyone recognizes that Latin poetry owes its existence to acts of translation from literary texts produced in the Greek-speaking world. In chapters 2 and 3 I take as a cue the narratives of migration of its early practitioners to Rome and expand on exclusively text-bound approaches by considering the effects that migration may have had on their self-perception, their translations, and others' perception of both. In the remaining chapters I work out the strategies that Cato adopted in order to overcome the limitations that derived from his status as *homo novus*. In chapter 4 I look at how he disavowed poetic agency and yet redeployed poetic forms by anchoring them to schemes of speech and action associated with an ancestral past and including pre-poetic forms generally bracketed under the rubric of the *carmen*. In chapter 5 I scrutinize how

---

1. For a useful survey of definitions of subjectivity, see Hall 2004.

Cato differentiated his writing activities by relying on the ritual practices that sustained his attainment and exercise of social and political authority. My attempt to bring authorial subjectivity into play from a variety of viewpoints ushers in the body as an additional factor to consider and is warranted by what we find in the texts. Let me offer here two examples.

In a fragment attributed to Ennius and preserved by Aulus Gellius we learn that the poet claimed to have "three hearts," *tria corda,* because he knew how to speak Greek, Latin, and Oscan (or Messapian).[2] This image reveals a subjectivity that is empowered by an emotional identification with multiple cultural and linguistic sites. At the same time, it reflects the variegated environment of second-century B.C.E. Italy.[3] But if we turn our attention to another Ennian fragment, the emotional equality that this image bestows on those different sites breaks down before the relative sociopolitical prestige that each enjoys. In keeping with the plurality of Ennius' heart, the fragment reads: *nos sumus Romani qui fuimus ante Rudini,* "we are Romans who once were Rudians."[4] This fragment not only alludes to Ennius' geographical relocation to Rome, but also proclaims his midlife promotion to Roman citizenship. This new identification supersedes his association with the civic community of Rudiae and 'nests' his Greek heart into the newly acquired identity.[5] Rather than disappearing, this heart informs his self-fashioning as a poet, his choice of Greek-derived formal and thematic frameworks, and the multiple processes of Romanization that figure in his poetry. In the *Annales* the dynamic relationship between Ennius' "three hearts" produces a bifurcated trajectory: as the poem endorses the expansionistic and political successes of the Roman leaders in Italy and beyond, it also opens up alternative perspectives on his and others' perception of being in the world.[6]

Cato too experienced migration; however, his subjectivity was distinctively different from that of the poets. Born in 234 B.C.E. in Tusculum, fifteen miles south of Rome, Cato belonged to an elite family that is thought to have acquired Roman citizenship in 268 B.C.E. with the rest of the Sabines. This means that he enjoyed from birth the right to embark on a politi-

---

2. Gellius 17.17 = *Op. Inc. Frag* 1Sk. Suerbaum (1968: 140–41) suggests Messapian instead of Oscan and locates this declaration at the end of the *Annals.*

3. For a recent assessment of the centrality of *cor* in Ennius' fragmentary corpus, see Gowers 2007.

4. Ennius, *Ann.* 525 Sk.

5. I am borrowing the concept of 'nesting' from hierarchy theory whereby each level of the hierarchy contains different elements and subsumes them within. For a reflection on 'nested identities,' especially in their relation to space, see Herb and Kaplan 1999.

6. For recent discussions of the latter trajectory, see Elliott 2007 and Keith 2007.

cal career in Rome and could look to the inclusive policy that had long regulated the cooption of new bodies into the urban aristocracy. And yet an obstacle remained: the advantages traditionally enjoyed by men whose ancestors had held the highest offices and who were identified as *nobiles*.

The most recognized way by which Cato negotiated his successful career as an 'insider outsider' was to draw on his Sabine origins.[7] By projecting on them the old-time virtue that had made Rome great and by purporting to incarnate it, he was able to counter what he saw as the corrupting influence of Greek culture and to displace the monopoly that the *nobiles* held on pristine morality and hardy customs. Cato's perception of himself and his agency was mediated through a twofold identification with Sabine and Roman sites and drew force from a polemical displacement of 'Greekness.'[8] The latter move could not be clearer than in a fragment of the so-called *Ad Filium:*

> Dicam de istis Graecis suo loco, Marce fili, quid Athenis exquisitum habeam, et quod bonum sit illorum litteras inspicere, non perdiscere. Vincam nequissimum et indocile esse genus illorum. Et hoc puta vatem dixisse: quandoque ista gens suas litteras dabit, omnia conrumpet, tum etiam magis, si medicos suos huc mittet. Iurarunt inter se barbaros necare omnis medicina, sed hoc ipsum mercede faciunt ut fides iis sit et facile disperdant. Nos quoque dictitant barbaros et spurcius nos quam alios Opicon appellatione foedant. Interdixi de medicis.[9]

> I shall speak about those Greeks in the proper place, Marcus my son, as to what I found out in Athens and what benefit there is in looking into their writings, not in learning them thoroughly. I will demonstrate that their race is most despicable and intractable. And reckon what follows as pronounced by a *vates:* whenever this race will give its literature, it will corrupt everything; all the more so, if they will send their doctors here. They have taken an oath among themselves to kill all the barbarians by their medicine, but they do this very thing for a fee, so that they may be trusted and destroy easily. They also speak of us all the time as barbarians, and they insult us more filthily than others by calling us Opici. I have forbidden you to deal with doctors.

---

7. Dench 1995: 85; Cornell 1995: 393; Blösel 2000: 53–54; Farney 2007: 109–10.

8. In *Laws* 2.5 Cicero speaks about municipal men as having two homelands (*patriae*): one by place (*locus*) and one by right (*ius*). For further considerations about this duality, see Farney 2007:1–38.

9. Pliny, *NH* 29.14 = Cato, *Ad Filium* 1 C&Sbl.

This fragment opens by featuring Cato's 'speaking I' addressing his son and promising him to deal with the Greeks on another occasion. Through this deferral, Cato situates the Greeks in an Athens construed as a peripheral site that he has self-confidently examined and represents their writings as objects that are both alien and alienable.[10] The alienable features that Cato attaches to Greek literature are here made prominent in his choice of *dare* (to give). Produced by a despicable and fickle race, these writings—he warns his son—are good to be inspected (*inspicere*) but should not be learned thoroughly (*perdiscere*). Paratactically adding to it, Cato ominously predicts that Greek literature holds the potential to undo (*conrumpere*) everything and equates his pronouncement to that of a *vates*. As a figure of pre-poetic Roman song shunned by Ennius in a famous fragment of the *Annales,* the *vates* becomes in this context a prop for empowering Cato's own self-positioning.[11] In what follows, Cato abruptly shifts his focus from literature to medicine and characterizes Greek doctors as conspirators and assassins operating under the disguise of paid professionals. The language of destruction (*necare, disperdere*) that he uses at this point recalls the ruinous power (*conrumpere*) previously attributed to Greek literature. The echo ushers in the unfamiliar idea of reading as affecting the body through the mind and suggests that Cato's distinction between *inspicere* and *perdiscere* does not rest on a different degree of attention paid to texts, but on the extent to which what is read comes to be incorporated. When viewed vis-à-vis Cato's positioning, Ennius' self-reference in bodily terms sheds some of its metaphorical dimension and brings to the forefront from a different direction the shared perception of the body as the vehicle through which an individual constructed and expressed his place in the world. Consequently, an approach that takes account of forms and themes as practical templates that affect and are affected by authorial subjectivity allows us to grasp the impact of embodied experience on the choice of forms, themes, and textualities in ways that a strictly textual interpretation cannot.

---

10. See Dench 2005: 324–26; Dupont 2005. The question of ownership in relation to Greek literature comes vividly into play in Horace, *Ars* 128–35 where Greek literary texts are defined as *communis* (128) and *publica materies* (131) that through poetic manipulation and translation become an area of *ius privatus* (131).

11. Ennius, *Ann.* 7.206–7 Sk. Cato's adoption of *vates* as an authoritative prop counters the negative overtones that are made manifest in Livy's narrative of the Bacchanalian affair of 186 B.C.E. (39.8–18), suggesting changes in their social location and a tightening of control over religious practices. See Gildenhard 2007b: 87–92; Wiseman 2006; Habinek 2005a: 227–28; Gruen 1990: 34–78. The rejection of the *vates* is central to Ennius' poetic self-fashioning and is treated in that relation in chapter 3.

My third argument is that in early-second-century B.C.E. Rome, writing helped to differentiate poetry and prose from everyday, unmarked activities; however, in their reciprocal differentiation and the social value accorded to each, a decisive role was played by modalities of writing and reading. This argument builds upon my claim that thematic and formal choices are expressions of diverse subjectivities and calls attention to the relationship between texts and acting agents. By focusing on this relationship, I consider texts as aesthetic artefacts and deal with them as material objects whose production and consumption are practical exercises that acquire significance when viewed in relation to the production and consumption of other texts. As such, I concentrate on diverse writing and reading practices and how they are strategically played off against one another to generate the perception that the writing activities of the agent and the reception of his texts are privileged in their import and consequences.

One of the distinctive features of early poetic writings is that they were produced primarily with a view to their being performed by the author himself or by professional performers during occasions that were temporally and spatially marked off from the everyday. In the case of poetic drama, we can safely say that these occasions were integrated in civic festivals organized and regulated by individuals who exercised sociopolitical authority. As for other early poetic texts, we are unable to proceed with the same confidence. Nothing prevents us from thinking that these may have been objects of reading acts similar to ours; however, a fragment attributed to the *carmen de moribus* in which Cato looks down upon poetic encroachments on convivial gatherings offers some ground for speculating that some poetic compositions were consumed in those contexts or, at least, in exclusive situations which Cato represents as bearing convivial features.[12] I expand on this more fully in chapter 3. The point that I would like to convey here is that the alien and alienable features that Cato attributes to Greek writings illuminate something significant about the relationship between authority and authorship in the Roman context. If we take the case of Ennius, we may say that he gained authorial success by translating from Greek literature and by situating himself in a longstanding series of reading events. But if we look at Ennius' authorship through Cato's lens, we can see that his poetic success granted him a limited agency. For one thing, Ennius constructed his authorship by relying on the kind of intake of Greekness and Greek literature that Cato

---

12. I am referring here to Gellius 11.2.5 = Cato, *carmen de moribus* 2 C&SB. Modern constructions of ancient reading are discussed in Parker 2009 (but the evidence he discusses dates to the late first century B.C.E. onwards).

rejects. Although we may choose to ignore Cato, it is important to keep in mind that Ennius enjoyed a lesser social standing and had to confront the perception that Cato promoted. Second, Ennius' positioning in the world was largely dependent on his poetic crafts and their favorable reception.[13] I call this quality of poetic writing 'scriptic.' The texts attributed to Cato, on the other hand, consist of what I call 'transcriptions.'

The term transcription has been used by Florence Dupont to define the relationship between orality and textuality whereby a text purports to encode "an utterance whose written reality *pretends* to be a transcription."[14] In Dupont's view, when written texts present themselves as fixing ritually or socially codified oral performances, the fiction bestows form on a text that otherwise would not have any. Expanding on Dupont's focus on fictionality and speech, I suggest that Cato conceived of the texts that he produced as transcriptions of speech acts and social events that were conducive to his accrual of sociopolitical authority. In turn, the sociopolitical authority that he accumulated over the course of his career opened up for him the possibility of redeploying paradigms of speech and actions that were recognized as having the power of ordering the universe, the community, and the household. Through the interplay of these factors Cato avoided the predicaments attached to poetic writing; at the same time, he extended his control over the reception of his transcriptions by leading readers to acknowledge his self-assertions as authoritative.

In the remaining pages of this introductory chapter I present the genealogy of my approach in relation to what I see as the most significant methodological debates that have taken place in the Anglo-(North) American scene of Latin studies in the last decade or so. The first relates to the rift between formalisms and historicisms in the study of Latin poetry and the second to the so-called 'invention of Latin literature.'

Form and History

One of the most enduring binaries structuring the study of Latin literature is the opposition between poetry and prose, where poetry constitutes the positive term primarily by virtue of its dependence on metrical laws and

---

13. Dupont 2009 and Farrell 2009 explore this element in different ways. But see also Pierre (2005: 241): "Le poète romain, quant à lui, n'est, d'un point de vue social, qu'un scripteur. Pour autoriser socialement son poème, il doit donner du poids: le poème sera reconnu comme publiquement valide, uniquement s'il est autorisé par un *auctor* qui le diffuse et le garantit."

14. Dupont 2009: 147; the emphasis is mine. Cf. also Dupont 1999: 61–63 and *passim*.

formal sophistications.¹⁵ In the nineteen-eighties and nineties the study of intertextuality developed around this hierarchical model, becoming the primary tool for interpreting Roman poetry. Born as a reaction to the monopoly of New Criticism in the Anglo-(North) American world and as a redress to the crisis of traditional historicism in Italy, intertextual studies called into question the unity of a text and located meaning in the relationship of a text with prior texts and in the codes to which it belongs. One consequence of this new trend was a positive re-evaluation of Latin poetry's "belatedness" with respect to Greece; another was an increasing interest in Augustan and Imperial poetry; yet another was a greater awareness of the constructed nature of literary interpretation and, consequently, of the critic's own ideological framework as a determinant in the process of reading.[16]

In the late nineties a number of concerns about interpretations focused on intertextuality began to arise from within the ranks.[17] Exemplary, in this respect, is Stephen Hinds' *Allusion and Intertext: Dynamics of Appropriation in Roman Poetry* (1998). In this book, Hinds reflected on how to distinguish between allusion and accidental confluence of words or commonplaces. He also raised the issue of how to treat authorial intention, stressing that from the point of view of interpreters, however conjectural, the alluding author is still instrumental, still "good to think with."[18] By turning next to the role of reading, Hinds used as a case study the archaic Roman poets and demonstrated the extent to which readings of them in antiquity keep informing our literary histories. Finally, he focused on the status of a text under examination in relation to the texts alluded to, asking what hierarchies structure their relationship—in other words, which of them constitutes the master-text.

In 2001 Lowell Edmunds published *Intertextuality and the Reading of Roman Poetry* as a response to Hinds' methodological reflections. Discussing the nature of allusions, Edmunds claims that they should be regarded as "pleasing or intriguing, often unordinary, uses of language that convey or portend some meaning valuable to the reader."[19] Following this trajectory, Edmunds dismisses the possibility that a poem may actually perform something in the world and proposes that it is "the

---

15. I should like to point out that the formation of Greek prose has received much more attention; see, e.g., Wardy 1996; Goldhill 2002; Kurke 2006 and 2010.
16. The best treatment of the "New Latin movement" is to be found in Fowler 1995. See also Fowler 2000.
17. A. Barchiesi 1997.
18. Hinds 1998: 119.
19. Edmunds 2001: xiii.

poet's adoption of a persona, his speaking in a fictional voice, that gives a poem its special status outside the ordinary uses of language."[20] As for the issue of authorial intention, Edmunds maintains that the very difficulty of introducing information about ancient authors from outside the poems downgrades intentionality to nothing more than "the scholar's rhetorical add-on at the conclusion of an interpretation."[21] To Hinds' reconstruction of how the earlier Roman poets were reduced to the status of "archaic" by ancient readers and to his wondering about what vantage point we should be taking, Edmunds reacts by characterizing this sort of exercise as purposeless since Hinds himself is located in "a new era of reception."[22] Ultimately, Edmunds articulates the interpretation of Roman poetry as an aesthetically-based reading practice that finds validity in what he calls the "Latin sub-community" and the "conventions of its discourse."[23]

While drawing attention to some genuine pitfalls of Roman studies, Edmunds' conceptualization of intertextuality is not as impermeable to historicism as it may seem. In fact, his strong resistance to looking outside texts and his equally strong penchant for the aesthetic are undermined by the way he locates the founding moment of a "reading culture." Although he acknowledges the *recitatio* and the reading of texts at elite dinners as ancient contexts of literary reception, he claims that the late first century B.C.E. witnessed the development of a new type of reading, one centered on a cognitive and/or aesthetic experience.[24] In doing so, Edmunds reinforces the high value traditionally granted to poetry, raising Augustan poetic texts to the status of master-texts and excluding by default any other texts chronologically or generically located elsewhere. Moreover, he constructs a locus of origins for the type of reading that he promotes by implying that intertextual analyses of Augustan poetry are the very discourses and conventions that structure the Latin 'sub-community.' Accordingly, Edmunds is pulled towards historicism after all, demonstrating that, even when aesthetically conceived, reading practices do structure social subjectivities and communities.

Somewhat fortunately, as Edmunds points out, Latinists have always been open to productive self-reflections and to entering into dialectical relationship with contemporary trends in the humanities.[25] In 2003

---

20. Edmunds 2001: 37.
21. Edmunds 2001: xii.
22. Edmunds 2001: xix.
23. Edmunds 2001: 168–69.
24. Edmunds 2001: 31, 108–9.
25. Edmunds 2001: 168.

Edmunds organized at Rutgers the conference *Critical Divergences: New Directions in the Study and Teaching of Roman Literature.* The papers delivered on that occasion and now published in *TAPA* 2005 are a signal indication of this fruitful, twofold engagement. One useful fact that emerges from these papers is that the rift between formalism and historicism that preoccupies all Latinists alike is not at all monomorphic. Indeed, as Alessandro Barchiesi alerts us, the ways in which it is articulated are still contingent upon generational positionings, local traditions, and professional demands inherent to the scholarly landscape in which individual Latinists seek (or are forced) to abide.[26] Consequently, it is important not only to interface the two approaches, as Barchiesi has it, but also to move beyond the politics of theoretical binaries altogether in a manner that valorizes classical studies in spite of global economies, local hierarchies, and whatever crises of critical thinking arise inside and outside academia.[27] If the study of allusions applied to Augustan poetry has been teaching us that texts are relational in nature and that reading is, no matter what, a practice able to structure subjectivities as well as communities, the transnational dimension of the postmodern and globalized world should make us wary of any individual or communal attempt to either homologize or hierarchize ancient practices in ways that elide the specific antagonisms and accommodations that informed them.

To articulate the relationship between text and context, inside and outside, form and history, is a multifaceted task; as such, it calls for a constructive and concerted effort. As the contributions to the Rutgers conference suggest, the careful study of words and phrases can and should be supplemented by a number of lateral approaches; these include the reading of texts falling outside the genre of the text under observation, a comparably close analysis of artefacts, and the reconstruction of how texts have been read/interpreted across time. The point is that there is so much that we do not understand about the ancient world and the way we relate to it that it is absurd to think that any given critical engagement with any given ancient material will provide an answer to all the questions. Critical approaches are not critical because they contain answers, but because they help us to constructively identify a phenomenon by the very act of moving close to it.

In his contribution to the Rutgers conference Thomas Habinek observes that, just as today, "to read" in the Roman world is "a practice,

---

26. A. Barchiesi 2005: 137 and note 5.
27. Connolly 2005.

entailing a specific, historically constituted set of relationships of body to voice, speaker to listener, male to female, master to slave, owner to object, and so on."[28] Habinek's shift of focus to the body complicates current binaries by adding a further variant. In his book *The World of Roman Song: From Ritualized Speech to Social Order* (2005), he invites us to move from text to language and from literature to song. By relying on the fruitful analytical work done on archaic Greek poetry, Habinek identifies a classificatory system based on the opposition between *cano* and *loquor* within the Latin language.[29] As opposed to the unmarked *loquor*, Habinek argues that *cano* and its derivatives relate to the establishing of a relation between the singer, the constituted social world, and the cosmic whole through ritualized speech. In this sense, ritualized means "made special through the use of specialized diction, regular meter, musical accompaniment, figures of sound, mythical or religious subject matter, and socially authoritative context."[30] Included under the same rubric as *cano* is *dico*, in the sense of "to express with authority" or "to insist upon the validity of."[31] *Cano* and *dico* are song in that they both constitute a marked form of *loquor* and relate to the voice of a person with special access to sources of authority. The difference between them turns upon what is stressed: *dico* "emphasizes the validity or authoritativeness of the utterance," implying an asymmetrical relationship between speaker and addressee, while *cano* points to its aesthetic characteristics and performance context.[32]

In contrast to both *cano* and *dico*, *canto* stands a notch lower, qualifying a musical performance to someone else's tune or the singing of a song authorized by another singer.[33] As for poetry, *poema* describes a poetically devised output in Ennius' *Annales*, appears once again in Lucilius to define a small portion of a larger poem called *poesis*, and reemerges in Horace in relation to the "fashioning that goes into its production rather than the authority that sustains it.[34]" And prose? This form of speech would come into the song system through *dico* in two ways. Starting from the political, social, and cosmic authority assigned to song, Habinek argues that oratory, philosophy, and dance are "aspects of song that struggle to be differentiated from and within the realm of special speech. By promoting the power of *dicta*, oratory and philosophy in particular derive

---

28. Habinek 2005b: 84.
29. Habinek 2005a: 2.
30. Habinek 2005a: 61–62.
31. Habinek 2005a: 63.
32. Habinek 2005a: 69–70, 72. See also Habinek 1998b.
33. Habinek 2005a: 67.
34. Habinek 2005a: 80.

their authority from the impact of ritualized language beyond the bounds of ritual, yet their practitioners use that authority to reshape the condition of its production."[35] Elsewhere, Habinek describes prose as secondary to song, owing its derivative status from "a loosening of the bonds, a progressive limitation of the marked elements that characterize song."[36]

In Habinek's account, the Roman evaluation of speech is closely tied to the relationship of the performer's voice to the body. The relationship between embodied performance (*mimesis*) and textual symbolization (*semiosis*) is central to Latin literature, while the break in the relationship, privileging the latter, is articulated as the liberation of voice from body.[37] Habinek's most persuasive examples center on the *ludus poeticus,* or "poetic play," as it is conjured up in a number of texts historically ranging from Catullus to Horace. Poetic play is constructed as an exercise in submission to bodily discipline, including social patronage, metrical laws, and the labor of writing.[38] In this the poet, struggling to establish his own autonomous and, therefore, authoritative voice, enters upon a process of self-empowerment. Transcendence from bodily constraints, however, is not so easily achieved. In this sense, Horace hints that his own *ludus* may turn into a more permanent state akin to enslavement.[39] As Paul Allen Miller aptly summarizes in his review of *Roman Song,* Horace helps us see that the "the ultimate dream of aristocratic Roman manhood is for *carmen*—the ritualized speech that constitutes the community as a living unity—to assume the status of *dictum,* authoritative speech freed from the scripting and embodiment of play (*ludus*)."[40] To my mind, Habinek points to an alternative vantage point from which to observe how Rome's cultural history was affected by the correlation between different strategies of ritualization and specific sectors of society. One aspect of poetry that Habinek mentions very briefly is that the origins of Roman poetry were historically bound up with nonelite and/or alien cultural agents.[41] This fact deserves more focused consideration.

Although scholars working across different fields are increasingly convinced that individual and collective identities are socially constructed

---

35. Habinek 2005a: 94.
36. Habinek 2005a: 92–93.
37. Habinek 2005b: 86–87.
38. Farrell (2009: 164–85) has recently added to the discussion by focusing on a number of anxieties that emerge in Catullus and other near contemporary poets in relation to poetry's dependency on the papyrus roll, a writing material perceived as a corruptible object meant to be given as a gift to others. Cf. also Pierre 2005: 241–42.
39. Habinek 2005a: 110–50.
40. Miller 2006: 608.
41. Habinek 2005a: 80, 82.

(and I take this as a given), less attention has been paid to how cultural expressions are shaped by these identities and how they are perceived accordingly. My work illustrates that Latin poetry's historical association with socially secondary individuals is, to a large extent, responsible for the perception of aesthetic discipline and poetic writing as exercises in bodily submission. Centuries later, Horace manifests the inescapability of this perception in his *Epistles*. While Habinek emphasizes that Horace presents his delivery of philosophical precepts as speech unconstrained by the rules of poetic engagement, I find it important to stress that the poet continues to constrain his speech within the bonds of the hexameter and constructs a written artefact of poetic design, expressing formally and materially the inescapable predicaments of Latin poetry's origins.[42] To recognize these predicaments has several advantages. One of these is the possibility to observe that the markedness of Roman poetry does not derive from its fictionality alone. Another is the opportunity to reflect on the limitations that we impose on ourselves by thinking about literature solely in terms of the poetic. Still another is the chance to approach anew the formal and written features of Latin prose and to develop alternative perspectives on Roman aestheticism.

In her review of *Roman Song,* Michèle Lowrie contests Habinek's methodological move of including writing under song as a vehicle for performance because it rules out the fact that "the Romans understood writing to provide certain advantages over song."[43] By underscoring that writing is a mechanism for the creation of an aesthetic artefact, Lowrie points out that, as opposed to song, which needs recontextualization, writing along with the category of literature allows for temporal longevity and ritual decontextualization. For Lowrie, in other words, writing helped construct objects aesthetically conceived (i.e., literary texts) that exceeded the moment of the utterance and allowed for the transcending of the speech act beyond its performance occasion and for its splitting off from the sacred at the same time. As a result, literature would have provided "a space in which to think about what song does, its powers, its limits, without always needing to actually engage in it."[44]

Lowrie's criticism, although inherently sound and insightful, betrays a widespread methodological flaw: the tendency to conflate writing, literature, and poetry. This conflation valorizes Roman poetic texts by imbuing them with an autonomous potency that they did not otherwise possess

---

42. Habinek 2005a: 148. See now Farrell 2009.
43. Lowrie 2006.
44. Lowrie 2006. A fuller articulation of this statement can now be found in Lowrie 2009.

regardless of any resistance to or reflection on the limits of song that these texts bear. Accordingly, to focus on the relationship between cultural practices and social hierarchies as I do can appear provocative, even heretical. Yet, I suggest that the study of this relationship reveals that the temporal longevity and the ritual decontextualization attached to poetic writing—as well as the space for reflection that it created—was intellectually powerful but performatively limited.

One of the most telling and well-known reflections on the limits of poetic writing can be found in Horace *Epistles* 1.20. In this poem Horace dramatizes his separation from his book of poetry as if speaking as a master to his manumitted slave. While reproaching the book's eagerness to cross the threshold into the public eye, he comes to liken the circulation of his poetry to prostitution. In this way, Horace reveals that the publication of a poetically manufactured text is bound up with acts of appropriation performed by a readership that the author cannot fully control. Horace's abbreviated biography attached at the end of the poem reinforces the message. By claiming that he has been able to win the favor of eminent men despite being the son of a freedman, Horace asserts his social superiority over other non-eminent individuals; at the same time, however, he admits the failure of his poems to promote him to the same social level of his favorite readers and addressees.[45] Accordingly, he makes conspicuous the social constraints that loom large over poetry as a cultural practice and stresses that poetic authorship went hand in hand with a process of dispossession. Underlying this relationship is what I call the 'scriptic' nature of poetic texts.

In her article "Reading as a Man: Performance and Gender in Roman Elegy" Mary-Kay Gamel observes that when scripts are performed control is dislocated from the author to the reader/performer, producing a contradiction: "the words spoken by performers both do not belong to them (because written by someone else) and yet do (because they come from their bodies)."[46] By taking stock of Gamel's observations, we can better comprehend Horace's quandary. To write poetry opens up the possibility of acquiring authorship; authorship, however, is not always a synonym for authority. In the case of poetry, this is strictly linked to a movable text that is alienated from its producer at the moment of reception. Although Gamel is thinking of public performance, Cato's representation of Greek literature in his address to his son suggests that the same alienating pro-

---

45. Oliensis 1995.
46. Gamel 1998: 86.

cess could well apply to private readings of texts.[47] The most conspicuous strategies adopted by poets to secure the most successful reception for their poems and the highest degree of authorial success for themselves were aesthetic artfulness and metrical sophistication. By the same token, the more authorial success the poet achieved, the more his texts were subject to appropriative acts carried out by their readers/performers. As such, when critics disqualify intentionality altogether and construct intertextuality as a matter that lies exclusively in the hands of readers, they evoke the limits of poetic agency and the power of Roman poetry to empower those who appropriated it.[48]

The case of the *Res Gestae* by Augustus can serve here as a nice contrast. In the paper that she presented at Rutgers, Lowrie confronts the occurrence of *auctoritas* in Augustus' text and calls attention to the relationship between social agency and cultural representation. Taking as a starting point Benveniste's definition of *auctoritas* as "a power that brings things into being by its exercise," Lowrie notes that this power emanates from the individual but is also granted to that individual by his followers. What this means is that "people only confer this sort of power on people with certain qualities (charisma) and the qualities can only find a field of operation once they are recognized."[49] Accordingly, she proposes to view *auctoritas* as a performative kind of political power that operates beyond the sphere of law; at the same time, she points out that, because *auctoritas* thrives on being actualized, cultural representation constitutes an active sphere of engagement of *auctoritas* itself.[50] To drive home her proposition, Lowrie suggests that with the *Res Gestae* we are dealing with a text that had the power of keeping *auctoritas* performatively in play because it was an account of how Augustus had actualized his own. What Lowrie does not fully elaborate in that context is that the *Res Gestae* is a text that could do so because its author was a social agent that enjoyed *auctoritas* in the first place.[51] This means that the strategies that Augustus adopted to make his *Res Gestae* a direct and enduring manifestation of his *auctoritas* depended on possibilities and limitations that were not at all the same as those experienced by poets.

In keeping with recent trends in the interpretation of Augustus' inscrip-

---

47. For the modern preoccupation over public performance vs. private reading, see Parker 2009.
48. See already Martindale 1993: 3–4.
49. Lowrie 2005: 42–43. For a discussion of *auctoritas* with a focus on Augustus, see Galinsky 1996: 15–42.
50. Lowrie 2005: 43.
51. For further explorations, see Lowrie 2007 and 2009.

tion, one may begin by suggesting that the *Res Gestae* drew its performative power from the architectural contexts in which it was located.[52] In this sense, Augustus would have capitalized on the well-established role granted to monuments in publicizing and preserving the reputation and accomplishments of the commemorated beyond their deaths.[53] Following the existing monumental tradition, he used writing to communicate things that could not be portrayed through visual devices by producing a list of offices held, military and political achievements, the names of temples and buildings sponsored, people conquered, and the like. As Greg Woolf points out, in monumental writing lists serve the purpose of situating the person commemorated by the monument as a whole in a nexus of relationships, human and divine.[54] Interestingly, to set the stage for such conclusions, Woolf turns to Horace *Odes* 3.30: *Exegi monumentum aere perennius* ("I have built a monument more lasting than bronze") and comments:

> monuments, the *Ode* implies, if they lasted long enough and were prominent enough, would preserve the fame of the commemorated, acting like mnemonics to trigger memories and perhaps speech. Once evoked, the deeds and qualities of the monumentalized, would be rehearsed, whether orally or in silence, and admired, and he or she would not "perish utterly."[55]

While Woolf uses Horace's poem to illustrate the mnemonic qualities attached to monuments, I would like to emphasize what the poem suggests about the power of poetic writing vis-à-vis monumental writing. In light of Horace's reflections on poetic authorship in *Epistles* 1.20, *Odes* 3.30 reveals that a poetic text can be said to be monumental only to the extent that it triggers the memory of its author's poetic skills and his success in having eminent men authorize his poetic creations.[56] But Horace's perspective sheds light also on another, hardly acknowledged, aspect of monuments.

On the one hand, by forcefully trumpeting that his poetry is a *monumentum* Horace is seeking a long-lasting public visibility; on the other, he

---

52. See especially Elsner 1996 and Güven 1998. As for recent editions, see Ridley 2003; Scheid 2007; Cooley 2009.

53. For anxieties about the corruptibility of monuments, see Fowler 2000: 193–217.

54. Woolf 1996: 26–28.

55. Woolf 1996: 25

56. Hardie (2007) has recently discussed Horace's use of Ennius as a mirror for trumpeting his poetic innovations and reflecting on his dependency on social superiors. Not surprisingly, Hardie finds *Epistles* 1.20 and *Odes* 3.30 teeming with Ennian allusions.

implicitly longs to avoid what he fears in *Epistles* 1.20, namely, that his poems may end up in the wrong hands. In this respect, what monuments allow that poetry does not is to obtain the highest degree of publication and the least degree of indiscriminate appropriations. This is because the insertion of writing into an architectural structure renders the text not only conspicuous but also unmovable. Moreover, even though monumental writing presupposes a wide readership, only individuals enjoying a certain degree of *auctoritas* themselves were in the position of reenacting the exploits listed in the text. That is, they would have used the accomplishments reported on the inscription as standards against which they could construct, measure, and expand their own *auctoritas*.

Augustus' *Res Gestae* can be described as a signal example of monumental writing which manifests its distance from poetry by pointing to writing practices performed by socially authoritative individuals and texts that had the power to sublate deeds and actions from the author's quotidian existence in such a way as to produce the perception that those actions were privileged in their scope and repercussions. Moreover, the *Res Gestae* helps us conceive how a text accrued social value when it excluded indiscriminate appropriations and allowed its socially authoritative author to enter the competitive arena of the Roman upper-class. And, if the study of Roman poetry has taught us something about the importance of form, the style of Augustus' *Res Gestae* exemplifies that Latin prose was not artless or natural; on the contrary, it deployed formalities that were perceived as a practical manifestation of *auctoritas*. For this reason, any serious work on Latin prose requires us to readjust the current notions of literature and song, and to consider the formation of Latin prose vis-à-vis its poetic counterpart.

If we understand literature solely as aesthetic writing, and if by aesthetic we mean only poetic, then the exclusion of Latin prose from the category of literature is inevitable. Likewise, if writing constitutes one of the ways in which speech is ritualized and turned into song, but only when it is used to produce a script for a performance to come, then a great number of prosaic texts will find no place in Habinek's classificatory system either. Such exclusionary conceptions of literature and song fail to account for the formal features of Latin prose and the social interpretation of the activities (including writing) that went into the construction of prose texts.

I contend that prose texts, like poems, were written objects that required a great deal of formal elaboration on the part of their authors. The same can be said about the nature of prose as song. Prose was marked speech by virtue of its association with socially authoritative individuals engaged in actions construed as extraordinary and, therefore, ritualized. Its textualization should thus be viewed as an equally extraordinary event and, once again, ritualized. What is difficult about Latin prose is that its formalities cannot be reduced to univocal and measurable schemes as these are based on the replication and invocation of speech patterns and behavioral templates associated with most diverse song types. Moreover, these replications and invocations were not affected by the same rules of social engagement and textual embodiment that loomed over poetry. In this sense, my study illustrates that the beginnings of Latin prose are interlaced with Cato's mastery and subordination of a wide range of cultural and social traditions in ways that did not limit but rather empowered a subjectivity that was, from the start, relatively more empowered than that of the poets. With this in mind, let me return briefly to Habinek's treatment of prose.

As I mentioned above, Habinek describes prose as emerging from the loosening of the bonds of song and the progressive limitation of the marked elements that characterize song. Habinek qualifies this description by way of pinpointing the entangled relation between the production of song and the order of the universe that Manilius unfolds in his work. Commenting on *Astronomica* 1.22–24, Habinek calls attention to use of *verba soluta* to mean words of prose. In relation to the order of the universe, Manilius understands them as "loosened from their own proper patterns"; in turn, he represents these patterns as those that connect words to the order of the cosmos, elaborating an interrelation that is as old as Roman song itself.[57] I would note, however, that Manilius' definition of prose rests upon two parallel ploys: the downgrading of prose to quotidian speech and the rounding up, if not equation, of poetry to song. In other words, Manilius disconnects metrical patterns from bodily constraints and augments their lesser social value by investing them with cosmological performativity. Yet, as Habinek notes, Manilius operated by "the dispensation of Caesar."[58] Consequently, measured against an "un-dispensed" notion of poetry, the phrase *verba soluta* stands for words that are unconstrained by the social and formal bonds of poetry and yet are tied to socially and formally ritualized practices. Paradoxically, one of Manilius' strongest claims, that the universe itself "desires to disclose the heavenly census through (his) songs" (*cupit aetherios per carmina pandere census,* 1.12), brings into view the instrumentality of poetry vis-à-vis the ritualized

---

57. Habinek 2005a: 92.
58. Habinek 2005a: 93.

terrain from which Latin prose sprouted and grew: his songs expose but do not affect the pecking order of the cosmos. As Manilius knew well, censorial practices were grounded in speech and writing practices, which, carried out by authoritative individuals (like Augustus), fell outside the poetic sphere. By observing prose from outside the narrow confines of the poetic, my study contributes to the reciprocal expansion and integration of literature and song as hermeneutical tools in at least two ways.

First, Habinek's distancing from the long-standing correlation of the term *carmen* with a primitive and unitary system of verbal ritualization calls attention to the urgency of rethinking Roman pre-poetic and non-poetic practices. Already in the late nineteen-sixties Bruno Luiselli noted that the surviving corpus of non-poetic and pre-poetic *carmina* is characterized by diverse types of linguistic formalization. Indeed, he distinguished between two registers of formalized speech according to their sphere of use. For Luiselli, the legal *carmina* appear to be less formalized and can be defined as "humble"; the religious *carmina,* on the other hand, are more formalized and, therefore, express a more "elevated" register. In the same study, Luiselli also pinpointed a stylistic evolution within each register and argued for the secondary relation of legal *carmina* to those falling within the area of the sacred, finding external corroboration in the *Tabulae Iguvinae*.[59]

Although one can contest that Luiselli's analysis suffers from a hierarchical and evolutionistic pattern typical of the Italian tradition, his study indicates that when looking onwards from an earlier period the term *carmen* relates to specific, albeit varied, strategies of speech formalization. Juxtaposing longer and shorter compositional segments, manipulating figures of sound, and stringing together two or three words are strategies that find no match in the Hellenistic tradition. Moreover, they characterize speech acts performed alongside and together with embodied activities that had the power of affecting reality in ways that poetry did not achieve on its own and that Habinek leaves unexplored. To be sure, the 'aura' that these strategies retained and accumulated over time and in spite of sociopolitical changes confirms that what is generically called '*carmen*-style' was perceived as a vital way of connecting the polity and its people to the cosmic whole that sustained them as well as an empowering ploy for objectifying reality for cognitive endorsement by all.[60] In this sense,

---

59. Luiselli 1969: 123–71. For the parallel with the Iguvian Tables, see especially pp. 168–71.

60. See Norden 1986: 172–73; Palmer 1961: 346–57; Timpanaro 1988: 257–61; von Albrecht 1989: 9–20; Courtney 1999: 1–11. I am here using the term 'aura' by referring to the

the fact that *carmen*-style was used outside the sphere of legitimate power (that is, magic largely speaking) and that this outside sphere was tightly policed constitute a signal expression of the performative potency that it was believed to possess.[61] Accordingly, the traces of *carmen*-style that we read in Cato's prose texts are better interpreted as the most visible (for us) signs of his achievement of *auctoritas* and his ability to uphold it. The practitioners of poetry would indeed mimic or parody this way of speaking and acting; however, the sociocultural value accorded to their mimetic acts was undercut by their lesser standing and by their exclusions from the most significant contexts of social performance. These included, among others, the speakers' platform in the forum, the Senate house, and the law courts.

Second, my analysis of early Latin prose in this book reveals that prose emerged out of a multiform process of expansion that stretched and extended the confines not simply of ritualized speech, but ritualized practices as well. By building on Lowrie, I suggest that thanks to its scriptic nature poetry offered new sociocultural possibilities by divorcing the speech act from its author and its original occasion. At the same time, however, I propose that the redeployment of the *carmen*-style outside the sphere of ritual by individuals enjoying *auctoritas* indicates an expansion and redeployment of social prerogatives and corresponding activities. As Elizabeth Meyer has recently demonstrated, one of these activities involved the production of *tabulae*. Embedded in actions undertaken on behalf of the legitimate and desired sociocosmological order, *tabulae* presented compositions bearing *carmen*-like features and constituted the final embodiments of the new reality that they helped create.[62] To retain their performative power, the uses of the *carmen*-style and the modes of textual production attached to them were guarded at all times. Nevertheless, the continuous creation of in-group hierarchies within the upper crust of Roman society required agents to invent ever new ways to make their speech acts special and their activities extraordinary. Prose, I argue, was both a consequence and an expression of these dynamics; but to compre-

---

meaning given by Walter Benjamin ([1936] 1969) in relation to the unique existence of a work of art within a particular context and by the history that it accumulates over time.

61. On this specific point, see most recently Meyer 2004: 103–7. In his recent thesis, Maxime Pierre (2008) argues that *carmen* is an utterance that carries its authority within itself, i.e., it has an authority that is not derived from the social authority of its author. I owe this reference to one of the readers for The Ohio State University Press; however, I have not been able to consult it myself. The first sign of policing the *carmen* is to be found in the so-called Twelve Tables (7.3).

62. Meyer 2004.

hend them one needs to remain open and inquisitive. In factual terms, it means that the closer a piece of prose resembles daily speech, the more one should be on the lookout for the alternative ploys of differentiation that are at work; the more prose formally reproduces socially lesser types of song, the more one needs to consider the hierarchies expressed by such mimetic appropriations; the more the modalities of prose text production are assimilated to poetic writing, the more we need to be wary of intra-elite relations and the stakes that such a ploy encodes.

Through a close analysis of the texts attributed to Cato the Censor, I tackle their link to preexisting authority-loaded practices and the then emerging tradition of poetry; at the same time, I investigate the sociohistorical contingencies that triggered the emergence of prose and shaped its impact. For a start, I delineate how Cato expanded linguistic and practical schemes associated with performances that took place in contexts permitting the sole participation of social agents engaged in the ruling, organization, and management of the community. Therefore, I pinpoint how he both displayed and augmented his achievement of *auctoritas* by using his ritual mastery and by stretching the spatial and temporal boundaries of the ritualized activities that sustained the construction of his own *auctoritas*. Second, I describe how Cato disavowed the encroaching presence of poets and other alien cultural agents in the life of the Roman ruling class and yet took hold of cultural forms introduced by them in such a way as to propose cultural mastery over alien and socially lesser cultural traditions as an added expression of *auctoritas*. A corollary to this twofold ploy was Cato's redeployment of writing from censorial, legislative, and pontifical activities. Although everyone acknowledges that the Romans had long engaged in these writing practices, their impact on our understanding of the Roman literary phenomenon and the generic distinction between poetry and prose is often overlooked by those who, in the last two decades, have engaged in the debate over the so-called "invention of Latin literature."

"The Invention of Latin Literature"
Orthodoxies, Debates, and Models

To a certain extent, the discussion about the emergence of a literature in Latin that is going on in the Anglo-(North) American scene of classics finds its starting point in Nevio Zorzetti's publication of two articles in the early nineteen-nineties. In these articles, Zorzetti discussed the scholarly debate of the previous one hundred years and encouraged a renewed look at the *carmina convivalia* evoked by Cato the Censor and a few later authors.[63] On the basis of these evocations, Zorzetti argued that B. G. Niebuhr was wrong to think that they had anything to do with epic lays or ballads belonging to a popular tradition; rather, they were linked to a musical culture supported by clusters of aristocrats joined together in *sodalitates*. By comparing them to the Greek *hetaireiai* (aristocratic drinking clubs), he suggested that the *sodalitates* elaborated an exclusive lore of exemplary memories and a didactic system expressed in musical forms and enacted during their convivial gatherings. In this sense, the scraps of *sententiae* and *praecepta* that are often associated with the figure of the *vates* and that come to us either anonymously or attached to specific names or proverbialized in popular tradition are a manifestation of the system of *sapientia* articulated in those exclusive contexts.[64] Moreover, Zorzetti pointed to a cultural evolution coinciding with the formation of the *nobilitas*, the new political class that emerged after the so-called Struggle of the Orders in the fourth century B.C.E.[65] The valorization of individual achievements in the service of the *res publica* and the increasing importance of public recognition reshaped the cultural practices previously linked to the *sodalitates* and their *convivia*. The cultural forms that until then had exclusively been produced, circulated, and transmitted within convivial settings by *sodalitates*, were now diverted to the public space of the *urbs*.

Zorzetti described this shift in this way:

> public life absorbed a remarkable number of elements which had previously existed within the closed traditions of *sodalitates*, and were not displayed in the public sphere. The heroes, cults, and values of the *gentes* became the property of the State and of the people. . . . Roman oral traditions then experienced their homeostatic adjustment, in the selection and superimposition of earlier memories . . . and also in their enrichment through the competition between the *nobiles* to contribute each from his own traditions to the image of the city.[66]

---

63. Specifically for a survey of the scholarly debate, see Zorzetti [1984] 1990: 289–95.

64. For *sententiae* and *praecepta* attached to names, Zorzetti ([1984] 1990: 300) quotes App. Cl. fr.6 Morel; for the anonymous ones, *Inc. Sent.* Morel p. 6. For those passed into the popular tradition, Zorzetti ([1984] 1990: 304 and note 43) cites Horace, *Epist.* 1.1.62, Gellius 4.5, Macrobius, *Sat.* 5.20.18.

65. For a discussion of this term and a view on the historical and ideological formation of the so-called *nobilitas*, see Hölkeskamp 2004: 11–48.

66. Zorzetti [1984] 1990: 302.

Zorzetti named this phenomenon "theatralization" and argued that the invention of the curule aedileship, the organization of the *Ludi Romani* in 366 B.C.E., and the *ludi scaenici* in 364 B.C.E. are indicative of the civic appropriation of cultural resources belonging to the *gentes* and their *sodalitates*.[67] Moreover, he proposed that at that time the members of the ruling group or possibly their *iuvenes* became involved in the rituals themselves.[68] In other words, Zorzetti maintained that even in the new political configuration, the *sodalitates* upheld their social distinction through rights of cultural production, performance, and preservation. Social distinction was guaranteed because the ruling class organized these public festivals and co-opted the performers from its ranks; in turn, the festivals conspicuously alluded to the exclusive possession of resources that made individual contributions and the performance of rituals possible in the first place. In other words, the "spectacles" demonstrated that each performer belonged to the privileged class by making visible to the whole *urbs* that he had access to the exclusive lore, the *sapientia,* that sustained the community. In a way, the *nobilitas* generated and enacted a collective representation, an "imagined community" (the *res publica populi romani*) that they shared with the *populus* as viewer.[69] The *populus,* on the other hand, watched its rulers performing the lore of the city and, by virtue of their watching, legitimated its rulers' assertions of authority and power. Finally, Zorzetti concluded that after "theatralization," the more sophisticated Hellenistic music, represented by the early Latin poets, replaced traditional music so that the decline of the previous aristocratic lyric culture intersected with the beginning of "the age of the Hellenistic professionals."[70]

In his 1998 *The Politics of Latin Literature* Habinek built upon Zorzetti by proposing that the emergence of Latin literature in the second half of the third and first half of the second centuries B.C.E. should be conceived as a cultural revolution aimed at redressing the "identity crisis" that troubled the ruling aristocracy at the time.[71] Confronted by the numerous challenges to its authority generated by Rome's transformation from a city-state to an imperial capital, the ruling aristocracy supported a cultural shift, which

---

67. For the *Ludi Romani,* see Dion. Hal. 7.70–73, and for the description of the *pompa circensis,* see Fabius Pictor, fr.16 P2. For the *origines scaenicae* as presented by Livy 7.2.8–13 and Livy 6.42, see Zorzetti [1984] 1990: 295–98.

68. For the participation of young aristocrats, besides Livy 7.2, see also Dion. Hal. 7.71 at least for the performance of the *Salii* and Valerius Maximus 1.1.9.

69. For the concept of 'imagined communities,' see the classic treatment of Anderson 1991.

70. Zorzetti [1984] 1990: 305.

71. Habinek 1998a: 34–68; "identity crisis": 35.

Habinek calls "a revolution in the sociology of literary production" and defines in the following way:

> Three developments define this revolution: reliance on writing, professionalization of performance, and importation of performers. Whereas archaic literary culture seems to have been characterized by performances that were not necessarily transmitted in writing, the new culture was intimately connected with the preservation, importation, and circulation of texts.[72]

This new culture benefited the ruling aristocracy in two complementary ways: by codifying an exclusively aristocratic tradition and by valorizing this tradition against other sources of authority. But although literature eventually helped resolve the aristocracy's malady, at least initially it clashed against and competed with pre-existing forms of acculturation. These were oral in nature and hinged on the aristocratic and musical tradition envisioned by Zorzetti.[73]

In his 2005 review article of the *Handbuch der Lateinischen Literatur der Antike. Erster Band: Die Archaische Literatur* published in 2002 and edited by Werner Saurbaum, Denis Feeney identifies Zorzetti and Habinek as the promoters of a paradigm change and the founders of a 'new orthodoxy.'[74] For Feeney, the German handbook participates in it by drawing on the same alluring but faulty analogy between archaic Greece and Rome, and prospers from a model of development from oral to literate imported from Greek studies. Feeney interprets this paradigm shift as a return to a nineteenth-century style of scholarship that, by deferentially mimicking Hellenism, has as its goal the recovery of "the same spontaneity and authenticity wistfully imagined in Greek culture."[75] Consequently, he sweeps the issue of the *carmina convivalia* aside and capitalizes on the works of Hellfried Dahlmann and Nicholas Horsfall in order to offer the following methodological prospect: later authors, being in a position of ignorance similar to ours, constructed what was 'before literature' either by analogizing or by calquing Greek accounts.[76] Thus, Feeney observes that even if the search for an original Roman culture may not be its driving principle, the 'new orthodoxy' does not do anything more or less than embrace an interpretative model that was in place already in antiquity.

---

72. Habinek 1998a: 36–37.
73. Habinek 1998a: 34–68.
74. See also Gildenhard 2003b.
75. Feeney 2005: 233–35.
76. Feeney 2005: 234–35. Dahlmann 1950; Horsfall 1994: 50–75, repeated in Horsfall 2003: 33, 72–73, 96–98.

Moving towards the *pars construens* of his review, Feeney calls attention to and elaborates on the pitfalls that derive from stressing the continuity between the pre-literary and the literary periods and from disregarding Rome's Italian connections. To claim historical continuity obscures the fact that "no society in the ancient world other than the Romans took over the prototypical forms of the institution of Greek literature as the basis for a corresponding institution in their own vernacular."[77] Lack of historical contextualization, on the other hand, suppresses the fact that Rome had been running an empire for at least a generation 'before literature' and that in mid-Italy Greek culture had long enjoyed a high prestige.[78] Accordingly, he proposes an alternative definition of originality and points to a number of phenomena, which—he correctly warns—can be easily simplified or homogenized.[79] To drive his point home, Feeney underscores the Romans' oscillating relationship with Greek culture as representative of 'otherness' and invokes Emma Dench's work to comment upon the way in which they could take up or put down the Greek role to distinguish themselves from the other Italians or to culturally promote themselves in relation to the Greeks. For Feeney, the initial lack of participation in the new literature by the Roman governing class is a signal expression of mirroring/distancing dynamics similar to those deployed by Taussig in his work on the Cuna Indians.[80] Moreover, Feeney looks back to his 1998 book *Literature and Religion at Rome* and spends a few words on the poets themselves; they were the multilingual *semigreci* who, by coming from Greek, Oscan, Messapian, and Umbrian towns, in fact created Latin literature. Borrowing Mary Louise Pratt's concept of 'contact zone,' Feeney remarks that these poets explored the interstices between the competing cultures of central and southern Italy.[81] He concludes by describing the poets as 'cultural brokers' who, by moving outwards from Greek culture, acted at its margins as mediating agents at a time of heightened cultural exchange.[82]

The overall tone of Feeney's criticism is symptomatic of how, in this debate, rifts and splits come to be created: each new contribution grows stronger by targeting others and by deconstructing their methodological weaknesses. To a certain extent, the pattern is very much in line with an existing trend that, as Barchiesi points out, responds to the pressures put

---

77. Feeney 2005: 230.
78. Feeney 2005: 231, 238.
79. Feeney 2005: 239.
80. Feeney 2005: 237–39; Dench 1995; Taussig 1993.
81. Feeney 2005: 239 citing Pratt 1992.
82. Feeney 2005: 239, deriving the phrase "cultural brokers" from Woolf 1998.

on professional academics since the late nineteen-seventies to discover something new. Because in the field of classics, the chances of finding fresh material are undoubtedly slim, the solution has been a compromise: to oppose and innovate upon the approaches and ideas of the previous generation.[83] In the field of Roman studies, where we witness even among younger classicists a strong interest in finding new ways to interconnect historicisms and formalisms, those who dare to participate in the debate over the beginnings of Latin literature need to deal with some added complications.[84] In this respect, Feeney's intervention makes clear that the formation of intradebate 'orthodoxies' has much to do with establishing the value of two sets of evidence, that is, what does not find an explicit expression in the literary archive and what falls outside the poetic. As for the first set of evidence, Feeney is at his best when, in unravelling the fallacies that go along with using Greek *comparanda,* he reconsiders the literary and linguistic work achieved by the earlier poets in the backdrop of Rome's Italian connections. As for the second, his renewed allegiance to 'literature' as a fully suitable hermeneutical tool and his narrow focus on poetry displaces the pathbreaking work of Erich Gruen and Sander Goldberg in the early nineteen-nineties and the areas of investigation that Habinek's *The Politics of Latin Literature* has opened up in the last ten years or so.

Differing somewhat in their approach to the sources (sociohistorical and literary, respectively), Gruen and Goldberg used the works of the early poets to make a case for the uncontested emergence of Roman culture in the Hellenistic world as an offshoot of military successes. Rather than being careless of Greek cultural achievements, Gruen maintained that the Romans exploited Greek culture as a means of enriching their own cultural heritage and as a foil for articulating a specifically Roman "national identity." In doing so, Gruen was able to counter the notion that the early poets served the needs of individual households or political factions and to argue that there were never philhellenic and antihellenic parties or movements in the first place.[85] By expanding on Gruen's contribution, Goldberg focused on epic and qualified the partnership between poets and the elite as one resting on the same communal intents and intellectual endeavors: "Roman aristocrats provided the subject and much of the audience of early poetry. The poets' claim to strength lay not just in recounting their achievements

---

83. A. Barchiesi 2005: 137.
84. For a sign of this interest, see "Historicisms and Formalisms," a Graduate Student Conference held on April 25, 2008 and organized by the Princeton Graduate Students. Website: http://www.princeton.edu/~classics/conferences/2008/histform.
85. Gruen 1990: 79–123.

but in creating a context that declared and confirmed their significance."[86]

The greatest merit of Gruen's work was to reevaluate Cato the Censor's ambivalence towards the Greeks and their culture. Goldberg added to it by calling attention to the aesthetic qualities of early Roman epic in a field that at the time was dominated by the study of Augustan poetry. What seems to have been forgotten in the last decade or so is that the picture drawn by Gruen and Goldberg levels out the fraught accounts that we have about the activities of individual poets (Naevius, in particular) and the expressions of resistance voiced by Cato the Censor through the invocation of ancestral convivial practices. For Gruen, Cato invoked these practices to oppose Hellenistic poses which, adopted by some members of the elite, did not match the Roman character and were opposed to the construction of a specifically Roman identity.[87] Goldberg, on the other hand, rejected their historicity together with Niebhur's hypothesis and Macaulay's elaboration of 'bardic ballads' and moved his attention to the Ciceronian context in which Cato's evocation is couched.[88]

Although sharing with Gruen and Goldberg the notion that language and literature are concerned with constituting national identity, Habinek gave further attention to the intimate relationship of literature with the Roman elite by emphasizing their acculturating work.[89] His attention to semantic details in specific textual contexts helped him show that the professionalization of culture, the creation of a literary dialect, the invention of a moral and cultural tradition, and the expropriation of Greek symbolic capital were not uncontested after all.[90] Moreover, he located the primal scene of Latin literature outside the poetic and argued that the process of evaluation that it claimed as its main feature is instantiated in the Preface to Cato's *De Agricultura*. For Habinek, Cato lifted the etymological association of *existimo* "I appraise" from the semantic area of economic calculation and constructed for it the metaphorical meaning of "I judge, determine" in the new area of literature in such a way as to replace *laudo* "I praise," a verb squarely connected with pre-literary convivial practices. In so doing, Cato manifested the tensions produced by a deep cultural anxiety over the ambiguity of value. At the same time, he established a disparity between aristocratic evaluation and mercantile practices attached to other social groups.[91]

---

86. Goldberg 1995: 30–37, 113–25.
87. Gruen 1992: 52–83.
88. Goldberg 1995: 46.
89. For Habinek's understanding of language, literature, and national identity see, Habinek 1998a: 44–45.
90. Habinek 1998a: 39 with reference to Cicero, *Brut.* 71.
91. Habinek 1998a: 46–50.

The greatest and least remarked merit of Habinek's argument was to point to prose as a neglected area of inquiry. Indeed, by repositioning a largely misapprehended text like the *De Agricultura,* he called attention to the emergence of prose as something more than an epiphenomenon of poetry or, worse, as a somewhat infelicitous literary experiment.[92] In turn, he raised the value of early Latin prose as a cultural form worthy of study in its own right and revealed that when its earliest attestations come into the picture the literary phenomenon assumes very different contours; as a result, the ability to interpret this phenomenon becomes tantamount to the willingness to push further the terms of the discussion and step outside familiar ground.

Looking at Early Latin Poetry through Cato's Prose

As I mentioned above, the unsuitability of Greek precedents as methodological *comparanda* has been remarked upon in various ways in relation to both the question of the *carmina convivalia* and the shift from oral to literate to which it has been applied. What has not been said is that the same holds true for many aspects of the Roman cultural tradition and for reasons that have less to do with its constant engagement with Hellenism than with the methodological predicaments that this engagement produces. Put in extreme terms, any Greek pattern or motif that we find in the Latin literary materials is the product of a cultural and linguistic reprocessing that makes better sense if we take into account the sociocultural hierarchies of legitimation that loomed over the choices available to their authors at the time of their production. This is not to say that Greek literary practices had no capacity to offer alternative or even contrasting spaces for reflecting on the world at any given time or that they have no explanatory value for understanding these materials. To be more precise, it means looking beyond and around the poetic in an attempt to identify and assess more accurately the complicated dynamics of mirroring and distancing that, as Feeney points out, structure both the early formation and the history of Latin literature.

Enlarging our purview on late-third- and early-second centuries B.C.E. Rome need not involve forging an originary Latin matrix or proposing a de-Hellenized account of Rome's cultural history. Rather, it helps address the perplexity that arises when we encounter textual materials bearing fea-

---

92. See Astin 1978: 198 and more recently Dalby (1998: 22), who defines Cato's *De Agricultura* as an "irritating handbook."

tures that do not easily fit Greek precedents and that encompass a polemical resistance to the near contemporary emergence of Hellenized cultural forms in Latin. Methodologically, to approach these materials without the support of Greek models is rather uncomfortable, mostly because the textual tradition of (say) the *Odyssey* or the Greek lyrics, however discontinuous, legitimates an untroubled conceptualization of their poetic counterparts in Rome.[93] Granted that, it is clear that when the varied nature of Roman cultural forms is interrogated from outside the comfort zone of the Hellenistic frameworks, to define the specificity of Latin literature becomes a thorny business and to locate its beginnings an elusive task.

As a longstanding participant in the discussion, Goldberg takes up the latter challenge in his *Constructing Literature in the Roman Republic: Poetry and Its Reception*. By focusing on poetry alone, Goldberg proposes that 'literature' did not exist at Rome before a sufficiently large and critically sophisticated reading public emerged, and until the available texts had been collected, commented upon, and canonized. For Goldberg, this process culminated with figures like Cicero and Varro, but was initiated and carried forth by rhetoricians and teachers who showed aristocratic readers how to appreciate and use them for their own purposes. Thus, he argues throughout that "when Cicero refers to *litterae,* he often means 'literature' in something very much like the modern sense of texts marked by a certain social status, where literary denotes not simply an inherent aesthetic value but a value accorded them and the work they do by the society that receives them."[94] Contributing to a renewed discussion about the performance dimension of Roman comedy, Goldberg pays special attention to the transformation of dramatic texts from mere scripts for performance to literary (i.e., organized and canonized) materials meant to be consumed by a reading public.[95] In the process, he adds to the discussion concerning the *carmina convivalia* and Roman epic.

First of all, Goldberg contends that the archaeological remains cannot help us come to terms with the historicity of the *carmina convivalia* evoked (but never heard) by Cato, nor do they allow us to prove that the early Romans had anything like a 'sympotic culture' from which literary epic developed. Second, by sifting through the argumentative layers that make up Cicero's testimony, he emphasizes that Cicero is the one responsible for making the *carmina convivalia* invoked by Cato in the

---

93. In this respect, the response to Habinek's *Roman Song* written by Feeney and Katz (2006) resonates with undue bitterness.
94. Goldberg 2005: 18.
95. For a thorough reassessment of the textual nature of comic scripts, see Marshall 2006.

Origines the progenitors of epic. Finally, Goldberg reads a fragment from the *carmen de moribus* (preserved in Gellius 11.2.5) where Cato conjures up ancestral judgments to form an attack on poetic encroachments on banquets alongside Polybius' moralizing passage about the extravagance that the young Scipio Aemilianus avoided (Polyb. 31.25.5). Through their juxtaposition, he proposes that the *convivia* that both Cato and Polybius so strongly criticized could not have been the sites for the performance of epic, either before or after the late third century B.C.E., as Jörg Rüpke has it.[96] Accordingly, he concludes that in the early second century B.C.E. poetry was receiving respect and that Livius Andronicus, Naevius, and Ennius provided a model for the later construction of Latin literature thanks to "their inherent merits and the consciousness of their achievement."[97]

Goldberg's intervention complicates the applicability of the category 'literature' to late-third- and early-second-century B.C.E. cultural practices.[98] At the same time, it denies validity to the archaeological record for gauging the historicity of Cato's *carmina convivalia* and their relationship with literary epic. Methodologically, Goldberg's interpretative project carries some important assumptions. Foremost among them is the idea that 'literature' comes to exist and becomes socially relevant only when texts undergo a certain type of reading and are accorded a certain type of value. Such an assumption remains a viable and worthy point of departure for a historicizing inquiry into an attitude towards texts that is relevant to us classicists; however, it is unsatisfactory when references to other cultural forms are rejected because they are not germane to our historicizing projects. While it is true that we will never be in the position to construct exact narratives about the content and form of early Roman convivial songs, it is nevertheless hard to deny the testimonial value that the archaeological remains hold. Although nowhere proving the historicity of Cato's evocations (in fact, this is their least important aspect), they do bear witness to a long existing, even if varied, relationship between aristocratic status and exclusive banqueting.[99] In this respect, the archaeological data help us see that archaic Rome was part of a cultural *koinè* that, by including Etruria and Latium, was founded on the gentilician organization of society. In this society the *convivium* was constituted as something distinguished

---

96. Rüpke 2000.
97. Goldberg 2005: 1–19; citation from p.15. As for speculations about epic's early reception, see Goldberg 2005: 22–28.
98. Goldberg 2005: 19. See also the review by Farrell 2007.
99. See Zaccaria-Ruggiu (2003) for a thorough discussion of the material evidence also in relation to the spaces allocated to the *convivium* within the house. For a more general discussion, see Habinek 2005a: 40–43.

from everyday eating and drinking through the strategic and ever changing combination of actions, songs, and objects. By these same means, the *convivium* concretized the prerogatives and responsibilities of a peer group composed of heads of *gentes* by entitling it to a disproportionate share of the community's resources.[100] The visual representations of *convivia* found in the so-called Second Regia at Murlo (590–580 B.C.E.) and the terracottas known as the type Roma-Veio-Velletri (530–525 B.C.E.) give substance to the centrality of convivial practices by featuring not only food and drinking but also performances of songs and players of musical instruments. Moreover, these scenes are part of complex cycles and occupy a position as relevant as depictions of races, weddings, assemblies of seated individuals, and arrayed armed men. As such, these materials testify both to the enduring centrality that the *convivium* enjoyed in central Italy for the definition of the aristocracy and the paradigmatic role that the practices of this aristocracy played in the structuring of social relations.[101] In light of these precedents, the fact that poetry figures in the early second century B.C.E. debate over conspicuous consumption and in connection with convivial practices is not at all surprising. Indeed, it suggests that in some elite quarters poetry was perceived as a practice that upset intra-elite relations and created in-group disproportions that affected the rest of society. This perception prompts a more nuanced understanding of Cato's invocation of ancestral banqueting and makes evident that the tendency to polarize the discussion in terms of oral versus literary does not do justice to ancient preoccupations. The notion of 'scenario' developed by Diana Taylor offers in this respect a practical way out for returning to the ancient materials with a less restrictive attitude.

For Taylor a 'scenario' is an embodied repertoire of cultural imaginings or schemes that are associated with physical locations. Formulaic and portable in nature, the schemes that make up a scenario have the power of structuring environments, behaviors, and practices; as such, they can also engender most diverse cultural expressions (poems, narratives, performances, films, and so on). These schemes remain powerful at each reactivation and remain so irrespective of whether or not they are 'mediatized' through objects, bodies, or texts. Furthermore, each reactivation of a

---

100. Habinek 2005a: 43. For a most recent reassessment of the *gentes,* see Smith 2006; for the role played by the *gentes* in the formation of city-states and their endurance throughout Rome's history, see Terrenato 1998; 2000; 2001; 2006; 2007.

101. Zaccaria-Ruggiu 2003: 18–19 and *passim* with thorough iconographic analyses. Cf. also remarks by Grandazzi 1997: 188–89. More on the Roman banquet can be found in Dupont 1999: 104–10.

scenario presents different combinations of formulaic elements while the manipulations that occur from one reactivation to another make visible or invisible societal anxieties as well as individual accommodations. Thus, Taylor explains:

> The discoverer, conqueror, 'savage,' and native princess, for example, might be staple characters in many Western scenarios. Sometimes they are written down as scripts, but the scenario predates the script and allows for many possible "endings." Sometimes, people may actually undertake adventures to live the glorious fantasy of possession. Others may tune in regularly to television shows along the lines of *Survivor* or *Fantasy Island.* The scenario structures our understanding . . . [the] framework allows for occlusions; by positioning our perspective, it promotes certain views while helping to disappear others. In the *Fantasy Island* scenario, for example, we might be encouraged to overlook the displacement and disappearance of native peoples, gender exploitation, environmental impact, and so on.[102]

Borrowing from Taylor, I understand Cato's invocation of ancestral convivial practices as the activation of a commanding scenario. Featuring a peer group composed of elite males, this scenario envisions them reclining at a banquet and performing in turn, without the mediation of texts and with outsiders excluded. By using this scenario as a benchmark, I follow the trajectory followed by poets and poetry from the volatile spaces of drama to more exclusive sites of social interaction. Viewed through the lenses of the convivial scenario, the linguistic and metrical recodification pursued by the poets, their intertextual allusions, and their strategies of self-presentation emerge as embodied ploys mediated by texts and deeply implicated in histories of geographical displacement and social affirmation. While it has been argued that, because of its fictional nature, poetry eschews any identification of the persona with the author, I propose that fictionality constituted one of the ways in which the poets could stretch the boundaries that limited their social agency.[103] In this sense, the convivial scenario invoked by Cato helps us analyze individual positionings in relation and in contrast to one another and in such a way as to remain sensitive

---

102. Taylor 2003: 28. Because Taylor does not state it explicitly, I find it important to stress that the last twenty years have witnessed an increasing interest in precisely the nature and workings of 'embodied schemes.' See especially Bourdieu 1990; M. Johnson 1990; Lakoff and Johnson 1999; Lakoff 2008.

103. Edmunds 2001: 37.

to the authoritarian nature of Roman social hierarchies at a specific time.[104] This is because the use of scenario as a methodological tool allows us to keep an eye on the critical distance that stands between the social actor and the cultural representations that he produces or the social actor and the patterns of behaviors attached to his standing in relation and in contrast to the ways other social agents handled the same distances. Clearly, every reconstruction of an overall picture joining together heterogeneous handlings of formalized languages and embodied schemes, and the parallel mapping of how these handlings intersected with the fluidity of Roman social relations remains just that, a reconstruction. Even so, through this reconstruction we will have identified a network of positions that relate to one another and capture the varied correlation between social subjectivity and cultural agency.

In chapter 2 I reconsider the formation of the Roman poetic tradition. By stressing that poetry was a practice linked to individuals relocated just like the texts that they translated, I suggest that the rhythmical, generic, and linguistic recodification that the poets performed bears the signs of their 'migratory subjectivity.' In the mid-nineteen-nineties Carol Boyce Davies coined this notion to describe black women's writings and to emphasize how moving across geographical and cultural boundaries can be itself an empowering and liberatory process.[105] By using this phrase, I aim to move away from discourses of cultural inferiority and superiority, center and periphery, to focus on the construction of poetic agency in relation to geographical and linguistic displacements as well as local negotiations and relocations across social divides. To sustain my argument, I concentrate on Plautine metatheatricality and the fictional character of the clever slave. Ultimately, I suggest that they both constituted mimetic spaces for reflecting on diverse social subjectivities and cultural agencies vis-à-vis the hegemonic and expansionistic drive of the Roman ruling class. A close look into the virtuoso and scriptic dimensions of Livius Andronicus' translation of Homer's *Odyssey* concludes the chapter and serves to lay the foundations for a renewed approach to epic.

In chapter 3 I turn to the epics of Naevius and Ennius. The concern with authorship that these poems communicate calls for a more detailed

---

104. As McCarthy (2000: 18–19) nicely puts it, "Roman society is fractured by division within divisions within divisions, each one marking out difference as well as marking out a hierarchical relation. These mutually complicating divisions include gender, juridical status, census, rank, geographical provenance, wealth, and cultural/intellectual achievement. Furthermore, each of these bases of assigning value . . . establishes a finely calibrated scale on which each person is placed above some and below others."

105. Davies 1994.

inquiry into the relationship between authorship and authority. One of my arguments is that, from the poets' perspective, epic was appealing not only because it boasted an enduring tradition in the Greek world but also because it envisioned solo performances and scenarios in which the figure of the poet is endowed with the faculty of deploying elite memories. Accordingly, I propose that the reprocessing of Greek epic allowed the poets who operated in Rome to negotiate their entrance into more exclusive spheres of social exchange and to manipulate elite desires of self-representation to their own advantage. In this sense, the idea that the early epic poems were born as scripts performed by their authors in social settings envisioning a chosen public takes nothing away from the likelihood that they were also objects of more public or private readings, nor does it jeopardize the value of our own reading practices in any way. After all, Goldberg's argument about the later construction of Latin literature as a practice centered on the reading and explication of these texts carried out by both authors and rhetoricians confirms that early poetry envisioned performances based on scripts across the board.[106]

Cato's ethnicized understanding of *litterae* deserves, in my view, as much attention as Cicero's for what it reveals about second century B.C.E. More broadly, Cato's distrust of the Greeks and his citations from Greek literature, his likely sponsorship of Ennius and his opposition to the progressive encroachment of poets on elite life emerge as some of the most visible signs of a larger and complex love affair between rulers and their 'others'. This love affair involved reciprocal mirroring, making the rulers' subjection of their 'others' problematic and the definition of authority both profound and disturbing. This is because, when mimicry comes into play, authority becomes increasingly dependent on strategic limitations expressed within the authoritative realm that are successful only in the measure that they enable the transformation of mimicked subjects into objects to be possessed.[107]

The formal analysis of Cato's prose that I pursue in chapter 4 reveals that as a *homo novus,* Cato compensated for his lack of an aristocratic past by exploiting the *carmen* tradition and by aligning his self-advancement with a series of relationships and oppositions that, by transcending the ordinary, invoked the coherence of the socio-cosmological order and vacated its aristocratic ascendency of familial specificity.[108] But Cato had also a vested interest in mimetic appropriations of alien and lesser traditions as ploys for

---

106. Based on Suetonius, *gramm.* 1.1.
107. See Bhabha 1994: 121–44.
108. On this aspect, see Blösel 2000.

constantly expanding his exercise of *auctoritas*. His expertise in handling different strategies of formalization helped Cato construct the self-assertions of his peers as divorced from the past and to represent their increasing reliance on nonelite cultural agents as an indication of failed mastery and, therefore, inability to rule. Viewed in this way, Cato's prose bears the signs of competing subjectivities even while signaling his practical ability to integrate and hierarchize very diverse cultural materials, practices, and frameworks through complex oppositions and homologies.

To acknowledge the embodied dimension of these dynamics as I do does not mean to give up our philological analyses; rather, it entails approaching written materials without stumbling on the slippery implications of extended analogies based on hyperliterary conceptualizations of textuality and the aesthetic. My analysis of how the formalities that characterize Cato's prose fold the body into the text illustrates that the 'aesthetic' or the 'literary' are not intrinsic or superior qualities; rather, they are two strategies among many whose relevance needs to be articulated in culturally and chronologically specific terms. For this reason, any inquiry into early-second-century B.C.E. Roman cultural practices cannot be deemed satisfactory unless the textuality of Cato's prose is taken fully into account vis-à-vis other types of textuality.

As I mentioned above, in his *Politics of Latin Literature* Habinek locates the primal scene of Latin literature in the Preface to the *De Agricultura* where the process of *existimatio* both evokes and replaces ancestral evaluative practices attached to *laudare* and the aristocratic *convivium*.[109] Thus, he explains:

> While *existimare* at an earlier stage of linguistic and cultural development means "to set a price on," in the concrete sense of assigning a monetary value, it now comes to signify assessment by the vaguer and more easily manipulable standards of goodness (*bonus*), reputability (*honestus*), and largesse (*amplissime*). Cato assigns to the inevitably controversial and ambiguous determination of a man's worth the simplicity of an economic evaluation. Yet in so doing he seeks also to establish a disparity between aristocratic *existimatio* and the tawdry processes of exchange and evaluation characteristic of other groups in society.[110]

While pointing in the right direction, Habinek's narrow focus on the economic meaning of *existimare* obscures its relationship with the specific

---
109. Habinek 1998a: 46–50.
110. Habinek 1998a: 49.

textuality of Cato's prose. Though highly fragmentary, the Preface to the *Origines,* the other foundational work attributed to Cato, amplifies the concept of *existimatio*.[111] On the one hand, Cato builds upon his invocation of convivial songs and the exclusivity of the convivial scenario; on the other hand, he likens texts produced by *viri clari* and *magni* to the financial accounts (*rationes*) that male Roman citizens wrote on *tabulae* and presented to the censor. Through this twofold strategy, Cato acted on his attainment of *auctoritas* and extended his privileged experience with the census beyond the confines of the ritualized actions and words that gave substance to its markedness. During the taking of the census, the *rationes* embodied the ability of male Roman citizens to manage their households and constituted the means by which these men were accorded responsibilities and privileges.[112] In the *Origines,* Cato conceives of *rationes* as texts meant to embody the words and actions of eminent men and to offer, like ancestral convivial songs, practical standards against which new generations of elite men could construct, measure, and expand their *auctoritas*. Ultimately, with the *Origines* we are projected into a world where writing did not stand in opposition to song, but it was the means whereby patterned words and actions, once textualized, were cast beyond the ordinary. In this respect, Cato's prose writing illustrates that textualization is not a linear process of evolution and that literature is neither a natural outcome nor, finally, a monomorphic phenomenon.

Chapter 5 builds upon what we read in the Preface to the *Origines* and explores how Cato's prose writings ultimately dovetail with what I call 'transcriptions.' As opposed to scripting, I show that transcription has to do with a type of *post-*performance textualization that allows the author to keep his *auctoritas* as a social agent performatively in play. My account of how Cato constructed his transcribing practices demonstrates also that these were not only an expression of his resistance to the encroachment of alien and nonelite professionals on the life of the elite. They were also purveyed as a resolution to the anxieties that derived from extending one's *auctoritas* through texts liable to be appropriated by an undifferentiated public and as a counterplay to those who, like Scipio Africanus, left no self-authorized memorials of their outstanding existence.

---

111. For general discussions of the *Origines,* see Sciarrino 2004a and Gotter 2009. A new edition of the fragments meant to replace Peter [1906] 1914 is in preparation under the direction of Tim Cornell. In this book I follow the edition of Cugusi and Sblendorio Cugusi 2001.

112. On census-taking and writing involved see generally, Nicolet 1980: 48–88; Lemosse 1949: 177; Gargola 1995: 76–77. On the marked aspect of writing on *tabulae,* see Meyer 2004: 91–92; on ritualized forms of reading, see Valette-Cagnac 1997.

I have organized the subject matter of this book into chapters that can be read in isolation so that the reader can exercise a certain degree of freedom; however, it is together that they make sense as a larger effort to map diverse positionings towards formalities and textualities in relation to social hierarchies and subjectivities. What follows in no way pretends to be an exhaustive account of early poetic and prosaic forms. My choice to focus on comedy and epic at the near exclusion of other poetic forms derives from the fact that in the former case we are lucky enough to have entire scripts and in the latter case the poets' engrossment with authorship merges with the special interest that epic enjoys in Latin studies. In reality, a more rounded account of early Roman poetry should include *fabulae praetextae* and *cothurnatae,* satire, the fable, and other even more obscure and highly fragmentary works (like, for example, Ennius' rendering of Archestratos' *Hedypatheia* or the *Euhemerus*). Likewise, my account of Cato's prose does not deal in detail with the content of his orations, the variegated compositions that make up the *De Agricultura* and the *Origines,* or, finally, with a number of writings generally bracketed under the rubric of *commentarii.* As I say at the beginning, my main goal with this book is to solicit new reflections on the complexity of the Roman literary tradition and to set the scene for a collective effort towards overcoming rifts and orthodoxies.

Chapter 2

Under the Roman Sun
Poets, Rulers, Translations, and Power

The most useful fact arising from the debate concerning the 'invention of Latin literature' is that the notion of a sudden fascination of an inferior (Roman) culture for a superior (Greek) one is no longer tenable. Not only does this notion rest upon a very essentialist understanding of culture and ethnicity, it also denies complexity to the intercultural exchanges that had been in place in Italy well before the end of the third century B.C.E. The archeological record has long demonstrated that, just as the Etruscans and other Italic populations, the Romans were greatly affected by Greek culture at large since at least the late eighth century B.C.E. The princely tombs of Etruria, Latium, and Campania, for example, speak of a very mobile aristocratic network which included the Greek colonies and whose hallmarks were conspicuous display and ownership of land.[1] In this context, the manufacture of pottery and metalwork shows throughout that the Hellenizing style was not perceived as something foreign and superior to be caught up with; rather, it was a common language that each craftsman interpreted in his own way.[2] In turn, Central Italy did not exist beyond the Greek horizon. From the sixth century B.C.E. onwards, the Romans and their neighbors featured large in both Greek poetry and prose.[3]

---

1. For a general discussion, see Cornell 1995: 81–118.
2. Holliday 2002: 7. For a sensible overview, see also Pallottino 1981 and, more recently, Cornell and Lomas 1997.
3. A concise and useful chronological survey is to be found now in Wiseman 2007b.

Over the course of the third century B.C.E., however, Rome's relationship with the Greek world shifted in new directions.[4] The victory over Pyrrhus in 278 B.C.E. ushered in a massive movement of spoils to Rome. Centuries later, Florus asserts that Curius Dentatus' triumph constituted a major turning point in triumphal display, witnessing the inclusion of statues and gold from Tarentum.[5] One needs to be cautious about retroactive periodizations, especially when they tend to oppose a primitive and simple past to a sophisticated and corrupted present.[6] Nevertheless, it is clear that the high prestige that "things Greek" had traditionally enjoyed intersected with their increasing availability through plunder. In turn, Rome's military success over Pyrrhus raised the stakes in the Italian-wide aristocratic competition and Greek paradigms came to be used as benchmarks for downplaying the competitors.[7] By the end of the third century B.C.E., the increasing concentration of material, human, and cultural commodities in the city and in the hands of its most powerful citizens had altered the system of migration and circulation once and for all. The translation practices that underlie the early formation of Roman poetry ought to be viewed as an offshoot and a manifestation of these larger social, political, and cultural trends.

In his discussion of the beginnings of Latin literature, Denis Feeney emphasizes the usefulness of Mary Louise Pratt's concept of 'contact zone.'[8] This concept, he argues, constitutes a constructive tool for gauging the multilingual and competitive environment of Italy from which the creation of Latin literature found some of its impetus. In her work Pratt explains that 'contact zone' refers to "the space of colonial encounters, the space in which people geographically and historically separated come into contact with each other and establish ongoing relations, usually involving conditions of coercion, radical inequality, and intractable conflict."[9] Borrowed from linguistics, the term 'contact' is used by Pratt to describe the improvised language that evolves from interaction, often in situations of trade. Finally, she specifies that at times a 'contact zone' overlaps with that of 'colonial frontier.'[10] Within Feeney's reconstruction, Pratt's understanding of 'contact zone' serves a twofold purpose: on the one hand, it helps

---

4. For general discussions, see Gruen 1990: 158–62; 1992: 227–31; Cornell 1995: 390–98; David 1997: 35–53.
5. Florus 1.13. 26–27.
6. See the Auditorium villa and the remarks by Terrenato 2001. For periodization in general, see Flower 2010: 18–34.
7. Feeney 2005: 236 with reference to the work of Dench 1995; 2005.
8. Pratt 1992.
9. Pratt 1992: 6.
10. Pratt 1992: 6–7.

him explain Rome's peripheral positioning in relation to Hellenistic culture, which at the time—he argues—was perceived as civilization pure and simple.[11] On the other hand, it sustains his emphasis on the multilingual cultures that flourished under the Roman *imperium* and the mediating role played by the poets who, by moving outwards from the Hellenistic world, acted as cultural mediators working at its fringes.[12]

What I find most productive in Pratt's notion is its strongly localized framework which becomes that much more powerful when it is applied to well-defined spaces of interaction.[13] In the case at hand, trying to identify these spaces opens up new interpretative paths. First of all, it allows for the possibility of moving away from discourses of cultural inferiority and superiority, center and periphery, by liberating the bilingualism or trilingualism of the early poets from fixed notions of language, culture, and identity. Second, it makes it possible to concentrate on how the poets' linguistic and cultural proficiency was dynamically interwoven with their migration *to* Rome and the translations that they performed *in* Rome. Third, from there we may observe how the poets' migratory subjectivity affected the strategies that they adopted in producing their translations and investigate the forms of action that belong to the translation process. Fourth, we may examine the agency that translating conferred on the poets by inserting into the frame the other agents that were involved in their translating activities. The more specific we are in defining the 'contact zones' in which the poets operated, the more are we in the position to explore the relations that existed between the cultural materials that underwent translation, the transfer agencies implicated, the individual translations that they produced, and the receiving public in their societal interlacements. Although our view is limited by the data available, by tackling these relationships we may assess better the cultural and social formations that poetry mediated.

In this chapter I attempt to identify some of the zones that in late-third- and early-second-century B.C.E. Rome figured encounters centered on poetic translations. By focusing on Plautus' comic scripts I examine how they encode diverse types of patterned speech and actions and how,

---

11. Feeney 2005: 237; 1998: 67–70. Cf. also Holliday 2002: 7–9 with the same underlying idea that Rome was located at the fringes of Hellenism building upon Veyne 1979.

12. Feeney 2005: 237, 239. If we look, however, at the alleged origins of the early poets, the outward movement envisioned by Feeney does not apply across the board. As for the difficulty of defining *imperium*, see Gruen 2004: 243–44 and more extensively Richardson 2008; Mattingly 2010.

13. For recent discussions of 'contact zones' as 'translation zones' that are both methodological and disciplinary, see Wolf and Fukari 2007; Apter 2006.

in turn, performances based on them mirrored back and forth the diverse worldviews of those involved in their production and reception. Later in this chapter I turn to Livius Andronicus' *Oduseia* and investigate what his translation of Homer's epic reveals about the agency of the early poets vis-à-vis that of their elite sponsors. My special interest in this latter nexus of agencies is driven by my larger aim to shed light on the asymmetries that the surviving poetic texts embed when viewed vis-à-vis Cato's prose writings. However, because any interpretation is itself mediated by the subjective frameworks of the interpreter, I find it important to preface my analysis with a few words about how my approach embraces some of the questions raised by our postmodern world and recent turns in the field of translation studies.

Contact Zones, Translation Zones

Our postmodern world is teaching us that any reterritorialization (and globalization indeed constitutes one form of it) leads to different but equally hierarchical structures of cultural circulation and new class formations. As Saskia Sassen argues, any city earns the stature of 'global city' in part by participating in a worldwide circuit of cultural commodities manufactured for its urban and wealthy professionals.[14] In turn, the global cities have become poles of attraction for immigrants and minority groups that service these professionals and create hybrid cultural products expressing both their displaced identity and their attempt to make the new environment their home. I do not think that the modern understanding of 'global city' provides us with straightforward analogies to account for the ancient situation. In fact, I would suggest that the extension of Rome's hegemony over Italy and the new role that the members of its ruling elite played in the process intensified expansionistic needs already in place. In light of these needs, the early poets were more than just cultural agents contributing to resolve the identity crisis suffered by the local aristocracy in the face of Hannibal's menace, as Thomas Habinek has it. They also did more than simply help this aristocracy catch up with the highly competitive cultural market-place of the Hellenistic Mediterranean, as Glenn Most remarks.[15] They were, first of all, social agents involved in the flow of resources that Rome's political and military ascendancy had produced.

---

14. Sassen 1991.
15. Habinek 1998a: 35; Most 2003: 388.

In recent years, the notion of diaspora has become a key term for representing the multiple identifications that characterize the lives of those who come from somewhere and establish their homes elsewhere, who assimilate to the norms and values of their new homes and remain trapped in a translation state of exilic dimensions. As Douglas Robinson puts it, "a diasporic culture is a global culture that is for ever displaced, in exile, living among strangers that become the familiar characters of our homes and places of work."[16] Viewed in this way, diaspora and, with it, the multilingualism and cultural hybridity of postcolonial contexts make translation in the most traditional sense impossible. For this reason, it is better to understand translation as a more or less empowering negotiation between cultural and linguistic divides and as a crucial and inescapable fact of life at the same time. Once again, we cannot map our modern experiences directly on the ancient situation.[17] What we can do, however, is to capitalize on modern insights by becoming more responsive to the migratory subjectivity of the early poets and the signs that this has left on the texts that we read today.

By emphasizing that poetry was a practice linked to individuals relocated just like the texts that they manipulated, I propose that the translation activities of the early poets were doubly 'performative.' They were cultural inventions largely based on the reprocessing of Greek literary materials, but they were also the means whereby their nonelite and alien inventors negotiated their adaptation to their changed reality. Those who in Rome held social and political power enter our purview because they were responsible for recruiting these poets and sponsoring their activities. In this respect, it makes sense to assume that some of their creative stimulus derived from demands sited within Rome's body politic. To think that these demands were linked to practices of conspicuous display is justified not only because these had long typified the Italian aristocracy, but also because later accounts invoke civic festivals as the contexts in which poetry made its first appearances. From a purely methodological point of view, my endeavor to assess the forms of agency that the early poets derived from their participation in civic festivals merges with ongoing attempts to demarginalize translation and translators alike.

In recent years the strongest challenge to the notion of translation and translators as 'secondary' or 'marginal' has stemmed from the acknowl-

---

16. Robinson 1997: 29. The field of diaspora studies is enormous and very much divided up into ethnic categories (African, Irish, Italian, and so on). In this sense, the articles gathered by Braziel and Mannur (2003) constitute a useful point of departure.

17. On the issue of generalization, see Tymoczko 2007: 200–206.

edgment that colonialism and translation practices have long gone hand in hand. In this respect, it is not at all surprising that some of the most radical conceptions of translation have come from former colonies around the world where the relationship with Europe used to be mapped on the metaphorical opposition between 'original' and 'translation.' What this metaphor has also suggested is that, from the point of view of the colonized, translation has always been a one-way process. Translations into European languages have served to make European expressions 'original' by denying or adapting the view of the colonized. Translations into the languages of the colonized, by contrast, have facilitated the imposition of European values and norms, once the most hostile resistance had been extinguished through bloodshed. Against this picture, translation theorists have been turning to 'translation' in order to reassess and reappropriate the term.[18] On the one hand, they have been scrutinizing how textual translations have been instrumental to the reinforcement of subordination and expropriation; on the other hand, they have been exploring the creative potential located in the in-between space that the translator invariably occupies.[19]

The shift of focus on the 'translation space' has most recently raised the need to go beyond source and target texts and to allow for the personal circumstances of the translator and the social networks in which he operates to bear on our analyses.[20] In dealing with early poetic translations we are forced into a textual encounter; accordingly, some questions about the poets' circumstances remain unanswerable. Regardless, to ask these questions is a way of factoring into the equation the poets' self-perception in relation to how others perceived them and the multiple agencies that affected and were affected by the cultural transfer that they performed. At a macroscopic level, we may contemplate the hierarchies governing the relationship between the source-culture (Greece) and the target-culture (Rome) and look at how the poets positioned themselves in relation to both. At a more microscopic level, we may understand the translation process as a form of interpellation that affects all the parts involved by binding them together. If so, early poetry offers the possibility to take into

---

18. Bassnett and Trivedi 1999: 5 and *passim*. See also the seminal studies by Rafael 1993; Cheyfitz 1991; Niranjana 1992; Robinson 1997.

19. Hose (1999) purports to adopt a postcolonial perspective, but speaks about the formation of a literary culture in Rome as a cultural colonization pursued by the politically weak followed by a struggle for emancipation from the colonial power of Greek culture. In other words, he projects colonial dynamics and postcolonial attempts to cultural self-determination back on the ancient situation by gesturing to and yet downplaying the historical fact that from the third century B.C.E. onwards Rome pursued and reinforced its political and military dominance over Italy and the Mediterranean.

20. See, most notably, Siméoni 1998; Pym 2003; Wolf and Fukari 2007.

account the power differentials that shaped Roman social relations at the time of its production and to consider how translating both limited and expanded the agency of each part.

A Scene of Beginning

Writing during the Augustan period, Livy dedicates a long paragraph in book seven of his history to the development of performance arts in Rome.[21] His account begins in 364 B.C.E. when a terrible plague hit the city. Livy reports that the Romans, incapable of containing the spread of the disease and won over by superstition, summoned a number of performers (*ludiones*) from Etruria and instituted the *ludi scaenici*. From there, Livy goes on to trace the evolution of stage performances to finally point out that from a healthy start the whole matter turned into a type of insanity "barely tolerable even in opulent kingdoms" (7.13). At this, one wonders what was so healthy about this beginning. By going back to the opening of Livy's digression with these words in mind, a compelling scene takes shape before our eyes:

> Sine carmine ullo, sine imitandorum carminum actu ludiones ex Etruria acciti, ad tibicinis modos saltantes, haud indecoros motus more Tusco dabant. Imitari deinde eos iuventus, simul inconditis inter se iocularia fundentes versibus, coepere; nec absoni a voce motus erant. Accepta itaque res saepiusque usurpando excitata. Vernaculis artificibus, quia ister Tusco verbo ludio vocabatur, nomen histrionibus inditum; qui non, sicut ante, Fescennino versu similem incompositum temere ac rudem alternis iaciebant sed impletas modis saturas discripto iam ad tibicinem cantu motuque congruenti peragebant.[22]

> Summoned from Etruria, professional performers (*ludiones*) danced to the accompaniment of the flute: they did not sing nor act out any imi-

---

21. For a philological treatment and discussion of scholarship on this troublesome passage, see Oakley 1998 *ad locum*.
22. Livy 7.2.4–7. It is not completely clear in Livy's text whether the relative pronoun *qui* refers back to the *iuvenes* or the *artifices*. I tend to believe that it refers back to the *iuvenes* and expanding on their activities, after explaining the lexical shift from *ludio* to *histrio* in relation to nonelite individuals engaging in dances and musical performances. Cf. Oakley 1998: 41 and 42 note 1. McC.Brown (2002: 26 note 4) rightly notices a contradiction in Oakley's commentary (who seems unable to decide whether the *histriones* are professionals or amateurs) and maintains that Livy is talking about professionals.

tation of songs (*carmina*); their movements were decorous and in the Etruscan style. Then, native youth began to imitate them, at the same time uttering jests in uncouth verses. Their gestures were suited to the voice. Once accepted, repetition improved quality. The native professionals (*artificibus*), because *ister* was the Etruscan word for *ludio,* were named *histriones*. And, they (the *iuvenes?*) no longer uttered verses akin to crude Fescennines, but rather began to perform medleys full of musical measures matched to (*discripto*) the sound of the flute and by moving in accordance.

In this scene, the young Romans meet the imported performers and start imitating their dancing bodies, while the imported performers do not imitate the youths in return and hold back from singing or mimicking *carmina*. Livy's narrow focus on encounters between alien professionals and native youth points already to the social amalgamation that in the long run this institution came to entail. Amalgamation, however, is also what Livy tries to exclude from his inaugural scene. Although the two groups engage with each other, lack of reciprocal mirroring helps to preserve social hierarchies and keeps the alien performers from affecting the practices of the local youth. This element, in turn, is reinforced by Livy's comments on the immediate outcome of this type of encounter. By repeatedly imitating the alien dancers, the young Romans learned to produce songs qualitatively superior. But when Livy chooses the verb *usurpare* to indicate intensive exercise, he uncovers the logic underlying his aesthetic appraisal. In fact, the verb highlights that the songs of the native youth improved only because the movement of cultural forms and practices was unidirectional and upwards. After this, Livy's syntax breaks down and we can hardly follow his zooming back to the performers and to the next developments. What we do catch, however, is that the performers become naturalized social entities (they are now called *vernaculi artifices*), although we soon realize that their new designation (*histrio*) keeps in view their alien origins.[23] Finally, Livy dwells on the *saturae* leaving syntactically ambiguous the identity of those who performed them. Apparently, these *saturae* are the *carmina* that the young Romans had initially kept for themselves, although now they are amplified by dance and melody, that is, the cultural forms seized from the alien performers.

Riveted by the moment of cultural expropriation, Livy constructs a

---

23. This etymology is shared by Valerius Maximus. 2.4.4; Plutarch, *mor.* 289 c–d (qualified as οἱ περὶ τὸν Διονυσιον τεχνῖται). Festus 89L and Isidorus, *Orig.* 18.48 derives them from Histria.

scene of beginning that emphasizes how alien cultural expressions and practices helped expand the cultural patrimony of free Romans. In this scene the process of cultural enrichment is represented as a two-step procedure: first, alien cultural agents are relocated into Rome in order to energize the communication between the civic community and the gods during a moment of crisis; second, by means of imitative practices the local youth takes hold of these new cultural expressions. As Thomas Habinek points out, "Livy's narrative is emblematic of Rome's relationship with outsiders, in particular the relationship of elite Roman males to their 'others,' throughout history."[24] But there is something else that we should not miss. Against this scene Livy projects a number of anxieties over the intractable problem of socially distinguishing cultural practices and forms when these move across perceived ethnic and social boundaries through mimicry. Indeed, in the attempt to catch expropriation in its purest form, that is, untainted by later developments, he also suggests how the Roman elite might have wished to imagine their relationship with their 'others' and their culture. In an ideal world, the 'others' are supposed to amplify instances of communication between the civic and the divine world by working in partnership with the governing elite. Besides that, they should take a place somewhere at the margins and, from there, deliver their cultural patrimony to the dominant group without asking anything in return. In other words, an ideal situation would involve a change of ownership that denies all forms of recognition or return to the first owners. Needless to say, Livy's wishful scenario stands far from cultural borrowing since, as a form of exchange, borrowing implies some sort of repayment for the good or service received.

To say that the Roman elite at large might have thought of outright theft as the best method for seizing the cultural patrimony of their 'others' means to acknowledge the proprietorial logic that sustained their cultural expansion. By following this logic, we also realize that historical reality deviated from ideals and presented forms of interaction between elite and nonelite different from it. The result of these interactions was appropriation nonetheless; but against the ideal parameter set by theft, elite cultural appropriations entailed two things at once: continuous negotiations with their 'others' and the emergence of culturally mixed expressions.

---

24. Habinek 2005a: 108.

The Recognition of Poetic Craftsmanship in Rome

Roman poetry owes its inception to a specific group of alien cultural agents that in the late third and early second centuries B.C.E. operated in Rome. According to Cicero, poetry made its first appearance in the guise of drama the year following the first capitulation of Carthage, when Livius Andronicus wrote and staged a play for the *Ludi Romani* celebrated in that year.[25] While it is easy to see that such a date does not correspond to a real beginning, there is plenty of evidence to suggest that it was around this time that poetically crafted drama became an essential element in public festivals, celebrations of military victories, temple dedications, and funeral games.[26] In a way, poetic drama came to fulfill a ceremonial and religious function somewhat similar to that which it had served in the Hellenistic cities. Its practitioners, however, came to occupy a social position significantly different.

Testimonies about the activities of the *technitai* or craftsmen of Dionysus point to the fact that this designation connected writers, actors, and musicians with a tradition based on the reperformance of written texts that went back to the theater of Dionysus and fifth-century Athens. Organized in guilds that did not fall under the jurisdiction of any rulers, these guilds traveled to all parts of the Hellenistic world and negotiated on equal terms with the cities or the royal houses that contracted their services.[27] Although some have posited a direct influence of these guilds and their members on the development of poetry in Rome, this hypothesis runs counter to the fact that explicit references to the hiring of *technitai* are scanty.[28] On the other hand, the sources indicate that many of the poets that began to work in Rome from the mid-third century B.C.E. onwards did not move to the

---

25. Cicero, *Brut.* 72–73. In this passage Cicero disparages Accius' chronology by which Livius Andronicus staged the first play at the *Ludi Iuventutis* in 197 B.C.E. after arriving as a slave in 209 B.C.E. Cf. also Cicero, *De Sen.* 50; *TD* 1.3; Gellius 17.21.42. For the reference to the *Ludi Romani,* see Cassiodorus, *Chron. ad ann.* 239. This last testimony talks about the production of both comedy and tragedy.

26. Cf. Taylor 1937: 285–91; Gruen 1990: 84.

27. Lightfoot 2002. For a recent reassessment of the cult of Dionysus, see Jaccottet 2003.

28. A point recently made by Brown 2002 (*contra* Gruen 1990: 87). Reference to their presence in Rome is limited to three occasions only: the Ludi celebrated by M. Fulvius Nobilior in 186 B.C.E., those celebrated by L.Scipio in the same year (Livy 39.22. 2 and 10), and those by L. Anicius in 167 B.C.E. (Polybius 30. 22). For a discussion of this last event, see also Edmonsons 1999. The limited presence of *technitai* does not exclude the possibility that early dramatic scripts were acquired from Hellenistic guilds and that the poets used the same arrangement techniques (cutting, expanding, or altering scenes). See Brooks [1949] 1981: 171; Traina 1970: 114–16; Gentili 1979: 18.

city by choice. Some are said to have come to Rome as prisoners of war (Livius Andronicus, Caecilius Statius, and Terence),[29] others seem to have been recruited by members of the Roman ruling elite in service abroad (Ennius).[30] As far as we can gather, only Plautus and Naevius migrated of their own accord.[31]

What is most important about these accounts is not so much their testimonial value but the narratives of more or less coerced relocation that they all share. Read symptomatically, these narratives point to the high profile that Rome was acquiring as a result of its increasing military and political hegemony and they encourage us to consider the specificity of the early poets' migratory experience.[32] In this respect, one could stress that the poets could soon rely on a guild (*collegium*) and from there promote their services just as their Hellenistic counterparts did; however, Festus indicates that as opposed to them, their guild was sanctioned by the governing class under special circumstances and came to be associated with the cult of Minerva:

> Scribas proprio nomine antiqui et librarios et poetas vocabant; at nunc dicuntur scribae equidem librarii qui rationes publicas scribunt in tabulis. Itaque cum Livius Andronicus bello punico secundo scripsisset carmen quod a virginibus est cantatum quia prosperius res publica populi romani geri coepta est, publice adtributa est ei in Aventino aedis Minervae, in qua liceret scribis histrionibusque consistere ac dona ponere in honorem Livi quia hic et scribebat fabulas et agebat.[33]

The ancients used the term "scribe" for both "public clerks" and "poets"; now, however, those who write public accounts on tablets are called "public clerks." Therefore, when during the Second Punic war Livius Andronicus

---

29. For Livius Andronicus taken captive in 209 B.C.E. there is an indirect reference in Cicero, *Brut.* 72–73 referring to Accius' *Didascalica*. Although Accius' chronology may be off, the narrative paradigm is what interests me. According to Gellius (4.20.13), Caecilius was a freedman and Jerome (*Chron.* p.138 Helm) asserts that he was an Insubrian Gaul, perhaps from Mediolanum. For Terence, see Nepos, *Ter.*1.

30. For Ennius, see Nepos, *Cato* 1.4.

31. For Plautus, see Plautus, *Most.* 769–70 although the reference is only limited to his Umbrian origins; for Naevius, see Gellius 1.24.2.

32. For later articulations of migratory subjectivities see, Philodemus (*Rhet.* 2.145 Sudhaus) who, together with Alexandria, mentions Rome as a pole of attraction for intellectual workers who move out of necessity, personal gain, or the glory of their country of origins. See also the case of Parthenius who, according to *Suda* π 664 = T 1 Lightfoot, arrived at Rome as a spoil of war and was freed on account of his education. In the introduction to his *Erotica Pathemata*, we can see that, apart from producing poetry himself, he also provided raw mythological material to be worked out by Cornelius Gallus into his elegiac poetry. See Fletcher 2011.

33. Festus L446.

had written a *carmen* which was sung by virgins, because the situation of the *res publica* of the Roman people began to turn out rather prosperously, the state assigned to him the temple of Minerva on the Aventine. In this temple scribes and actors could meet and make sacrifices in honor of Livius because he wrote and acted his plays.

In this passage, Festus suggests that the poets were socially clustered with scribes and their writing practices socially mapped on preexisting ones.[34] Moreover, Festus points to ritual as the space within which the absorption of poetry into society was mediated by reporting that the establishment of the *collegium* was a form of recognition bestowed on Livius Andronicus for his contribution to the celebration of a rite of expiation. This rite, Livy reports, had been motivated by Hasdrubal's crossing the Alps and by the destruction of the temple of Juno Regina on the Aventine in 207 B.C.E. To ward off civic turmoil, Roman officials drew on a number of resources: *haruspices* were called from Etruria and the matrons were urged to finance the rite with their own dowries by means of an edict of the *aediles*. The ceremony resulted in a major production and Livius' contribution entailed the performance of a hymn written by him and sung by young aristocratic women during the celebration.[35] But more can be said about Festus' narrative once we compare the elite involvement that it suggests with what Livy unfolds in his scene of inauguration. Whereas in Livy the performers are alien dancers who shun singing, in Festus the performers are young Romans who sing from a composition produced by an alien professional. At one level, Festus alerts us to encounters across social lines that both counter and solidify Livy's reservations about social and cultural mixing. At another level, he points to the shared understanding of rituals organized at moments of civic uncertainty as the original contexts around which and in which these encounters took place.[36] In the larger economy of the recorded circumstances that contributed to the rooting of poetry in Rome, both Livy and Festus share the understanding that the social integration of the poets intersected with their progressive entanglement in the project, however troubled, of expansion (political, social, cultural, and cosmological) of the Roman ruling elite.

---

34. For the presence of scribes in Etruria and Latium, see Colonna 1976 and, more generally, Harris 1989: 149–74.

35. Livy 27.36.3–4. Ps.-Acro on Horace, *Carm. Saec.* 8 (via Verrius Flaccus) talks about the commissioning of another hymn performed in 249 B.C.E. Some have linked it to Livius Andronicus (Gruen 1990: 83 note 17).

36. For the socioemotional background of crisis as the trigger for the establishment of poetry, see Habinek 1998a: 39–41.

At about the time when the temple of Minerva became the site of the new guild, Rome witnessed a burgeoning of poetic dramas and an intense exploration of cultural forms falling outside of drama itself. Trying to fit them within a system neatly codified in earlier (Greek) or later (Latin) discussions of literary genres does nothing more than throw into relief the vast array, or rather, disarray of cultural materials that these wordsmiths were able to manipulate. Perhaps a better way to tackle these texts is to focus on their mixed nature and to deal with the social relations that this mixture encoded. To do so, however, it is important to acknowledge that poetic texts were written with a view to being performed. Here I may seem to be merely stating the obvious since we are relearning how we think about early dramatic scripts by considering their performance aspect.[37] But our narrow focus on dramatic scripts as the only type of poetic texts to be performed has led in the past to discussions about the societal impact of (say) early epic that leave unexplained its specific dynamics.[38] Ancient narratives about early poetic activities tend to emphasize that the poets performed on stage or engaged in readings from their compositions.[39] To give some credit to these narratives does not deny that early poetic texts may have also been objects of solitary readings; rather, it helps us see how they began to circulate in more exclusive circles. For now, however, my focus remains on the ways in which the multifarious self-identifications of the earliest poets met with the project of multifold expansion in which Rome's rulers were engaged from the place that the Senate assigned to them and through the texts that they constructed.

In past years critics have insisted that the establishment of the guild in the temple of Minerva contributed to the social advancement of their members and granted them a great deal of independence.[40] This interpretation has had the merit of steering the discussion away from the idea that the poets strictly served the political interests of individual elite households or, otherwise, suffered State impositions. Even so, it is hard to believe that their relationship with the Roman ruling elite was based on purely intellectual interests and a shared vision of 'national identity.'[41] Rather than by their intellectual or nationalistic insights, the integration

---

37. See Goldberg 2005 but more pointedly Marshall 2006.

38. The increasing awareness of this problem is nicely attested by how Goldberg (2005) builds upon his previous contribution on epic (Goldberg 1995).

39. Livy 7.2.6–10; Val. Max. 2.4.4; Suetonius, *gramm.* 1.1. Cf. Duckworth 1994: 5–6.

40. Gruen 1990: 88–90 and *passim;* Goldberg 1995: 29–32.

41. This is basically the argument laid by Gruen 1992; 1990. For a recent assessment of Gruen's dependency on Cicero's representation of poetry in the *Pro Archia,* see Zetzel 2007: 9–13. Although focused on Ennius, see also Gildenhard 2007b: 84–85 and note 77.

of poets and actors in the social cityscape as craftsmen appears to have been sustained by an increasing elite investment in their creations. On this score, the wide range of testimonies about the emancipation of some poets from slave to free to Roman citizens suggests that what made this group of cultural agents special was their translational expertise.[42] This implies that the early poets' self-perception was affected by multiple factors. These include their physical migration to Rome from other parts of Italy, their progressive integration into the social fabric of Rome, their interaction with members of the Roman ruling elite, and their ability to navigate and manipulate diverse cultural traditions.

From our standpoint, traces of poetic subjectivity are to be ferreted out from the generic disarray that marks early poetic texts. At times these traces overlap with representations of the diverse worldviews of the people involved in the exchanges that sustained the creation process. At other times they are shaped by the themes explored and the occasions that hosted performances from poetic scripts. Accordingly, when we look at the early poetic material that has survived, often in a fragmentary state, it is crucial to observe the combination of different codes (be they metrical, thematic, or linguistic) that these texts bear. Equally crucial, however, is it to observe the choices that sustained their construction, the events that envisioned poetic performances, and the variety of agencies involved.

Poetry in the City

Festus suggests that the craftsmen who produced scripts and performed from them were integrated into Rome's social landscape thanks to Livius Andronicus, who wrote a hymn for a rite of expiation that took place in 207 B.C.E. For the most part, however, their activities were organized around dramatic spectacles inserted in the larger program of fixed as well as occasional religious festivals that took place in the civic space. Signaled by the appearance of the actors (*actores*) before the audience, the space in which the actors performed (*scaena*) was a makeshift construction. Once the actors left the audience's sight, no traces of the occurrence would remain in the cityscape.

Some years ago, Erich Gruen argued that erecting and dismantling the dramatic space constituted a ritual of power in itself and demonstrated the

---

42. So, for example, Livius Andronicus and Caecilius are freed (Jerome, *Chron. Olymp.* 148.2 for Livius and Gellius, 4.20.13 for Caecilius), and Ennius becomes a Roman citizen (Cicero, *Pro Arch.* 22. Cf. also Ennius, *Ann.* 524 Sk).

decisive authority of the ruling class over the artistic sphere.[43] Resistance to the construction of a permanent theatrical structure, however, also testifies to the challenges that poetic drama could have posed to this very authority if not properly channeled.[44] If hosted in a permanent building, it certainly would have become an institution of its own. Anxieties over such a prospect emerge in Scipio Nasica's intervention in the mid-150s. According to Livy, Nasica argued that a permanent theatrical structure would have been unprofitable and would have damaged public morality.[45] Just as profitability does not imply that it was a matter of mere economics, so too Nasica's appeal to morals does not really express a concern with the moral welfare of the Roman people as such. To erect and disassemble stages was a costly enterprise, a lavish expenditure that conspicuously pointed to the civic generosity of Rome's ruling class.[46] As such, locked within civic rituals orchestrated by the governing elite, poetic drama turned into a ceremonial accessory that celebrated the increasing hegemony of this elite and intensified its links with the divine realm. Contrary to our expectations, perhaps, the rulers' investments in the production of poetic drama derived less from what drama communicated than from what it allowed them to do.

What made poetic drama so incredibly appealing was the poets' ability to draw together cultural expressions existing in separate locations and different forms. In this sense, the surviving dramatic scripts can be best described as the outcome of two parallel acts of transformation. By translating theatrical texts generated in the Greek world, the poets contributed to the concentration of literary materials from other parts of Italy into an increasingly hegemonic Rome. But in the process of domesticating these materials, they also textualized the varied Italian song culture, which existed most exclusively in embodied form and included the Atellana and the Fescennine, among others.[47] Thus, early poetic texts had less to do with textual translation as such than with a thorough reworking and remapping of existing cultural materials mediated through writing. In turn, these

---

43. See especially discussion in Gruen 1992: 183–222, but also more recently Beacham 1999: 30.

44. A point made by Beacham 1992: 66, but from a different perspective than mine. Gruen (1992: 208) disagrees with the dangers of *stasis* signaled by Appian (*B.C.* 1.28) asserting that the suggestion is anachronistic.

45. Livy *Per.* 48. Information about this event can also be gathered from Valerius Maximus 2.4; Appian, *B.C.* 1.28; Orosius 4.21.4; Vell. Pat. 1.15.3; Augustine, *CD* 2.5.

46. For the high costs, see Tacitus, *Ann.* 14.21. My suggestion here departs from Gruen (1992: 209) who argues that "a permanent theater, whatever its advantages in cost and convenience, would represent a symbolic relaxation of that authority."

47. For the influence of the Atellana and the Fescennine, see Duckworth 1994: 3–16.

writings looked to the ritual occasions for which they were constructed in the first place. To come to terms with the relationship between poetry and ritual, one may start by considering the emotional work that comedy allowed the spectators to entertain.

Recent research into the comedies of Plautus has taught us to see that the beneficiaries of any pleasures that they provided were not only the less powerful or the disenfranchised members of the audience, but also the socially and politically dominant. As Kathleen McCarthy has recently argued, pleasure stemmed primarily from Plautus' capacity to combine and recombine the comic modes that were at his disposal: 'naturalism' (generally associated with his Greek models) and 'farce' (loosely linked to the Italian Atellan). 'Naturalism' placed stable identities beneath shifting appearances until, in the moment of recognition (*anagnorisis*), these identities surfaced once again. 'Farce,' by contrast, saw these identities as contingent and revealed this contingency through the tricks devised by the clever slave. Through the almost inextricable combination of and dialogism between these two comic codes, poetic drama in Greek dress (*fabulae palliatae*) helped fulfill the multiple and contradictory fantasies of the audience attending the performance. On the one hand, the audience found respite from the labor of domination and from the struggle involved in maintaining one's position in the larger scheme of social relations; on the other hand, because identities were finally restored so too were hierarchical relations dramatically confirmed and, I would add, divinely corroborated.

The effects that McCarthy describes are highly compelling since they point, among other things, to the pressures that slavery (as an institution bolstered by conquest) imposed on the dominant members of Rome's society. While expanding the social and economic standing of the Roman masters, slaves were constant reminders of a progressive loss of self-reliance. As we shall see, this inextricable contradiction emerges in Cato the Censor's *De Agricultura* where the mythology of the self-sufficient peasant/soldier that flickers in the Preface clashes against the representation of a farm run by slaves who fulfill the commands of the absent master. By transforming the social figure of the slave into a 'ritual object' or a 'talisman,' comedy expressed these pressures in a liberatory manner for the benefit of all.[48] But the anxieties of those masters who also ruled the community (and commissioned the writing and the performance of poetic drama) were multiplied by the pressures inherent in their project of

---

48. For these ritual transformations, see Habinek 2005a: 54 and McCarthy 2000: 19.

expansion. In a way, their successes were becoming more and more bound up with their capacity to draw on an increasingly diversified population with quite different cultural backgrounds. The creators of Roman poetic drama appear to respond to this additional set of concerns by manipulating sound patterns belonging to ethnically different traditions and transforming diverse perceptions of reality into civic song.

In her introduction, McCarthy remarks that Plautus' interest in the dialogism between diverse comic modes is the product of an attitude towards language shared by all the early poets. In her words, "it is a manifestation of a deeper principle, the consciousness of language as a separate system that is never exactly coextensive with its function as a means of communication."[49] Plautus, then, as well as the other poets, did not use the phonetic aspect of language to convey meaning but to pit sound patterns against each other. This concentration on linguistic sounds independent of the meaning that these sounds expressed can still be traced in the scripts that have survived. Focusing on Plautus' mastery of phonetic iterations, Alfonso Traina has counted 2,283 *hapax legomena* and has systematized them according to categories derived from classical rhetoric: alliteration, homoioteleuton, figurae etymologicae, paronomasia, and so on.[50] This interest in phonetic repetition is often bracketed under the larger rubric of conventionality and stylization and invariably attributed to the tradition of the comedy in Greek dress in which Plautus participated.[51]

In Plautus' comedies as well as in other forms of poetic drama, phonetic repetitions are not the only way in which speech is organized. For if the verbal sounds of one word reverberated on other words in the syntagm, syntagms were constrained by quantitative meters that were repeated from line to line and changed according to a specific pattern. Iambic senarii served plain dialogues; iambic, trochaic, and anapaestic septenarii and/ or octonarii characterized sections chanted to musical accompaniment; Greek lyric meters of various types were used for songs strictly speaking.[52] Accordingly, we are dealing with two ways of patterning speech

---

49. McCarthy 2000: 8.

50. Traina 1977: 130–31. He also notes (pp. 163–65) that Plautus is not interested in onomatopeia except when he mimics the modes of tragedy (*Amph.* 1094; 1062). The same case is made by Mariotti (1952: 44) in relation to the tragedies of Livius Andronicus. The only onomatopeia that we find in comedy relates to the beating of the slave (see list in Traina 1977: 164). In this sense, one could also say that tragedy and comedy ritualized two distinct sounds/ noises, transforming them into elements of song: comedy did it with the beating of slaves, and tragedy with the noises of battles. In this sense, one may want to consider also the blooming area of sound studies and the impact of soundscapes on experiences of the world.

51. See especially Wright 1974: 36 and *passim.*

52. Based on MacCary and Willock 1976: 35. But for a more recent assessment of the

sounds: one 'phonetic' and one 'quantitative.' Although merging into one another, these two formalized patterns were also distinctively linked to two different cultural traditions. Phonetic repetitions invoked Italian song genres;[53] quantitative patterns reached out to the Greek literary tradition, which organized speech around syllabic length and consistently avoided phonetic reiteration. To have a sense of how powerful the ethnic correlation between formal patterns and their mixture is, it may be useful to turn to the field of American studies.[54]

According to Richard Middleton, in the American musical tradition musematic repetitions are based on the reiteration of short units (musemes) and are opposed to the type of musical circularity that characterizes collective oral inventions. Discursive repetitions, by contrast, are based on the reiteration of longer musical phrases mixed together and contrasted in a hierarchical framework. In the American context, these two patterns are also historical and ethnic categories ('black' and 'white,' respectively), and their distinction or combination has always been mediated by the needs of distinct socioeconomic configurations.[55] In our case, it is virtually impossible to imagine how, during the performance of poetic dramas, the combination and reiteration of diverse sound patterns were impressed on the ears of its audience. Even so, we can safely say that the poets' manipulation of sound patterns attached to ethnically distinct traditions contributed to the creation of a 'contact zone' located within the socioculturally variegated environment of Rome and the realm of civic festivals at the same time.[56]

Years ago Giorgio Pasquali commented that all Plautus' characters spoke the same language; this language, however, stood far from the one used in everyday life.[57] To these remarks Traina added that just as in the composite Plautine world we find innumerable fragments of Roman reality, so too in the fleshy and hyperbolic expressions of slaves, pimps, and prostitutes the turbulent audience of Plautus recognized the core of their

---

division of comedy into arcs and their metric composition, see Marshall 2006: 203–44.

53. Habinek (2005a: 52–55) identifies convivial songs, love-songs, aristocratic braggadocio, prayer, military language, and precepts. Besides that, comedy includes parodies of other dramatic forms. Within tragedy critics have identified the language of religion, law, and public administration, see Jocelyn 1967: 38–43; Fraenkel [1922] 2007: 240–51.

54. See, for example, Lott 1993: 173–82.

55. Middleton 1986: 164.

56. As for sound effects it is worth remarking the ways in which Plautus and Terence made the metrical ictus coincide with the tonic accent of the word, a strategy that might have helped the domestication of Greek rhythms. For this issue, see Parsons 1999 *passim;* see also Stuertevant 1919.

57. Pasquali 1968: 314–28.

own language.⁵⁸ Focusing on the Greek models, others have pointed out that in Rome the metrical and lexical distinctions that in the Greek context had kept tragedy and comedy apart were completely blurred.⁵⁹ More recently, Habinek has argued that comedy absorbed into itself song genres that spill outside the simple Greek/Italic divide.⁶⁰ Taken together, these diverse impressions testify to the transformational powers of the poets and their effort to embrace sound patterns, cultural forms, and linguistic expressions belonging to the various peoples that lived under the Roman sun. In turn, the multiform communicative tool that the poets devised allowed the attending audience to enter a series of relations that looked to the divine world. The practice of *instauratio* makes the latter trajectory especially conspicuous: if the performance was interrupted or if there was some omission or mishap, it had to be repeated.⁶¹ The narrow focus on proper procedure manifested in this practice confirms that the 'contact zone' created by poetic drama had less to do with a specific physical location and more with the patterned speech and actions that concurred to create it.

It has long been recognized that when the impersonating actors performed on stage, their mixed way of speaking, singing, and dancing produced an environment located—to adopt Brooks' (borrowing from *Peter Pan*) felicitous expression—in a 'never-never land' that was neither Greece nor Rome.⁶² Sometimes, this 'never-never land' is explicitly constructed through rhythm and dance as, for example, in Plautus' *Maenechmi* (49–56), where the prologue speaker declares that he is going to Epidamnus on "(metrical) feet (*pedibus* 49)" without moving from the place on which he stands (i.e., the stage) (56). Other times this location is created in words more simply, as in *Truculentus* (1–8; 10–11), where the poet presents himself through the character on stage as the one erecting Athens without architects in the public space (*ager publicus*) of Rome. The construction of a 'never-never land,' however, is not limited to comedy alone. For example, in a fragment attributed to Ennius' translation of Euripides' *Medea* (214–18) the Roman audience is transported into that

---

58. Traina 1977: 169.
59. See most recently Hunter 1985: 15; Jocelyn 1967: 37–39. Cf. also Ribbeck 1897: 366–68.
60. Habinek 2005a: 44–47.
61. See Cicero, *De Har. Resp.* 2.23; Livy 7.2. See also, Terence's prologue to the *Hecyra*. Interrupted in 165 B.C.E. during the Ludi Megalenses, this comedy was reperformed in 160 B.C.E. at the funerals of Aemilius Paullus. Lebek (1996: 32–33) points to ritual procedure but insists on the economic effects of these reperformances, for if not entirely performed a script could be resold.
62. Brooks [1949] 1981: 275.

same location when on stage the formidable character of Medea addresses the women of Corinth as "rich and most distinguished matrons."[63] A trick of translation can be seen here to both domesticate the mythical location represented on stage and induce a social group within the audience to become judges of Medea's actions. The constructedness of the 'never-never land' created on stage and the ways in which it was built by linguistic, musical, and bodily means calls for larger considerations about the relationship between the world on stage and the world outside of it.

One way to go about this relationship is to deploy Victor Turner's understanding of drama as a type of "cultural performance" that works as a "magic mirror" that makes "ugly or beautiful events or relationships which cannot be recognized as such in the continuous flow of quotidian life in which they are embedded."[64] Following Turner, it may be said that the poets combined diverse song traditions and stylized the quotidian experiences of the spectators in order to create a make-believe world prearranged in writing.[65] By relying on these writings the actors engendered a space through their speech and actions that reflected back on the spectators diverse perceptions of reality.[66] For our purposes, the 'reflexive' possibilities ushered in by poetic drama are more easily detected in the metatheatrical moments scattered throughout the Plautine corpus.

Metatheater Reconsidered

Coined by Lionel Abel in 1963, the term metatheater has accrued over time a wide variety of meanings.[67] At a very basic level, metatheater refers to any force in a play which challenges the idea of theater as being nothing more than an uncomplicated (or naturalistic, if you want) mirror against

---

63. To be sure, this address is included in a line that is hard to reconstruct because embedded in the body of a letter addressed by Cicero to Trebatius (Cicero, *Fam.* 7.6.1). Jocelyn (1967: 357–61) discusses the various attempts that have been made to determine the original line and notices Ennius' marked translation of the Greek γυναῖκες into *matronae* rather than into *mulieres* noting that "the Corinthian women are bound to their mates by *iustum matrimonium* and hence protected by all the majesty of the city-state's law and custom. Medea, by implication is only a *concubina* (361)."

64. Turner 1988: 22.

65. Turner's model has undergone major criticisms but it has also triggered some very productive reflections over the position of the observer. To get a sense of both, see Taylor 2003: 8–12; Bell 1997: 72–76.

66. It should be noted that this mirroring allows us today to identify class ideologies and social phenomena at large; for this sort of sociohistorical investigations, see Leigh 2004; Gruen 1992; Konstan 1983.

67. Abel 1963.

which the spectators view themselves and identify with the actions of characters. By sharpening our awareness of the artificiality of theater and by revealing the boundaries that separate theater from life, metatheater would help the spectators focus their attention on the illusoriness of life and prompt them to consider the theatricality of life itself. The notion of metatheater was first applied to Plautine comedy by Marino Barchiesi in an article published in the early seventies. In that article Barchiesi suggested that the breaks in the dramatic illusion that we find scattered in Plautus' scripts served as moments of reflection on the history of the text's creation and its construction from previously existing plays.[68] In the mid-eighties Niall Slater argued that Plautine metatheater reveals an acutely self-conscious awareness of the constructedness of both the characters and the play, and contributed to the articulation of comic heroism.[69] Incarnate in the clever slave (*servus callidus*), this heroism manifested itself in this character's ability to control the plot and other characters. Recently William Batstone has disputed that Slater's conceptualization of metatheater as an exclusively theatrical matter divorces Plautine theater from the life of ancient spectators: metatheater – Batstone reminds us—is based on the perception that "all the world's a stage" and in Plautus this perception meets with a non-theatrical and specifically Roman view of life theatricalized.[70] By taking Batstone's remarks as a cue, I would like to look at two passages of the *Curculio* to consider the forms of actions that the break of the dramatic illusion permitted. In the first passage the character of the choragus goes out of his way to describe the social types that inhabit the forum:

> Edepol nugatorem lepidum lepide hunc nactust Phaedromus.
> halapantam an sycophantam mágis esse dicam nescio.
> ornamenta quae locavi metuo ut possim recipere;
> quamquam cum istoc mihi negoti nihil est: ipsi Phaedromo
> credidi; tamen asservabo. sed dum hic egreditur foras,
> commonstrabo, quo in quemque hominem facile inveniatis loco,
> ne nimio opere sumat operam si quem conventum velit,
> vel vitiosum vel sine vitio, vel probum vel improbum.

---

68. M. Barchiesi 1970.
69. Slater 2000: 9-12. Gutzwiller (2000: 103–4) argues against Slater's association of metatheatricality with the Atellan farce. For my purposes, the origin of this technique is less important than what this technique allowed the poets to do.
70. Batstone 2005: 31; however, for larger considerations about Roman "theatricality," see Dupont 1985 and, more recently, Dupont 2000 with a focus on the relationship between actors and orators.

qui periurum convenire volt hominem ito in comitium;
qui mendacem et gloriosum, ápud Cloacinae sacrum,
ditis damnosos maritos sub basilica quaerito.
ibidem erunt scorta exoleta quique stipulari solent,
symbolarum collatores apud forum piscarium.
in foro infimo boni homines atque dites ambulant,
in medio propter canalem, ibi ostentatores meri;
confidentes garrulique et maleuoli supera lacum,
qui alteri de nihilo audacter dicunt contumeliam
qui ipsi sat habent quod in se possit vere dicier.
sub veteribus, ibi sunt qui dant quique accipiunt faenore
pone aedem Castoris, ibi sunt subito quibus credas male.
in Tusco vico, ibi sunt homines qui ipsi sese venditant,
[in Velabro vel pistorem vel lanium uel haruspicem]
vel qui ipsi vorsant vel qui aliis ubi vorsentur praebeant.[71]

By Pollux, Phaedromus has nicely found himself a nice liar here. I don't know whether I should call him a con man or a shyster. I am afraid I won't be able to get back the costumes I rented out; but I don't have business with him: I entrusted them to Phaedromus himself; still I'll keep watch. But while he is away, I'll point out where you can find any kind of person, so that nobody spends too much effort if he wants to meet someone, someone with or without vices, someone good or bad. Anyone who wants to meet a perjuring fellow should go to the comitium; if he wants to meet someone who lies and boasts, he should go to the shrine of Venus Cloacina. Let him look for rich profligate husbands under the walls of the basilica. In the same place will be male prostitutes, and the one who get promises of money; the ones who contribute to group meals are at the fish market. At the bottom of the forum good and rich men stroll about; but in the middle, near the gutter, are the pure pretenders. The ones who are arrogant, talkative, and spiteful, who brazenly speak slander against someone else on no grounds, and who have plenty that could truly be said against themselves, are just above the Lacus Curtius. In the shadow of the old shops are those who give and receive money at interest. Go behind the temple of Castor and Pollux: right there are those you would be a fool to trust. In the Vicus Tuscus are the people who sell themselves; on the Velabrum [you can find] a baker [or miller] a butcher or a seer, or those who themselves cheat or offer others a place where they can cheat.
(Trans. Moore)

---

71. Plautus, *Curc.* 462–84.

The choragus, here, is a character drawn into the world on stage from the world outside of it. By following his indications critics have recently charted the social types elicited in speech on the spatial configuration of the forum and have pointed out that some of them present features that we also find in comic stock characters (the *miles gloriosus,* the *senex amator,* the *adulescens,* the *leno,* and so on).[72] The identification of the forum itself as one possible performance location has led C. W. Marshall to argue that the play was performed in the Comitium, an area of it formally defined as a sacred space or *templum.*[73] Whereas Marshall counts as a counterargument the fact that a dramatic performance would have been inappropriate for the sacredness of the place, I think that his reconstruction calls attention to the too often forgotten ritual dimension of poetic drama.[74] On this score, the choragus' speech may well suggest that the insertion of poetic drama in a public space already ritualized constituted one of the ways in which poetry accrued special status. If so, the socio-topographical map that the choragus unfolds makes clear that metatheater did not simply serve to break the dramatic illusion and reveal the constructedness of the play; it also helped generate an interface between the world created on stage and that of the spectators. This interface allowed the latter to participate in both the dramatic action and the communication with the divine that the *ludi* sought to establish. Accordingly, the reflecting 'contact zone' arranged by the poets in their scripts and realized by the actors on stage emerges here as mediating between and bestowing power on multiple perceptions of reality.[75] This fact encourages us to examine the kind of agency that poets and actors derived from their participation in the *ludi* and how this too was reflected upon the dramatic 'contact zone' and reflected back outside of it.

Clues about this latter mirroring process can be found in another moment of the *Curculio:*

> Dáte viam mihi, nóti [atque] ignoti, dúm ego hic officiúm meum
> facio: fugite omnes, abite et de via decedite,
>   ne quem in cursu capite aut cubito aut pectore offendam aut genu.
>   ita nunc subito, propere et celere obiectumst mihi negotium,
>   nec <homo> quisquamst tám opulentus, qui mi obsistat in via,

---

[72]. See Moore 1998: 131–39, 219–22 but also the more definitive intervention of Marshall 2006: 40–47.

[73]. Cicero, *De Rep.* 2.11.

[74]. Marshall 2006: 47.

[75]. Marshall (2006: 245–79) does an excellent job at balancing out the poet's agency in composing the script vis-à-vis the improvisational interventions of the actors.

nec strategus nec tyrannus quisquam, nec agoranomus,
nec demarchus nec comarchus, nec cum tanta gloria†,
quin cadat, quin capite sistat in uia de semita†.
tum isti Graeci palliati, capite operto qui ambulant,
qui incedunt suffarcinati cum libris, cum sportulis†,
constant, conferunt sermones inter se<se> drapetae,
obstant, obsistunt, incedunt cum suis sententiis,
quos semper videas bibentes esse in thermipolio†,
ubi quid subripuere: operto capitulo calidum bibunt,
tristes atque ebrioli incedunt: eos ego si offendero,
ex unoquoque eorum exciam crépitum polentarium.
tum isti qui ludunt datatim servi scurrarum in via,
et datores et factores omnis subdam sub solum.
proin se domi contineant, vitent infortunio.[76]

Known or unknown, make way for me, while here I execute my commission; fly all of you, be off, and get out of the way, lest I should hurt any person in my speed with my head, or elbow, or breast, or with my knee. So suddenly now am I charged with a business of quickness and dispatch. And be there no person ever so opulent to stop me in my way, neither general, nor any tyrant, nor market-officer, nor demarch, nor comarch, with their honors so great, but that down he goes, and tumbles head-first from the footpath into the carriage-road. And then those Greeks with their cloaks, who walk about with covered heads, who go loaded beneath their cloaks with books, and with baskets, they loiter together, and engage in gossiping among themselves, the gadabouts; you may always see them enjoying themselves in the hot liquor-shops; when they have scraped up some trifle, with their covered pates they are drinking mulled wine, sad and maudlin they depart: if I stumble upon them here, from every single one of them I'll squeeze out a belch from their pearled-barley diet. And then those servants of your *scurrae*, who are playing at catch-ball in the road, both throwers and catchers, all of them I'll pitch under foot. Would they avoid a mishap, why then, let them keep at home.
(trans. Riley; slightly modified)

This passage represents the arrival of Curculio on stage. While performing the role of the *servus currens,* the character describes the people that he imagines to be crossing his path by methateatrically drawing into the frame

---

76. Plautus, *Curc.* 280–98.

a number of social types crowding the contemporary cityscape of Rome.⁷⁷ In this context, the group that stands out is composed of Greeks, ethnically typified by their foreign apparel, their books, their way of moving about, their habits, and their food.⁷⁸ Needless to say, these constitute also some of the visible markers that contributed to characterize the performing actors; as such, ethnic characterization here emerges as yet another poetic strategy of mirroring and inclusion that parallels the poet's manipulation of diverse languages, sound patterns, cultural traditions, and subjective perceptions of reality. On one level, just like the formation of the verbs *pergraecari* and *congraecari* in other plays, the characterization of Greeks as 'others' here reflects on cross-cultural encounters experienced by the audience and thematizes the dynamics of attraction and disdain that they triggered.⁷⁹ On another level, the visual identification between social actors and fictional characters indirectly conveys a larger claim: poetic drama lies open for all to see whatever the 'others' hide, steal, do, and chat about in real life and transforms their 'otherness' into a benign and empowering addition to civic life. More, however, can be said about the mirroring game played in this passage once we turn our attention to the other two social types described at the beginning and at the end of it.

At the very start Curculio strikes a defiant pose by fictionally warning those who stand on a higher station to get out of his way. The warning could be read as an interpellation of those in the audience who exercise sociopolitical authority in Rome; however, by characterizing them through a jumble of Greek words connected to public offices, Curculio reduces the consequences that such an outrageous behavior would provoke if the identification were taken at face value.⁸⁰ Towards the end of the passage, Curculio singles out nonpoetic performers as slaves of *scurrae* who are only able to imitate each other in an undifferentiated space of the cityscape (*in via*, line 296).⁸¹ Taken together, the confrontational characteriza-

---

77. For the hypothesis that the actor performing Curculio may have been moving among the audience, see Wiles 1991: 59–60.

78. Generally identified as "intellectuals" in Leo 1913: 146; Zweerlin 1990: 242–43. Cf. also Gentili 1979: 95.

79. For *pergraecari*, see Plautus, *Bacch.* 812–13; *Most.* 22–24, 64–65, 959–61, *Truc.* 88–88a; for *congraecari*, see *Bacch.* 742–43. On the Greek population in Rome, see Kaimio 1979: 22–25 (which argues for a primarily servile population during this period) and Noy 2000: 223–25. My focus on the Greeks here does not imply that these are the only ethnic "others" that we encounter in Plautus' comedies. See Richlin 2005.

80. For hyper-hellenization, especially in relation to the tricks played by the clever slave, see Moore 1998: 50–66 *passim*. I should also like to point out that the character of the *servus currens*, because of its inherent outrageousness, is later censored by Terence, *Heaut.* 30–32.

81. On the *scurrae* as performers, see Corbett 1984; Petrone 1983: 170–75.

tions woven into Curculio's speech call into play an implicit comparison between the power that the insertion of poetry in the program of civic festival conferred on their practitioners and the power wielded by the various social types methateatrically drawn into the dramatic space. In what follows, I expand on metatheater by considering the specific agency that the poets derived from translating Greek textual materials.

Poetry as the Art of Translating

In Plautus the technical term used for translation is *vertere*. As James Halporn put it some years ago, the relationship between early poetic drama and its Greek 'originals' conjured up by this verb could be called "the Homeric question of Latin studies."[82] To be sure, it is since the publications of Friedrich Leo (*Plautinische Forschungen zur Kritik und Geschichte der Komödie*, 1912) and Eduard Fraenkel (*Plautinisches im Plautus*, 1922) that critics have been trying to assess the degree of faithfulness and/or originality of the Roman tradition vis-à-vis their Greek precedents. Thanks to these types of assessment, Roman poetic drama can now be approached as a poetic form worthy of being studied on its own merit without forcing Latinists to take an apologetic stance towards its 'secondariness.'[83] But if at this juncture we are to fully understand the nature of this 'secondariness,' we might also want to recognize that any interest in qualitative comparisons between Greek 'originals' and Latin 'translations' is a byproduct of a long and conflicted history fought over the Greek literary tradition.[84]

In relation to comedy, this historical trend surfaces most clearly in Quintilian where the author comments on Plautus, Caecilius, and Terence by stating that "deprived of the advantage of writing in Attic Greek, they were only able to aspire to achieving a mere shadow of their originals."[85] In Gellius the qualitative comparison between a passage from Menander and a passage from Caecilius' *Plocium* leads him to consider the latter a very poor rendering of the 'original.'[86] By taking this history as normative, a case can be made for the early poets being responsible for changing the rules of Roman engagements with Greek culture by making its literary

---

82. Halporn 1993: 191.
83. In this sense, it is significant that in looking at Plautine drama in its own right McCarthy (2000: 9 note 12) underscores only in a footnote that her use of 'secondary' does not imply any lesser value.
84. For a general discussion, see Bain 1979.
85. Quintilian 10.1.99.
86. Gellius 2.23.

tradition a resource worthy of competing for. In this respect, the historical shipwreck of the 'originals' curiously places us in a position that is not much different from the one occupied by the earliest audience since our access to them is similarly mediated.[87] Although there is no doubt that these early recipients were somewhat familiar with the 'originals' manipulated by the poets, one may suppose that they hardly met them as textual entities.[88] Eventually, the elite sponsors overcame their dependency on poetic mediations by putting their hands on them and by acquiring the transformational skills of the poets. Initially, however, the poets thrived on their advantage.

Standing outside the drama proper and introducing the dramatic action, Plautine prologues tend to present an impersonating actor luring the audience into the performance to come.[89] On those moments, the poet shows off by proxy the Greek origins of his plots in the same way as victorious generals paraded their foreign spoils during their triumphs.[90] With the unfolding of the play the initial focus on the poet's handling of Greek 'originals' shifts onto the ability of the clever slave to improvise plots and schemes; at times, remarks about the clever slave's mastery of the comic game dovetails with considerations about the dramatic skills of the poet. For this reason interpreters have long understood the fictional construct of the clever slave as a special locus of poetic self-reflection.[91]

In a much-studied scene of the *Pseudolus* the identification poet/clever slave emerges when Pseudolus addresses the spectators and comments on his attempt to devise a plot to cheat money from Simo:

> Sed quasi poeta tabulas quom cepit sibi,
> Quaerit quod nusquam gentiumst, reperit tamen,
> Facit illud veri simile quod mendacium est
> Nunc ego poeta fiam: viginti minas

---

87. In Terence, *Eun.* 19–22 we find represented the process of evaluation through which a script went before their staging; the magistrate in charge relies exclusively on the poet's presentation of it.

88. The case made by Gentili (1979) about the longstanding Southern Italian performance tradition is a case in point in relation to the Roman audience exposure to it. For performances in Greek in Rome in the late Republic, see Cicero, *Ad Fam.* 7.1.

89. For appeals to the audience's responsiveness to return favors, see Plautus, *Amph.* 20–23; 46–49; *Asin.* 14–15; *Cas.* 1–2; for their martial successes, see Plautus, *Amph.* 75–76; *Capt.* 68; *Cas.* 88; *Cist.* 197–98; for moral uprightness, see Plautus, *Amph.* 64–85; *Cist.* 199–200.

90. For references to Greek originals and advertisement of poet's translating activity, see Plautus, *Trin.*18–19; *Asin.* 11; *Merc.* 9–10; *Cas.* 32–34; *Miles* 86–87; *Poen.* 52–53. For the parallel, see Connors 2004: 204 and McElduff forthcoming.

91. For the concept of "comic heroism" drawn from the clever slave's adoption of martial language to describe his feats, see Fraenkel [1922] 2007: 159–72 (building upon Plautus, *Pseud.* 703–705a); Slater [1985] 2000: 16–17. Cf. also M. Barchiesi 1970.

> Quae nusquam sunt gentium, inveniam tamen.⁹²

> But just like a poet, when he takes up his tablets,
> Searches for what is nowhere but still finds it,
> Making what is a lie seem like truth
> Now I will become a poet: I'll find
> The twenty minae that are nowhere.

Here Pseudolus assimilates himself to the poet and asserts that if his job inside the world of fiction is to find (*invenire*) money that does not exist anywhere, the job of the poet outside of it is to find cultural materials to summon onto his tablets in order to lay the foundations to the verisimilar world realized on stage.⁹³ As William Fitzgerald has aptly observed, the link between the poet and the clever slave construed here is later expanded to include the relationship between the poet and the audience:⁹⁴

> suspicio est mi nunc vos suspicarier
> me idcirco haec tanta facinora promittere,
> qui uos oblectem, hanc fabulam dum transigam,
> neque sim facturus quod facturum dixeram.
> non demutabo. Atque etiam certum, quod sciam,
> quo id sim facturus pacto nihil etiam scio,
> nisi quia futurumst. Nam qui in scaenam provenit,
> novo modo novom aliquid inventum adferre addecet:
> si id facere nequeat, det locum illi qui queat.⁹⁵

I suspect that you suspect that I am promising all of these exploits just to amuse you while I perform this play, and that I won't do what I have said that I would do. I won't break my word. Though, as far as I know, I don't know how I'll do that, only that I will. For anyone who comes on stage must bring some new invention in some new fashion; if he can't do that, then let him give space to someone who can.

In this typically metatheatrical moment Pseudolus continues to play the same game of identification by linking the poet's pressure to find ever new material to show on stage to the compulsive desire of the audience to enjoy

---

92. Plautus, *Pseud.* 401–5.
93. On this comedy, see also Fitzgerald 1995: 56–58; 2000: 44–46; Sharrock 1996; Slater 1985 [2000]: 12–13.
94. Fitzgerald 2000: 45.
95. Plautus, *Pseud.* 562–70.

more and more instances of poetic drama. In an earlier passage, however, when Simo suspects that Pseudolus is colluding with the pimp, Pseudolus indirectly expands on the pressure factor by indirectly exposing the poet's dependency on the vouching authority of his superiors:

> Aut si de istac re umquam inter nos convenimus
> quasi in libro quom scribuntur calamo litterae,
> stilis me totum usque ulmeis conscribito.[96]

> Or if we cannot find an agreement about this matter, then as if letters in a book which are written with a reed, scribble all over me with rods.

Fitzgerald has pointed out that with these words Pseudolus brings into the purview of the audience the precarious position that the clever slave shares with his creator by suggesting that the ultimate power to write the script does not reside with the poet but with those who exercise their authority over him.[97] Thus, if in the world of fiction the poet's creative power met with the clever slave's cunning, in the real world the poet confronted himself with the hierarchies that shaped life in Rome. Insofar as the poets engaged in the business of entertainment and at this point shared with actors the same *collegium,* it is not unreasonable to think that they too suffered *infamia* and, therefore, were liable to corporal punishment from which other citizens were legally protected.[98]

In the Plautine corpus the most explicit reflection on those liabilities is spawned from yet another moment of identification between poet and clever slave in a passage of the *Miles Gloriosus:*

> illuc sis vide,
> quem ad modum adstitit, severo fronte curans cogitans.
> pectus digitis pulsat, cor credo evocaturust foras;
> ecce avortit: nixus laevo in femine habet laevam manum,
> dextera digitis rationem computat, ferit femur
> dexterum. ita vehementer icit: quod agat aegre suppetit.
> concrepuit digitis: laborat; crebro commutat status,
> eccere autem capite nutat: non placet quod repperit.
> quidquid est, incoctum non expromet, bene coctum dabit.

---

96. Plautus, *Pseud.* 544–46.
97. Fitzgerald 2000: 47.
98. Cf. Fitzgerald 1995: 57. For a legal overview of *infamia,* see Greenidge [1894] 2002; for larger implications, see Edwards 1993: 123–26; Dupont 1985: 95–110.

ecce autem aedificat: columnam mento suffigit suo.
apage, non placet profecto mi illaec aedificatio;
nam os columnatum poetae esse inaudivi barbaro,
cui bini custodes semper totis horis occubant.
euge, euscheme hercle astitit et dulice et comoedice.[99]

Just look at him, how he stands there with bent brow, considering and cogitating. He is tapping his chest with his fingers. Intends to summon forth his intelligence, I suppose. Aha! Turns away! Rests his left hand on his left thigh, and his right hands reckons with his fingers. He hits his right thigh and so vehemently: his plan is having a hard birth. Snaps his fingers! He's in distress. Constantly, changes his position! Look there, though; he is shaking his head—that idea won't do! He won't take it out half baked, whatever it is, but give it to us done to a turn. Look though! He is building–supporting his chin with a pillar! None of that! I don't fancy that sort of building, not for a minute. For I happen to have heard that a foreign poet has a pillared face and a couple of custodians always lying on him hour after hour. Glorious! A graceful and comic pose!

(trans. Nixon; slightly modified)

In this passage Periplectomenus describes the bodily postures that the clever slave, Palaestrio, assumes in the process of devising a scheme. The description sets in motion a 'deictic' trajectory that breaks the boundaries of fiction and points to a poet under custody located outside the dramatic action.[100] In past years, the allusion has been understood as an explicit reference to the incarceration of Naevius for lampooning individual aristocrats; however, in his 1970 article on metatheater Marino Barchiesi points out that the portrayal could also be understood as yet another crucial moment of poetic self-reflection over the compositional process.[101] If so, these lines more directly thematize the poet's concern with appeasing his superiors and his perception of them as presences haunting the creative process. Apart from that, it would appear that the 'first generation' of poets had a rather free approach to their sources.

---

99. Plautus, *Miles* 200–13.
100. Here I use the adjective 'deictic' loosely, building upon the study of *deixis* in Greek materials and its cultural work elaborated by Bakker (2005) on linguistic grounds. Note that in our passage the boundaries of fictionality are crossed at the intersection with the deictic *illaec* (210).
101. M. Barchiesi 1970: 124–27. For a more thorough discussion of Naevius, see chapter 3.

In a passage from *Mostellaria* Tranio, the clever slave, reflects on Plautus' relationship with his Greek 'originals' in the following way:

> si amicus Diphilo au Philemoni es
> dicito is quo pacto tuos te servos ludificaverit
> optumas frustrationes dederis in comoediis.[102]

> If you are a friend of Diphilus or Philemon, tell them how your slave has cheated you: in comedies you will give them excellent deceptions.

William Anderson has argued that in this passage the roles of the slave Tranio and the poet are fused together so that they each taunt their masters, Theopropides and his Greek predecessors respectively.[103] But given that Plautus likes to present the clever slave as the master of the dramatic game, it would be more precise to say that the fusing of the clever slave with the poet's self discloses the particular investment that the poet had in translating Greek 'originals.' By admitting to have been found in them Tranio sustains Plautus' aggressive use of his sources as reservoirs of raw materials; by proclaiming to be the prime manifestation of the poet's translational skills, he frames a case for respect on his behalf from his superiors. In my view, the fluid manner in which poet and clever slave merge into one another makes this metatheatrical instance a case in point for understanding their identification in general as highly dynamic as the poet's perception of his selfhood.

Perhaps, one way to go about grasping the slippery relationship poet/clever slave is to think of identification in terms of 'projection' and 'introjection.' Formulated to describe children's mental development, these notions feature large in object-relations theory and have been extended to explain mental processes in adults.[104] To put it rather simply, projection in adults is generally regarded as a defense response based on displacing and attributing threatening or undesirable qualities of the self to an object. Introjection, on the other hand, relates to the self who replicates behaviors, attributes, or other aspects of the surrounding world that are perceived as desirable and attractive. In psychoanalysis these two mechanisms are recognized as being intimately connected and as promoting an individual's sense of self-esteem in the fluctuations that shape the relationship of the self with reality as the self perceives it.

---

102. Plautus, *Most.* 1149–51. On this passage, see Anderson 1993: 33.
103. Anderson 1993: 33.
104. For a useful overview of object-relations theory as developed from Freud onwards, see Greenberg and Mitchell 1983.

If we take the clever slave as the object to which the poetic self relates, its slavishness can be described as a projection of the negative attributes that make up the poet's social alterity and its cleverness as an introjection that allows the poetic self to overcome those very attributes. In our case, however, the poetic self's stake in the dynamic relationship between projection and introjection is complicated by the role that slavery as an institution plays in the conception of the clever slave as an object in the first place. As variously recognized, Roman masters conceived of their slaves as both nonhuman and human, as objects through which they could aggrandize themselves and as subjects with the power to do what they themselves could not (or were not allowed to) do.[105] Accordingly, Plautus appears to be using the clever slave to extend himself on stage and assert his control over his Greek sources. By the same token, because mastery has a lot to do with the ability to harness the subjectivity of inferiors to one's will, the triumphing language that the poet puts in the mouth of the clever slave promotes the perception of the poet's cultural mastery as a version of sociopolitical power. His superiors are thus invited to exercise this power by using the poet as a surrogate.

Outside the Plautine corpus, the assimilation between cultural and sociopolitical power is explicitly explored in a fragment from Naevius' *Tarentilla*:

Quae ego in theatro meis probavi plausibus
Ea non audere quemquam regem rumpere:
Quanto libertatem hanc hic superat servitus![106]

What I had approved in the theater with my plaudits no king can ever dare
to destroy: by how much does servitude here surpass that freedom!

Generally assigned to the clever slave, the speaking 'I' featured here exploits the reciprocal identification poet/clever slave in order to construct the world on stage as the place in which the freedom of the underdog to do whatever is denied to top dogs finds its fullest realization. The applauses of the audience metatheatrically absorbed into the dramatic frame confirm the poet's success in having his recipients conform to his will and vouch

---

105. Finley 1980; Bradley 1994 *passim;* for a reflection on slavery along these lines, see McCarthy 1998: 183–87.

106. Naevius, *Com.* frg. 72–74 Ribbeck. According to Marino Barchiesi (1970: 126) this passage should be read next to the allusion to the incarcerated poet in the *Miles Gloriosus.* By understanding it as a reflection on the misadventures of the poet Naevius, Barchiesi suggests that Plautus sent a rather nonheroic message of political disengagement to the clever slave speaking in the *Tarentilla.*

for his claim to a share of power. Although circumscribed by the boundaries of fiction, this power is nonetheless projected outside of them as a mark of unquestionable distinction.

It is a common assumption to understand the literary aesthetic that shapes Plautus' comedies as common property of the poets who engaged with the *comoedia palliata,* that this aesthetic was 'traditional' in the strictest sense of the word. My analysis suggests that this tradition was also open to the use of fictional constructs for self-reflexive purposes.[107] This is not to say that early poetic texts are transparent windows through which we can now look at the life of their authors.[108] Rather, it only means that the clever slaves who on stage devised schemes to meet the desires of their young masters give us clues as to how these early poets deployed their linguistic and cultural expertise in order to stretch the social constrictions that limited their agency in Rome. Slater has coined the phrase 'mobile sensibility' in order to refer to the clever slaves' ability to understand the wishes and the beliefs of their masters without necessarily espousing them.[109] I suggest that this sensibility dovetails with explorations of the power that resided in the opaqueness of the poets' alterity with respect to the distinguishing source of their craftsmanship (Greek 'original' texts) and the migratory subjectivity that informed their being in the world.

The Inauguration of Epic

The highly fragmentary state and the lack of contemporary evidence about its reception makes the interpretation of Livius Andronicus' *Oduseia* problematic; even so, its first line reveals that Livius engaged in an identificatory game very similar to the one that we see played out in comedy:

Virum mihi, Camena, insece versutum (*Ody.*1)

Sing to me, Muse, of the man of twists and turns.

In his work *The Rhetoric of Imitation,* Gianbiagio Conte uses this line to point out that Livius the translator enjoys a conditional freedom and unprotestingly accepts the limits imposed by the original: "Livius Andronicus,

---

107. For an exploration of traditionalism, see Wright 1973; for a reflection on self-expression in comedy, see McCarthy 2000: 7–10.
108. For the issue of autobiographism, see Slater [1985] 2000: 118–20.
109. Slater [1985] 2000: 171.

in his translation of the *Odyssey*, shows his acute awareness of the position of the translator: he admits in his first line that his freedom is limited, showing a respect for the original that is almost obsequious."[110] Like other commentators before and after, Conte follows the tradition of comparing 'original' and 'translation,' and focuses on the degree of faithfulness of the latter by evaluating the coincidence between each lexical item. Accordingly, he remarks on the archaizing choice of *insece* for ἔννεπε, emphasizes the semantic parallelism between *versutum* and πολύτροπον, notices the alliteration *virum–versutum,* and considers the substitution of *Camena* for Μοῦσα.[111] More recently, however, Stephen Hinds has gone a little further:

> If we are prepared to allow to his [i.e., Livius Andronicus'] *incipit*-line the concentratedness of meaning commonly granted to an *incipit* in "new poetry," we may just see his artistic self-consciousness further demonstrated in a deft programmatic pun through which he defines his project and differentiates it from Homer's. "Tell me, *Camena*, of the man who was *versutus*." *Versutus* "characterized by turns" like the Greek πολύτροπος; but in particular characterized by the "turn" which he has undergone from the Greek language into Latin. *Vertere* is the technical term *par excellence* for "translation" in early Latin literature (as in *Plautus vortit barbare*); and here in this programmatically loaded context our poet introduces a Ulysses whom the very linguistic switch to which he owes his textual existence has been made part of his proverbial versatility, has been troped into his πολυτροπία.[112]

With these words, Hinds has raised the likelihood that in the very opening of his translation Livius staked out a very self-conscious claim of poetic authorship precisely where, according to Conte and others, he seems to make no claims to any. Indeed, it would appear that Livius attributed to Odysseus the very qualities that made up his professional selfhood and articulated his authorship through a mutual referentiality between his migratory subjectivity and the Homeric characterization of Odysseus as

---

110. Conte 1986: 82–83.

111. To be sure, Conte relies on the works of Mariotti 1952; Traina 1970. But for a more recent reenactment of this line of interpretation, see Goldberg 1995: 64. As for Livius as a nonfaithful translator, see Kytzler (1989: 43), for whom the line would appear shorter than the original. As for when he actually pursued this translation some critics think that he did before he began to produce drama (see, for example, Hardie 1920: 198), others afterwards (see Kaimio 1979: 212). Although I discuss epic after drama, in no way do I imply that they were developed at different times.

112. Hinds 1998: 61–62. In footnote 20, Hinds points out the conflicted interpretative history of Odysseus' epithet discussed in Pucci 1982, and its meaning as "of many turns of language."

the cunning traveler *par excellence*. The dichotomy between Livius the poet-translator and Odysseus the translated hero is thus erased and the locus of meaning displaced somewhere between the text that bears the translation and the worldviews that the text mediates.[113] Accordingly, just as in comedy, so too in Livius' epic the central character is exploited as an object of both projective and introjective identification and translation is represented as an occasion for playing with the gaps and boundaries that stood between perceived realities and fictional constructs. This fact is not at all surprising since Livius was also a playwright; in this respect, it is also not at all usurprising to find Pseudolus, in the homonymous Plautine play, characterized by way of the same adjective (line 1243). In my view, these homologies invite us to move beyond the strictly textual and take into account similarities and differences between poetic drama and epic from a performance perspective.

On one level, both genres are cultural forms based on the reprocessing of Greek literary texts, linguistic codes, cultural traditions, and embodied practices. On another level, poetic drama suggests that the textual outcomes produced by the poets acquired value just to the extent that they sustained and informed an encounter with an audience. The possibility that Livius produced his translation with a view of it being performed encourages us to think about the social configuration of the receiving audience, the contexts for which the text was initially constructed, and the fact that epic, if anything, implies a one-person performance. Since the text as it stands does not provide any secure evidence, to work with this possibility means to face the challenging task of navigating between later testimonies and the contemporary *comparandum* offered by poetic drama.

In the *De Grammaticis et Rhetoribus* Suetonius asserts that both Livius Andronicus and Ennius engaged in exegetical translations from Greek texts and in exemplary readings from their Latin compositions in both private and public spaces (*domi* and *foris*).[114] Although Suetonius' historical reliability is controversial, the contexts of reception that he conjures up coincide with what we know about epic in Greece during the archaic and

---

113. If we also consider that first lines worked also as titles to identify works (as Possanza 2004: 53 points out), perhaps Livius looked to advertise himself as translator in view of later receptions of his text as well.

114. Suetonius, *gramm.* 1.1: "Livium et Ennium dico, quos utraque lingua domi forisque docuisse adnotatum esse—nihil amplius quam Graecos interpretabantur aut si quid ipsi Latine composuissent, praelegebant." The use of *commentor* in Plautus *Poen.* 1: *Achillem Aristarchi mihi commentari lubet* seems to point to the same approach to texts. For Jocelyn (1967 *ad locum*) it is a verb related to performance techniques of actors.

the classical period.¹¹⁵ By obliquely relying on the Greek precedent and contemporary poetic drama, some scholars have stretched the reference to *foris* by insisting that Livius and the other early epic poets performed *in propria persona* during civic festivals.¹¹⁶ By capitalizing on Suetonius' indication of *domi* as the other context of reception, others have argued that Livius used his translation for educational purposes in the household of Salinator.¹¹⁷ Whereas the first hypothesis cannot be verified, the second relies on Horace who, centuries later in his so-called *Letter to Augustus*, asserts that when young he had to learn by heart the *Oduseia* through the mediation of a *grammaticus*:

> Non equidem insector delendaque carmina Livi
> esse reor, memini quae plagosum mihi parvo
> Orbilium dictare.¹¹⁸

> I am not in pursuit of Livius' songs and don't think that they ought to be destroyed, which I remember Orbilius dictated to me when a boy with his rod.

As Hinds acutely notes, these lines encode Horace's attempt to outwit Orbilius, who was also a well-known interpreter of archaic Latin poetry. Indeed, Horace takes a condescending attitude towards the poetic skills of Livius by choosing *insector* only to flaunt, through this very choice, his thorough understanding of the older poet's choice of *insece* in the first line of his poem.¹¹⁹ As crucial as it is for understanding Horace's poetry, the passage in itself does not provide any corroborating data in relation to the immediate reception of Livius' poem. In the light of this, a better start is to look at Horace's overall characterization of Livius' epic in his didactic poetry about poetry and from there reconsider the kind of authorial presence that the poem mediated.

In the *Ars Poetica*, Horace famously discusses the shortcomings of the "faithful translator" by offering his own version of the *Odyssey*'s opening lines:

---

115. For Suetonius' historical reliability, see Kaster 1995: 48–54.
116. The most explicit formulation of this view is in Wiseman 2007a: 40–41.
117. Jerome, *Chron. Olymp.* 148.2 (with reference also to the fact that because he taught the sons of Salinator he gained freedom). As for a purpose that went beyond teaching, see Gruen 1990: 84–85. See also Goldberg (2005: 46) on the limited circulation of the poem.
118. Horace, *Epist.* 2.1.71–73.
119. Hinds 1998: 71 and note 37.

> Dic mihi, Musa, virum captae post tempora Troiae
> Qui mores hominum multorum vidit et urbes.[120]

> Tell me, Muse, of the man who after the conquest of Troy
> Saw the customs and the cities of many men.

In a way, these lines can be read as a corrective commentary on Livius' seemingly faithful translation meant to displace the attention away from Horace's own investment in translation.[121] By leaving πολύτροπος untranslated, Horace debunks the self-referentiality inherent in Livius' choice of *versutus* and erases the old poet's claim to authorship. Moreover, by invoking the Muse he plugs his own translation into a composition structured in Homeric hexameters. In the economy of Horace's poetic project, these two moves are justified by the abbreviated history of Latin poetry inserted into his *Letter to Augustus:*

> Graecia capta ferum victorem cepit et artes
> intulit agresti Latio; sic horridus ille
> defluxit numerus saturnius, et grave virus
> munditiae pepulere.[122]

> Conquered Greece conquered her fierce victor in turn and introduced the arts into rustic Latium; and, it was in this way that the uncouth Saturnian ran dry, and refinement drove off the fetid smell.

In these lines Horace summarizes the dynamic relationship between military conquest and cultural fascination that shaped Rome's relationship with Greece from the late third century B.C.E. onwards. We are just able to take in the complexity of this relationship inasmuch as Horace quickly displaces our focus on to the civilizing effects attributed to the introduction of Greek *artes*. This would coincide with the hexameter superseding the Saturnian and the blotting out of "foul smell" from Latium.

As Maxime Pierre has recently pointed out, the aesthetic framework informing these lines rests on the representation of formalized speech that does not match Greek versification as shapeless and uncouth.[123] Even more

---

120. Horace, *Epist.* 2.3.141–42.
121. As for Horace's own poetic project, as Feeney 2002 points out, the poet never ventures to discuss Greek lyric.
122. Horace, *Epist.* 2.1.156–59.
123. Pierre 2005, see especially 232–36.

to the point, perhaps, Horace exploits here the disparaging association of non-Hellenized cultural forms with excessive rusticity and primordiality that we find more fully articulated in rhetorical texts from the first century B.C.E. onwards.[124] By building upon this association, he advocates the desirability of Greek *artes* and naturalizes their attributes by claiming that they are an essential component of Rome's civilizing mission. In the process, Horace suppresses not only the problems associated with the social secondariness of poetry's origins in Rome, but also the Saturnian's association with the sphere of power and authority. Interestingly, the later grammarians who attempted to find a fixed form for the Saturnian (to no avail) speculated about its Greek origins as well.[125] But when they did so, they acted in opposition to received opinion: from the late first century B.C.E. onwards this opinion linked the Saturnian to Saturn and the original site of Rome.[126]

The relationship with Rome attributed to the Saturnian that we find in later sources echoes Livius' aim at geographically anchoring his translation to the spring of the Camenae located somewhere close to Porta Capena.[127] In turn, it seems clear enough that Livius' choice of the Saturnian found its impetus in a more or less contemporary development. Around the same time, compositions in Saturnians were springing up everywhere in Rome. Some of these constitute perhaps the first manifestation of the Greek-based epigram; whatever the case, these compositions are all tightly associated with the dominant members of Roman society.[128] Indeed, the Saturnian frames textualized *dicta* and ritual songs performed by aristocrats as well as inscriptions representing the achievements and the moral qualities of individual aristocrats inside tombs and in more public contexts.[129] Against this backdrop, Liv-

---

124. Connors 1997.
125. McElduff forthcoming. For the Greek origins of the Saturnian, see Caesius Bassus, GL VI.265.8; Festus 432.13; Porphirius, ad Hor. *Ep.* 2.1.157. For a recent reassessment of the Saturnian in relation to remains of Faliscan, South Picene, Umbrian, and Oscan, see Mercado 2006 based on Parsons 1999.
126. For Saturn and Rome, see Virgil, *Aen.* 8.355–58; Varro, *LL* 5.42 (with reference to the Capitolium and citing the authority of Ennius). See also Luiselli 1967: 26 and *passim*.
127. The *Camenae* were connected with a sacred grove and a spring just outside Rome's Porta Camena or Capena (cf. Vitruvius 8.3.1). In Livy (1.19.5; 1.21.3) Egeria, the most famous of these deities, has an affair with Numa and whispers to him divine rites; subsequently, Numa dedicated a grove to her and the Camenae.
128. Van Sickle (1987) constructs his argument about the influence of Greek epigrams by focusing especially on the Scipionic elogia. See footnote below.
129. See Appius Claudius' *dicta* (*FPL* pgs.11–3); the *carmen saliare* and the *carmen arvale* (*FPL* pgs. 2–11); the Scipionic *elogia* (*CIL* 1.29–30; *CIL* 1.32; *CIL* 1.33; *CIL* 1.34) and the *elogium* of Atilius Calatinus (*FPL* pp.13–4); the *tabulae triumphales* of Acilius Glabrio and L. Aemilius Regillus (*GL* 6.265.29) and the inscription located in the temple of Hercules Victor in which the 146 B.C.E. victory of Lucius Mummius at Corinth was commemorated (*CIL* 1.541). As for recent remarks about the Saturnian as a form of speech linked to significant acts and

ius' translation bears the signs of a cultural operation that goes much beyond the mere translation of a text written in Greek into a text composed in Latin. For one thing, it reveals that Livius situated his handling of a longstanding and influential Greek tradition right within a nexus of Roman geographical and elite connections. Moreover, his virtuosity involved reducing the whole poem into a composition fitting a single roll and directly confronting the power of language as his superiors understood it.[130] Accordingly, any appeal to the authority of Homer and the Greek epic tradition on our part occludes the extent to which Livius actually overrode it.[131]

If we return to the first line of the *Oduseia* and use comedy as a benchmark, the fluid game of object relation that Livius plays with Odysseus appears to be based on the same instrumental approach towards Greek 'originals' that we find spelled out in Plautus. But while in comedy the proclaimed source of authorization is the success that the poet enjoys with the audience and the ritual context in which his craft is consumed, in Livius' epic the only source that we can detect is the Camena who is called to pursue/sing (*insece*) to the poet (*mihi*) about Odysseus and the poet at the same time. The power of this claim can be better appreciated if we also take into account the stereotypes of cunning and untrustworthiness that the Romans applied to the Tarentines.[132] If we do so, Livius appears to exorcise the negative characterization of his geographical origins by transforming it into a strategy of self-fashioning and by calling into play the performativity assigned to the Saturnian. Although we are not in the position to measure the immediate reception of Livius' poem, to think about the *Oduseia* as a solo performance sheds some interesting light on his poetic game.

In a theatrical performance the poet and the actor are distinct agents that meet each other through the fictional character. Put rather simply, the poet creates a character that the actor impersonates by adopting words and actions that conform more or less accurately to what the poet intended. As we have seen, in comedy the character of the clever slave takes on something of the poet's subjectivity, but the audience's encounter with it is mediated through the body of the actor. Accordingly, if the actor somehow bungles his performance, the poet has some space for dispelling from himself any negative consequence. If we think of Livius' epic as a solo per-

---

the *carmen* in general, see Meyer 2004: 54. A few important remarks on Livius' use of the Saturnian in relation to its weighty associations are to be found also in Possanza 2004: 51–53.

130. For the drastic reduction in length, see Goldberg 1995: 46.

131. Goldberg (2005: 20–21) takes this authority for granted even while highlighting the discontinuity of its success.

132. For a survey of the construction of these stereotypes, see Lomas 1997.

formance carried out by the poet *in propria persona,* the distance between the audience and the poet is reduced and the possibility that their encounter may not be felicitous increases the poet's stake. In case of failure, the only course of redress would have resided in his ability to renegotiate the boundaries between fiction and reality.

The ways in which later authors return to Livius and identify him as the fountainhead of Latin poetry may suggest that his exploration of epic was predicated on the privileged status that he had managed to achieve during his professional life in Rome. Certainly, during his performances he supported existing structures of visibility by turning his body into a source of entertainment and by playing with the ethnic stereotypes of his audience. And yet, he challenged normativity by appropriating for himself the socially loaded Saturnian and by equating the prestige of the Homeric tradition with his own cultural competence. This competence involved knowledge and understanding, but also the ability to negotiate sociocultural breakpoints and to untie the nodes of communication where conflicting interests come together.

Naevius continued to explore these breakpoints and nodes by creating an epic in Saturnians focused on the achievements of Rome's leaders and by inserting himself directly into the representational frame. Ennius followed by presenting himself as a reincarnation of Homer and rejecting the Saturnian in favor of the hexameter. In the next chapter, I explore the interventions of both Naevius and Ennius and read aestheticizing narratives such as that of Horace against the grain offered by Cato's representation of poetry. For the moment, I find it important to stress that by giving up the idea that the Romans met Greece only some time around the late third century B.C.E. and were seduced, there and then, by the cultural superiority of the Greeks, we let the poets and their sociocultural import take the center stage. What remains of their outputs allows us to observe that the social advancement of a small number of them and the valorization of poetry as a practice were linked to the anthropologically recognized fact that sociopolitical potency relies on a continual effort to capture someone else's inalienable possessions; to embrace someone else's ancestors, magic, power; and to transfer parts of these identities on to oneself and the next generation.[133] Through self-display and self-promotion the poets provided their elite sponsors with new means whereby to express their project of communal and individual expansion. At the same time, they turned themselves into highly prized resources for their sponsors to both court and exploit.

---

133. Weiner 1992: 48.

Chapter 3

Conflicting Scenarios
Traffic in Others and Others' Things

In 168 B.C.E., following his victory at Pydna, Lucius Aemilius Paullus brought Macedonia under Roman rule. Plutarch reports that on that occasion the library of King Perseus was shipped to Rome and became the private possession of Paullus, who donated it to his sons.[1] If we are to believe Plutarch's account, it would have been around this library that the Greek hostage Polybius staged in his *Histories* his first encounters with the young members of the powerful household of the Scipios:

> I have already explained how this friendship developed from the borrowing of books and from discussions around them; when the Achaean hostages were distributed in various cities of Italy, the sons of Lucius Aemilius were still young; Fabius and Scipio insisted with the consul that Polybius reside in Rome. This desire was met and the friendship of Polybius with the two young men became increasingly more intimate.[2]
> (trans. Paton—slightly modified)

As a way to illustrate the nature of his intimacy, Polybius represents the future conqueror of Carthage as a young man worried about not having the qualities that he needs in order to fulfill his inherited social role of

---

1. Plutarch, *Aem.* 28.11.
2. Polybius 31.23. 4–5.

patronus. To this concern, Polybius claims to have replied:

> I admire you when you say that you are pained to think that you are of a milder character than is fitting for the members of this family; for that shows that you have a high spirit. I myself would be delighted to do everything that is in my power to help you speak and act in a way worthy of your ancestors. As for the knowledge that I see you both looking for with great zeal and diligence, there will be no want of people ready to help both you and your brother; so great is the throng of people flowing nowadays from Greece. As for what you say you are troubled about, I believe that you could not find a helper and collaborator more up to the task than myself.[3] (trans. Paton—slightly modified)

What I find remarkable about this exchange is the resourcefulness with which Polybius plays for some control in a situation that was linked to his forced relocation to Rome and his loss of freedom. In the first part of his reply, he offers his expertise in speech and behavioral practices to help the young Aemilianus meet the standards required by his rank.[4] In the second part, he points to the great number of Greek immigrants present in Rome ready to provide the two brothers with what they seek, only to reassert that he is the man fit for the job.[5] In what follows, Polybius reveals the imperatives that prompted him to respond as he did:

> While Polybius was still speaking these words, Scipio, grasping his right hand with both hands, and pressing it warmly said: "if only I could see the day on which you, regarding nothing else as of higher importance, would devote your attention to me and join your life with mine; for then I shall at once feel myself worthy of my household and my ancestors." On the one hand, Polybius was very happy to see the desire and the affection of the young man; on the other, he was embarrassed when he thought about the high position of the family and fortune of its men. After this mutual understanding, the young man never left Polybius' side, and preferred his

---

3. Polybius 31.24.4–8.

4. As Habinek (1990: 172–74) notes, Polybius takes the freedom to provide "an unofficial progress report or an after-the-fact evaluation [whose] de-briefing would prevent the aristocrat from making a blunder in public or help him develop the qualities that would assist in the ultimate attainment of political, military, and religious honors." Cf. also Habinek 1998a: 50–51.

5. As a matter of fact, it is quite plausible that Aemilius Paullus had hired some of these Greeks for the education of his sons in various subjects, including rhetoric (see Plutarch, *Aem.* 6.4–5).

company to anything else.[6]
(trans. Paton—slightly modified)

Implicated in Aemilianus' emotional outburst is that he does not simply desire the help of Polybius; he wants the whole of him, his attentions and his life. As a matter of fact, Aemilianus makes clear that it would be only by fulfilling this desire that he would feel at peace with the obligations that he has towards his family and his ancestors. Accordingly, blinded by the admiration of which he has become the object, Polybius ends up expressing the sociocultural horizon within which his interlocutor operates: being a Roman aristocrat means to expand one's own self by taking a hold of 'others,' their land, their wealth, and whatever else these 'others' embody. In other words, Polybius' claim about his knowledge of aristocratic standards and his offer to sustain the young aristocrat are reinterpreted by Aemilianus within a logic of ownership whose roots lay in Roman imperialistic practices. These included bloodshed, plunder, and enslavement, but they also coincided with and indeed depended on the possessive fascination that Roman aristocrats felt for their 'others' and the 'things' that these 'others' possessed or embodied. In this respect, the episode recounted by Polybius calls attention to the fact that an 'other' could perceive this two-sided attitude and that, if given the opportunity, he would manipulate this attitude to his own advantage. With this, I may seem to be claiming that the feelings of friendship that developed between Polybius and Aemilianus were not sincere and genuine.[7] What I am proposing, by contrast, is that precisely because they were so, these feelings facilitated the change of cultural ownership that occurred during their encounters and made each of them "feel good" about themselves. What these feelings did not (and could not) have the power to do, however, was to blot out the hierarchical relations of power that kept each part involved apart. Accordingly, when considering a narrative such as the one written by Polybius, it is important to take into account two separate and yet related aspects: one, the exchange narrated ultimately advertises the power and enrichment of the dominant party; two, the lesser party has a stake in representing the exchange as an emotional affair satisfying for all.

Polybius' relationship with Aemilianus begins with Aemilianus' declaration of his possessive desire and takes off as soon as Polybius responds to this desire and begins to convey his knowledge to the former. In this

---

6. Polybius 31.24.9–12.
7. On the issue of sincerity and reality of emotions in friendship ties of various sorts, see Konstan 2005; in relation to Horace, see Bowditch 2001.

process of transfer, not only does Polybius validate Aemilianus' desire, he also acknowledges the power that Aemilianus holds over him. Yet the possessive love that Aemilianus feels for Polybius and the knowledge that he embodies is exactly what the Greek hostage is after. In fact, it is only when Aemilianus declares his love that Polybius gets the support that he needs in order to survive in Rome and pursue his literary ambitions. Hence, the exchange that Polybius portrays constitutes the prelude to a story of a highly lopsided, but also fully reciprocated love. This factor incites us to look beyond Polybius' narrative and to plumb more deeply the scenario on which it is mapped.

Diana Taylor has proposed that a scenario can be understood as a repertoire of cultural imaginings that are always embodied and bear the weight of accumulative repetitions. These have the power to structure social environments and behaviors as well as fictional performances and textualized narratives. For our purposes, the notion of scenario developed by Taylor is particularly helpful because it offers us the possibility to find an interface between what has been textually transmitted and the practices that we can no longer access.[8] For this reason, let me outline the steps that Taylor deploys in order to make the notion of scenario a methodological instrument for exploring the relationship between the allures of poetry as a cultural expression associated with professional 'others' and Cato's prose.

First, in order to recall a scenario we need to conjure up the physical location or scene. This can be the space of a dramatic action, a highly codified environment, an ordinary location, or, finally, an imagined site. Accordingly, the notion of scenario incites us to observe certain elements inherent in the text and to form an idea of where a certain cultural form was displayed or what contexts certain practices evoke. Second, in scenarios we are brought to deal with the body and how individual social actors manipulate a given environment and act out embodied schemes. In this sense, the scenario allows us to treat in the same way actors assuming a role in a fictional performance or narrative and actors adopting socioculturally determined behaviors in particular contexts by keeping actors and roles simultaneously in view. Third, in a scenario scenes and actions and/or behaviors are formulaic; as such, a scenario predisposes certain outcomes and yet permits inversions, occlusions, and changes. Regularities and deviations make us wary of the uneasy matches and areas

---

8. Taylor 2003: 29–32. See chapter 1 for a preliminary explanation of Taylor's notion of scenario.

of tension that are either exposed or suppressed from one emergence of a specific scenario to another. Fourth, by looking at how a scenario is transmitted over time and reemerges in various contexts, it is also possible to take into account the different media (e.g., writing, recounting, gestures, dances, songs) whereby a certain scenario is expressed, transmitted, and elaborated. Although the medium that I am exploring is writing, the use of scenario as a theoretical tool makes it possible to link up cultural imaginings with the social constraints that shaped actions and/or behaviors more generally, including those that guided textual representations and uses of writing. Finally, the scenario forces us, observers at a temporal distance, to situate ourselves in relation to the scenario that we are scrutinizing and to become wary of how we transmute ancient preoccupations into something that makes sense to us.

In the following pages I turn to Naevius' and Ennius' retranslations of Greek epic. Prompted by the sociocultural imperatives that Polybius' narrative so clearly exposes, the epics of Naevius and Ennius allow us to test the elite investments in poetry. Differences in the ways in which each of these poets inserts himself into the frame of their epics bring into view the tensions that accompanied these investments and our need to fully acknowledge the existence of pre- and nonpoetic scenarios. One such scenario loomed over Livius Andronicus' *Odusseia* and prompted his choice to transform the Homeric hexameters into Saturnian cola, an authoritative way of speaking associated with an exclusive repertoire; this repertoire included cultural imaginings as well. As we shall see, on a number of occasions Cato the Censor turned to this repertoire and from there he invented a convivial scenario that excludes the participation of professional 'others.' In this scenario the actors are the ancestors and, by extension, those who are in the position of claiming to be their successors; moreover, they meet at banquets and sing in turn the achievements and praises of the most distinguished among them.

Cato the Censor articulated an exclusive convivial scenario to defy the one promoted by the poets where the poet is the person vested with the faculty of constructing elite memories. Others (like Fulvius Nobilior) looked to the additional social prestige that they could derive from the poetic medium and, therefore, favored the collapse of one scenario into the other. In the backdrop of these divergent elite responses, the poets were soon forced into the limited role of cultural providers. From this position they flaunted their insights with the result of transforming themselves and the knowledge that they embodied into highly contested commodities.

The Naevian Scenario

In the *Bellum Poenicum*, Naevius built upon Livius Andronicus' groundbreaking translation of Homeric epic. He did so by recounting the military successes of Rome's rulers during the first war against Carthage within a mythological framework translated from the Greek tradition. Unfortunately, the remains of Naevius' epic are extremely scanty. Yet we know that, just like Livius, he managed to introduce into his script a few (or more?) self-referential lines. According to Aulus Gellius, Naevius spoke directly about his own involvement in the very war that he sought to represent:[9]

> M.Varro . . . stipendia fecisse ait (eum) bello poenico primo, idque ipsum Naevium dicere in eo carmine quod de eodem bello scripsit.[10]

> Varro asserts that he (i.e., Naevius) served in the First Punic War, and that Naevius himself said this in that song which he wrote about the same war.

In the last decade or so, critics have used this testimony to underscore that the *Bellum Poenicum* knew no patrons and that the poet did not do more than pride himself in the achievements of the Roman generals. This interpretation has been encouraged by a concerted effort to save Naevius from the accusation of having sustained the political aspirations of individual elite households. Thus, the veracity of the ancient tradition whereby Naevius suffered prison first and exile later has been overridden, and the more modern interpretation whereby the poet endured all of this because he outraged the Metelli has been dismissed.[11] As it stands, the nature of the evidence makes any attempt to reconstruct Naevius' life extremely conjectural. Even so, the formation of narratives focused on his arrogance should not be rejected altogether because together with the textual shards that represent his exchange with the consul Metellus (or his family at large), these narratives betray a set of anxieties over the intrusion of 'others' into elite life.

We know about this exchange from later commentators. The most

---

9. For a lively discussion of where this self-referential passage should be placed, see M. Barchiesi 1962: 261–62.

10. Gellius 17.21.45

11. Gruen 1990: 92–100 and Goldberg 1995: 33–37. For the reference to prison, see Gellius 3.3.15; often corroborated through Plautus, *Miles* 209–12 (as we have seen in the previous chapter) and Festus 32 L. As for his exile, see Jerome, *Chr. Olymp.* 144.

crucial is a scholiast's gloss on Cicero's allusion to it in *Verrines* 1.29:

> Dictum facete et contumeliose in Metellos antiquum Naevi est "Fato Metelli Romae fiunt consules," cui tunc Metellus consul iratus versu responderat senario hypercatalecto [*sic*], qui et Saturnius dicitur: "malum dabunt Metelli Naevio poetae."[12]

> There is an old saying of Naevius addressed wittingly and insultingly to the Metelli, "in Rome the Metelli became consuls by fate." At this the consul Metellus became angry and replied with a hypercatalectic iambic verse, which is called Saturnian: "The Metelli will do harm to Naevius the poet."

To a certain extent, ancient and modern narratives elaborated on this exchange of verses do nothing more than confirm the nature of the scholiast's report as a sketchy outline. The notion of scenario allows us here to reembody words and actions into the social actors and to draw from the details of their interaction the social values and the power relations on which this exchange is constructed.

First of all, the scene or the physical environment within which this exchange takes place is completely suppressed and so is the presence of any other social actors besides Naevius and the consul Metellus. The suppression elicits the imagining of this exchange as both immediate and intimate. In turn, the narrow focus on the verses and their movement from Naevius to Metellus and back promotes a specific view of the actors through the messages encoded in each speech act and in the actions/reactions that accompany these acts.

An element left generally unremarked is that the exchange is initiated by Naevius, who evaluates the political and military deeds of the Metelli by using an iambic senarius, a speech pattern typical of dramatic dialogues. This latter element has induced some to believe that the line belonged to one of Naevius' *fabulae praetextae*. Centered on Roman mythological and historical exploits, the *fabula praetexta* was a poetic genre that Naevius had brought onto the Roman stage, perhaps by reworking a preexisting performance tradition.[13] As already noted, this hypothesis is hard to corroborate since the scholiast defines Naevius' utterance simply as a *dictum*

---

12. Ps. Ascon. 215 Stangl; cf. also Caesius Bassus *GL* 6.266 (where the reference is not to the consul Metellus but to the family of the Metelli).

13. For the link between this poetic genre and preexisting performance traditions, see Wiseman 1998. For speculations regarding its context of performance, see Flower 1995. On the *fabula praetexta* in relation to the sacral dimension of *imperium*, see Zorzetti 1980.

and does not link it to any specific dramatic script or context.[14] This fact strengthens the impression that the implied setting is more exclusive than the theatrical environment.

Speculations about the Saturnian nature of Naevius' line have been rightly rejected on philological grounds.[15] Yet these speculations remain compelling because the line could also be read as a defective form of it.[16] With this, I am not advocating that Naevius actually produced this line or that this line is derived from his epic. Rather, I am arguing that in this narrative Naevius' attempt and failure to produce a Saturnian fits the traditional characterization of his arrogance: without permission to do so, he tries to mimic an authoritative way of speaking while referring to aristocratic exploits. His attempt misfires and what comes out is an iambic senarius. Though a speech pattern perfectly fit for the ritual context of drama, the senarius is here made to mark Naevius' nonelite standing. On the other hand, that this verse is meant to characterize an attempt on the part of the poet to boost his prestige finds confirmation in the scholiast's definition of this line as a *dictum,* if we accept that *dicere* and its derivatives refer to any speech act through which the speaker strives to take an authoritative position in relation to his/her interlocutor.[17]

As for the reply of the consul Metellus, it is normally assumed that he found Naevius' line outrageous because it implied that they had reached the consulship by sheer accident rather than by any worthy achievements.[18] Accordingly, Metellus turned against the poet and promised to punish him. Just as in Naevius' case, the speech pattern and the linguistic register inherent in Metellus' line contain relevant information. Scholars have noted that *malum dare* is a typical comic expression and that through it Metellus would have cast himself into the role of the comic master.[19] This reading is highly convincing as it points to what sociolinguists call 'accommodation,' that is, a speaker's adaptation to the language of his/her interlocutor.[20] But if we are to gauge the full effect of Metellus' response,

---

14. This is rightly pointed out by Goldberg 1995: 35.
15. E.g., Goldberg (1995: 35 note 17) rejects Flintoff's reading (1988: 598–99) by noting that though breakable into two uneven cola, the first colon lacks the so-called *caesura korschiana.*
16. As Jed Parsons pointed out to me, in Naevius' line "Metelli" is longer than "fato" (the first half-line should be longer than the second); the line, in other words, would work only if there were another word before "fato" that has dropped out.
17. Habinek 1998b: 71–73.
18. E.g. Gruen 1990: 98–100; Goldberg 1995: 35–37.
19. For the comic language inherent in the Metelli's line, see Gruen 1990: 100 and Goldberg 1995: 35.
20. On the notion of accommodation in socio-linguistic terms, see the fundamental work

the tendency to reduce its authoritative dimension ought to be slightly resisted. For if through this act of accommodation Metellus takes up the role of comic master, by means of a Saturnian he most authoritatively recasts the poet into the role of the comic slave who, however cleverly, is still to serve his superiors. In this sense, it is not at all irrelevant that in later discussions Metellus' line emerges over and over as the model Saturnian.[21] While this fact corroborates once again the historical relationship between the Saturnian and socially authoritative individuals, the larger notion of scenario allows us to grasp the specific scenario implied in the exchange as a whole.

By and large, the vignette offered by the Ciceronian scholiast cannot be understood as a faithful report of an actual episode of Naevius' life. What it does signal, however, is that the practice of representing the most significant activities of the ruling elite was a delicate issue, if not a privilege that some were unwilling to hand over unconditionally to the poets. Furthermore, if with the *Bellum Poenicum* Naevius situated his claim of authorship in the context of war, the poem included an attempt on the part of the poet to reap social prestige in a way comparable to those whose deeds he recounted. Accordingly, the scenario that informs the above exchange illustrates that some members of the ruling elite interpreted Naevius' strategies of self-presentation as a definite act of insolence, as if the poet had taken the liberty of speaking about the ruling elite as though he were a member of the class himself.

To put it in other words, what we read around and about Naevius indicates that poetry was a new medium and the prospects that it raised for the Roman elite were both enticing and disturbing. Poetry was enticing because it was a cultural practice that allowed them to use Greek literary materials in order to deepen and extend the cosmological dimensions inherent in their expansionistic drive. But poetry was also disturbing because the poets' attempts to garner social prestige by meddling in authority-building activities threatened the very prerogatives whereby the Roman aristocracy had long constructed and affirmed their authority. As in other traditional societies, these prerogatives were based on specific activities and constituted a type of resource that aristocrats guarded carefully and valued highly.[22] The changes in the epic scenario carried out by Ennius in his *Annales* make particularly explicit what we find condensed

---

by Giles and Powesland 1975.

21. Caesius Bassus, *GL* 6.265; Terent. Maur. *GL* 6.399.2497; Ad Fortun. *GL* 6.283.25.

22. For a discussion of how aristocrats define themselves in traditional societies through distinctive behaviors and activities, see Helms 1998:115–20.

in the Naevian narrative: first, the growing importance of poetry as a tool for articulating and evaluating the activities that defined the ruling elite as such; second, the anxieties of some elite over the encroachment of 'others' on their socially distinguishing practices.

Ennian Changes of Scenario

Cicero informs us that Marcus Fulvius Nobilior left for his Aetolian campaign in 189 B.C.E. accompanied by Ennius and other poets.[23] Two years later, Fulvius returned victorious but had to face the resistance of his personal enemies when they questioned his claim for a triumph, accused him of misconduct during the siege of Ambracia, reproached his ferocious plundering of the city, and produced witnesses in support of their accusations.[24] Despite this hostility, Fulvius obtained public recognition for his achievement with a splendid triumphal procession.[25] Furthermore, he restored to the citizens of Ambracia the private property that he had confiscated and consigned the rest of the booty to the *pontifices*. By this time, the *pontifices* regularly separated sacred items from profane: while the former were supposed to be reconsecrated, the latter were to be privately distributed or publicly displayed.[26] In this sense, Cicero and Eumenius (a third-century C.E. panegyrist) confirm that, after his triumph or during his censorship in 179 B.C.E., Fulvius rededicated a group of sacred objects, the images of the nine Muses that he had brought from Ambracia, in a new temple. This temple is known as the *Aedes Herculis Musarum*. Situated in the Campus Martius, it became the new meeting place for the poets.[27] Finally, Servius adds that Fulvius transferred into his new religious establishment an altar attributed to Numa and dedicated to the Camenae invoked by Livius Andronicus. This shrine was originally located outside Porta Camena (or Capena), but after being struck by lightning it had been temporarily housed in the temple of Honos and Virtus.[28]

The relationship between the Camenae and the Muses instantiated

---

23. Cicero, *Tusc.* 1.3 and *Pro Arch.* 27.
24. Livy 38.9.13, 38.43–44, 39.4–5; Polybius 21.29.6–30
25. Livy (39.5.15) records that at the triumph 785 statues in bronze and 230 statues in marble were displayed.
26. For a recent contribution on Fulvius Nobilior's contested triumph, see Witzmann 2000. For a discussion of the role of the *pontifices* in this period, see Gruen 1992: 110.
27. Cicero, *Pro Arch.* 27; Eumenius, *Pan. Lat.* 9.7.3 Baehrens.
28. Servius *A*.1.8. Note that Servius refers to the *aedicula Musarum,* not *Camenarum.* A slip which scholars are quick to correct.

in Fulvius' temple has long been explained in light of poetic discourses. For example, in his magisterial edition of Ennius' *Annales* Otto Skutsch pointed to a textually problematic line in which the poet seems to be negotiating the transition from one set of deities to the other. In turn, he linked this transition to Ennius' metrical shift from the Saturnian of Livius Andronicus and Naevius into the hexameter, on the one hand, and to Fulvius' religious establishment, on the other.[29] In this view, the coincidence between Fulvius' rededication of statues of the Muses and Ennius' invocation of them is interpreted in Horace's terms, as the sign of a partnership between the general and the poet in the larger project of paving the road to more refined cultural forms and the submission of Rome to the cultural power of Greece.[30]

Although interested in the relationship between poets and the elite, the multiple attempts that have been made in the last decade or so to correct this reading share a relative disinterest in their entanglements with what the poets in antiquity sought to promote. So, for example, it has been argued that rather than rejecting the Camenae, Ennius and Fulvius were accomplices in absorbing them into a larger Greco-Roman concept. Indeed, their explicit link with the hoary Camenae would have allowed the Muses to grow into the deities overseeing the celebration of 'national' exploits.[31] By debunking a strictly political interpretation of the *Annales*, this reading leaves unexplained how the hoariness of the Camenae would have ratified this shift and builds upon a scenario in which the poet is unproblematically vested with the power of immortalizing elite memories.

By adopting a more literary approach, other critics have defended the poetic skills of Livius Andronicus and Naevius, and have pointed out that Ennius was very much responsible for constructing his poetic

---

29. The transition Camenae–Muses would take place in Ennius, *Ann.* 487 [*sed.inc.*] Sk: "Musas quas memorant nosce nos esse Camenae." This fragment presents numerous textual problems. For bibliographical references and traditions of interpretation, see Gruen 1990: 117–19. As for the connection Camenae–saturnians and Muses–hexameters, see also Ennius, *Ann.* 206 Sk, accompanied by Varro, *LL* 7.36. For further reflections, see Sciarrino 2004b.

30. Skutsch 1985: 144. Consider also the imagery of light that Skutsch uses elsewhere in relation to Greece: "the Muses, mountain spirits at first, then goddesses of music, poetry, and dance, had under the bright sun of Greece become the patrons of all intellectual pursuits. This, then, is Ennius' claim: he writes not as one darkly inspired, but in the full light of knowledge as a master of craft" (1968: 5).

31. Though simply put, this is the opinion of Gruen (1990: 117–18; 122). Much of his reading is based on Cicero's celebration of poetry in the *Pro Archia*. A countering attempt to this trend is in Zetzel 2003 and 2007. See also Gildenhard (2007b: 85 note 77) who rightly notes that "the outlook of the epic is 'national' (or 'civic'), but this perfectly matches the interests of Ennius' patron."

predecessors as "archaic" and "hirsute," that is, "unpolished."[32] In these reappraisals, however, the association between the Camenae and the prepoetic song tradition is left completely unexplored. Furthermore, by calling attention to later readings of Ennius' archaization and rustication of his predecessors, these readings blur the larger and more immediate picture. A closer examination of how Ennius manipulated the epic scenario that he had inherited from his predecessors brings to light how Ennius satisfied Fulvius' investments in poetry and yet curbed the elite anxieties that the narratives about Naevius express. These anxieties, as I have pointed out, concern the encroachment of 'others' on the activities that characterized the ruling elite as such.

For one thing, Ennius' employment of the hexameter and his invocation of the Muses somewhere at the beginning of his poem are not self-standing literary devices nor do they express any particular nationalistic intent on the part of either Ennius or Fulvius, or both. Rather, they are the formal means through which Ennius reflected on his participation in Fulvius' feats of conquest. After all, it was before the poet's very eyes that Fulvius had plundered cult objects representing the Muses in Ambracia and had transported them to Rome.[33] Second, the *Annales* was also entangled in the reconsecration of these objects in the temple that Fulvius erected in Rome and in the messages that Fulvius sought to promote through it. In this sense, Ennius' very account fleshed out the conception of history and heroism unfolded in the *fasti* and the year-by-year list of consuls and censors that Fulvius had taken care to display in the portico of his religious complex.[34] Granted that, Ennius manipulated the Greek epic tradition in order to create for his audience a very specific perspective on his cultural agency and social subjectivity. Rather than provocatively situating himself in a nexus of Roman and elite connections like Naevius, he situated his cultural agency away from it and offered a representation of his social subjectivity in tune with his nonelite status.

---

32. Among recent appraisals of Livius Andronicus' and Naevius' poetry from an aesthetic perspective, see Goldberg 1995: 58–82. For the construction of early poets as "archaic" and "hirsute," see Hinds 1998: 62–63 and, less detailed, Leigh 2000. An excellent review of the debate is now in Gildenhard 2007b: 71–86. Much of what I say here corroborates Gildenhard's insights.

33. See Keith 2007 for a compelling reading of the Muses' importation in relation to successive narratives of forced female relocations to Rome (the Sabine women in *Annales* 1 and the destruction of Alba Longa in *Annales* 2).

34. For the *fasti* and the list of consuls and censors displayed in the temple, see Macrobius, *Sat.*1.2.16; for discussion, see Rüpke 1995: 39–44, 345–66. As for the link between the *Annales* and these lists, see also Gildenhard 2003a: 95–97. Rüpke (2006) goes as far as to suggest that the *fasti* themselves were Ennius' own creation.

After his invocation of the Olympian Muses and their beating feet (*Musae, quae pedibus magnum pulsatis Olympum,* 1.1 Sk), the poet goes on to describe his poetic investiture by reactivating a very powerful Greek-made scenario familiar to us from Hesiod and Callimachus.[35] But whereas in the Greek scenario the poet meets the Muses who bestow on him the power of song, in his dream Ennius encounters Homer in person (*visus Homerus adesse poeta,* 1.3 Sk) and finds out that the Greek poet's soul has migrated into his, that is, Ennius', body.[36] Whereas critics tend to focus on the literary and philosophical framework underlying this strategy of self-presentation, I would like to draw attention to what this ostensibly self-aggrandizing framework enabled Ennius to do.

First, the Greek-derived dream scenario allowed him to situate his poetic authorship within a profoundly non-Roman context and, therefore, to partially occlude the circumstances that prompted the construction of the *Annales,* namely, his participation in Fulvius' military campaign. Moreover, by presenting himself as Homer reincarnated, he reinvented his own migratory subjectivity in bodily terms and set forth an understanding of his selfhood as a conduit for Homer's relocation into Rome.

Ennius' strategy of self-presentation finds a formal expression in his adoption of Homer's hexameter and, therefore, in the aural perception of his script. If this were not enough, Ennius took also care to define his poetic craft by using the Greek-derived word *poemata* (*latos <per> populos res atque poemata nostra / clara> cluebunt,* 1.12 Sk). Accordingly, he would have encouraged his audience to perceive his poem as a written object of poetic design speaking about Roman elite memories in an uncompromising rhythm. Later in the poem, this framework is both expanded and reinforced.

In a fragment attributed to book 7, Ennius shuns the Saturnian by associating it with pre-poetic figures of song and by refusing to write about the war treated by Naevius (*scripsere alii rem / vorsibus quos olim Faunei vatesque canebant,* 7.206–7 Sk). It is generally assumed that in these lines Ennius looked to convey a sense of superiority by situating his predecessors in an uncouth past.[37] This reading would be warranted not only by Horace's history of Latin poetry in his *Letter to Augustus* but also by Cicero's citation of these lines in *Brutus* 71 and 75. In these places Cicero strengthens the association of *faunei* and *vates* with a preliminary moment of cultural

---

35. Hesiod, *Theog.* 22-ff. speaks about of the poet's encounter with the Muses on Helicon and their inspiration to sing; Callimachus at the beginning of his *Aitia* presents the same type of investiture and introduces the motif of the dream.

36. These elements are all discussed by Skutsch 1985: 147–67.

37. E.g. Skutsch 1985: 371.

development and locating Ennius in a superior phase of this development in order to set the stage for his own twofold endeavor: the transformation of Roman oratory into a primarily written practice and the presentation of his oratory as the ultimate outcome of a progressivist history.[38]

I propose to revisit this line of interpretation by paying more focused attention to Ennius' own writings. What stands out is that Naevius is not at all presented as a *faunus* or a *vates;* rather, he is refigured as someone who wrote about the First Punic war by using turns of languages (*vorsibus*) associated with *Faunei* and *vates*. In other words, Ennius includes Naevius in his poetry as a mere imitator of non- and pre-poetic song but does not accompany this inclusion with judgments of value on the tradition of which the Saturnian was an expression. As such, he does provide a framework by which to think about the history of Roman cultural practices, but it will be the work of later authors to construct the pre-poetic past as uncouth and primitive, and to oppose this past to a sophisticated and enlightened present.[39]

To better gauge Ennius' positioning in relation to Naevius', it may be worth taking into consideration other significant fragments even if their attribution to specific books is highly contested. The first, preserved by Servius (*ad Aen.* 8.361), runs as follows:[40]

Contra carinantes verba atque obscena profatus.[41]

Having spoken abusive and obscene words against those who tear apart with insults.

---

38. Interestingly, Cicero adds that, even if somewhat undeservingly, Ennius had downplayed Naevius' import (*Brut.* 75). It should also be noted that in *Orator* 171, Cicero draws on Ennius once again to support his rejection of "old things." On this passage, see Narducci 1997:157–73 For the ultimate outcome of the claims inherent in this passage, see *Cicero, Brut.* 292–96.

39. This type of reworking can be seen already in Lucilius (484–5M) who represents the Fauni in somewhat negative terms in relation to Numa. As for the same type of strategy at a time contemporary to Cicero, see Lucr. 4.580–82. Note that in Lucretius *vates* is used twice with a derogatory tone, 1.102–3; 108–9, while the figure of the poet is valorized (see especially, 5.1444–45). Cf. also the discussion by Wiseman 2006. For the positive recuperation of the *vates* at a later stage, see Hardie 1986: 11–32 and Gildenhard 2007b: 87–92.

40. For the problems associated with the fragment (which are many), see the few notes by Skutsch (1985: 716–17), which cannot be fully evaluated without considering other opinions. Most important contributions are Grilli 1965: 11–15; Reggiani 1979: 60–61; Flores, Esposito, Jackson, and Tomasco 2002: 175–81.

41. Ennius, *Ann. Sedes Incertae Frg.* 576 Sk. I should like to note that in the same Servian context, we find the following: "alibi "<at> (Flores) neque me decet hanc carinantibus edere cartis." Whereas Flores (2000: 74) inserts it right after 7.206–7 Sk, there is the tendency of reading this fragment as belonging elsewhere (the *Satires*). See also comments in Flores, Esposito, Jackson, and Tomasco 2002: 186–88. If Flores is right, the line would adjust the understanding of Ennius' attack on Naevius, specifying something like "nor is it right for me to lay open this matter (i.e., the First Punic War) with abusive writings."

Some years before Skutsch's edition, Alberto Grilli proposed to place this fragment in the opening of Book 7. In his view, *profatus* relates to the religious-divinatory sphere and would take Ennius as its subject. Consequently, in this line the poet would have cursed his enemies as a way of concluding his attack on Naevius and his supporters. Grilli supported his proposition by turning to the Hellenistic tradition and a parallel in Callimachus' virulent attack on the Telchines (*Ait.* 1.17–18 Pf). Rather than using a verb equivalent to *epitrúzein* to define the abusive language of his detractors, Ennius would have chosen a visual image associated with the agricultural world thanks to the link of the verb *carinare* to *carere* "to card wool." Moreover, in order to give a cohesive version of the entire section Grilli suggested that just as in Callimachus' *Aitia,* so too Ennius' attack is lodged in a dream setting that looks back to the beginning of the poem and slightly ahead to a claim to specialized knowledge:[42]

> Nec quisquam sophiam, sapientia quae perhibetur,
> In somnis vidit prius quam sam discere coepit.[43]

> Nor did anyone saw in a dream *sophia,*
> which is called *sapientia,* before he began to learn it.

Thomas Habinek has recently argued that these two lines anticipate the reevaluation of Roman traditions in accordance with Greek philosophy and testify to Ennius' intervention in "a roiling debate over the nature, meaning, and class identification of *sapientia.*"[44] In this view, the dream of *sophia* would have had the same relationship to the Pythagorean tradition as the process of metempsychosis that opens up the poem. Though highly compelling, the Pythagorean connection need not exclude the possibility that Ennius also bracketed under the rubric of *sophia* the Callimachean meaning of poetic *tekhnê,* as Grilli suggested.[45] Thus, if all points of view are taken into account, it could be said that Ennius rejected the *modus operandi* of Naevius and the like, echoing the Callimachean precedent. Not, however, as Grilli has it, to blame them for their attacks on his poetic intervention, but for their misappropriation of forms of elite self-expression that some elite preferred to keep outside the sphere of poetic competence. In this sense,

---

42. Grilli 1965: 13–14.
43. Ennius, *Ann.* 7.211 Sk.
44. Habinek 2006: 485–88. For the ways in which Cicero plays with the relationship of *sapientia* with *philosophia,* see Gildenhard 2007a: 97–106.
45. See especially Grilli 1965: 17–21.

like Skutsch, I think that if we want to place the line in the context of book 7 we need to read *profatos* in parallel with *carinantes* since it is hard to see how Ennius, who keeps his distance from the formal means that relate to the Roman world of nonpoetic song, could be prophetically speaking *obscena*. Accordingly, a better reading could be the following:

Contra carinantes verba atque obscena profatos

Against those who card words and prophesy obscene things.[46]

Adding up to Ennius' strategy of self-presentation, this passage would contribute to his claim over knowledge that looks to the Hellenistic world and that he declares to have acquired through a Pytagorean-oriented oneiric experience. Thus, just as through a dream he elaborates on his migratory subjectivity by presenting himself as Homer reincarnated, so too through a dream he sustains the incorporation of *sophia,* understood as philosophic knowledge and poetic *tekhnê,* into the elite tradition of *sapientia,* which at the time referred to aristocratic assertions of advisory competence.[47]

That Ennius strove to portray himself as someone operating differently from Naevius and the like by turning to the Hellenistic tradition is made clearer in two other fragments. In the first, he commits to the literary standards of the Alexandrian tradition *([cum] neque Musarum scopulos / nec dicti studiosus [quisquam erat] ante hunc . . . nos ausi reserare,* 7.208–10 Sk);[48] in the second, he plays with Livius Andronicus' translation of the first line of the *Odyssey:*

---

46. Ennius, *Ann Sedes Incertae* Frg. 576 Sk.
47. Habinek 2006: 485. For *sophia* as a byword for poetry, see, e.g., Solon 13.52; Xenophanes B 2.14; Pindar (*Ol.* 1.116, 9.38, *Pyth.* 1.12). Many thanks to Patrick O'Sullivan for pointing out to me these loci.
48. For a different reading and positioning of the line, see Flores 2000: 74 (with comments in Flores, Esposito, Jackson, Tomasco 2002: 188–91; the commentary by Tomasco remains somewhat elusive):

quom neque Musarum scopulorum <quisquam
    /scandebat>
nec <calamo> dicti studiosus quisquam erat ante
    /hunc

Translated into Italian as follows: "perché né delle Muse le rupi <alcuno saliva>, né <con la penna> studioso della parola alcuno era prima di costui." The insertion of *calamo* is intriguing especially in view of the emphasis that Ennius placed on his poetry as a textual artifact disengaged from Roman traditions.

insece Musa manu Romanorum induperator
quod quisque in bello gessit cum rege Philippo.[49]

pursue Muse with my hand what each
of the Roman generals carried out in the war against Philip,

In these two lines Ennius emends Livius' invocation to the Camenae and states that the subject of the poetry that will follow is "what each Roman general accomplished in the war against King Philip." More importantly, he pushes the meaning of Livius' *insece* from "sing" to "pursue" and, perhaps, goes as far to correct *insece* into *inseque*. What Ennius' ultimate choice was is hard for us to reconstruct since already in antiquity it was not at all clear which of the two verbs Ennius had chosen.[50] Yet the meaning of "pursuing/following" seems to be corroborated by the insertion of *manu*. Critics tend to translate *manu* into "by feats of valor" and, therefore to translate the line into something like "sing/pursue, Muse, what each of the Roman generals carried out by feats of valor in the war against Philip." I prefer to associate the noun with the initial verb and to understand *manu* as relating to the poet's own hand and, therefore, translate the lines as I do above. If not so, I would at least allow for the possibility that Ennius played with both meanings of *manu*, leaving open the possibility to choose between the two variants.[51] Giving space to this reading would do justice to the semantic shift identified in Ennius' allusion to Livius' *insece* and Horace's rendition of it into *insector* that we find in *Epistles* 2.1.71. Moreover, it would give further substance to Ennius' choice to disembed his voice and his poetry from the realm of Roman authoritative song by bringing poetic writing to the fore.

Recently Ingo Gildenhard has pointed out that Ennius' exploitation of conceptual resources generated in the Greek world should be interpreted as a claim of poetic authorship that is tantamount to an abdication of social authority. To support his argument, Gildenhard asserts:

---

49. Ennius, *Ann.* 10.322–3 Sk. For Ennius' clearly alluding to the first line of Livius' *Odyssey,* see already Gellius 18.9.3. As for the interpretation of this line as a "correction," see Skutsch 1985: 499.

50. Gellius 18.9.5. See also Hinds 1998: 59.

51. Skutsch (1985: 499): "used somewhat redundantly to denote feats of valour of which *manus* (pl.) is synonym in Virg. *Aen.* 6.683." A more compelling parallel is perhaps to be found in the lines from one of Naevius' comedies, preserved for us in Gellius 7.8.5: *etiam qui res magnas manu saepe gessit gloriose, / cuius facta viva nunc vigent, qui apud gentes solus praestat / eum suus pater cum pallio uno ab amica abduxit.* But compare also the use of *manu* in relation to poetry, authorship, and performance in Plautus: *apporto vobis Plautum, lingua non manu,* Plautus, *Men.* 3.

vates and *carmen* are charged terms in Rome: the former refers to a prophet or seer who functions as the mouthpiece of a deity possessing him; a *vates* is therefore a figure with privileged access to divine knowledge. The latter is commonly used in archaic Latin to refer to speech-acts that make a difference, in religious, legal, or moral terms. Ennius shrewdly dissociates himself from these problematic (since highly political) forms of power by resolutely situating his authority *as author* in the sphere of the aesthetic.[52]

In identifying Ennius' twofold strategy of self-presentation—his rejection of Roman authoritative song and his embracing of Hellenistic-based aesthetic—Gildenhard obliquely points to the scenario that I am trying to unearth and the elite anxieties that, as we have seen, are embedded in the narratives that we read around Naevius. Unlike Naevius, Ennius appears both to acknowledge and to assuage them. Just like Naevius, he focuses on the military and political exploits upon which the Roman elite had constructed their hegemony. Contrary to Naevius, he downplays his involvement in these activities, and avoids reproducing the Saturnian, a speech pattern evoking power and authority. With this in mind, I propose to pay renewed attention to how Ennius constructs his role in Roman society through the famous scene of the anonymous companion:

Haece locutus vocat quocum bene saepe libenter
Mensam sermonesque suos rerumque suarum
Consilium partit, magnam quom lassus diei
Partem fuisset de summis rebus regundis
Consilio indu foro lato sanctoque senatu;
Quoi res audacter magnas parvasque iocumque
Eloqueretur †et cuncta†malaque et bona dictu
Evomeret si qui vellet tutoque locaret;
Quocum multa volup
       Gaudia clamque palamque;
ingenium quoi nulla malum sententia suadet
Ut faceret facinus levis aut mala: doctus, fidelis,
Suavis homo, iucundus, suo contentus, beatus,
Scitus, secunda loquens in tempore, commodus, verbum
Paucum, multa tenens antiqua, sepulta vetustas
Quae facit et mores veteresque novosque †tenentem

---

52. Gildenhard 2003a: 103–4.

> Multorum veterum leges divomque hominumque
> Prudentem qui dicta loquive tacereve posset:
> Hunc inter pugnas conpellat Servilius sic.[53]
>
> Having spoken in this way, he calls upon someone with whom he often had the pleasure to share his table, his conversation, and his thoughts on private affairs, tired after spending a large part of his day in counsel in the broad forum and the holy senate; to this person he spoke rather openly about small and great matters and jokes, letting out good and bad things to say, if he felt like it and knowing that they were kept safe. With whom much pleasure
>
> Joys both private and public; the type of person whom no opinion, ill-considered or evil, can persuade to do wrong: learned, trustworthy, a charming man, pleasant, content with his lot, prosperous, shrewd at saying the right thing at the right time, helpful, a man of few words who preserves many ancient matters which have been buried by antiquity, who understands customs both old and new, and the laws of many ancient gods and men. He is cautious and capable of speaking up or keeping silent. In between battles Servilius turned to this man in this way.

This fragment sketches the interaction between Servilius Geminus and an unidentified man of lower standing. It is generally assumed that the fragment alludes to Ennius' relationship with Fulvius, or at least to his own circumstances.[54] What is more, the sketch is staged in a military camp between one battle and another. Accordingly, Ennius elaborates on his experience with war in order to do something completely different from what Naevius did through his *Bellum Poenicum*. Rather than elaborating the war scene to stake out a claim to social authority, against this setting he constructs a character involved in the life of a powerful Roman. This someone does not engage in the activities that distinguish a Roman ruler; his status is tightly bound up with the services that he is able to provide. He knows when to speak or keep silent and he provides the busy politician back at home and the active general at war with a safe venue by which to alleviate the burdens of power. Moreover, during his interactions with the Roman general and politician this someone lets out the cultural knowledge

---

53. Ennius, *Ann.*8. 268–86 Sk.
54. Skutsch 1985: 93–94, 447–62. See also Gellius 12.4, where this passage is presented as an example of proper behavior for an *amicus minor*. Gellius also ascribes to Aelius Stilo the interpretation that here Ennius is depicting his relationship with Fulvius Nobilior. This is generally uncontested, see Badian 1972; Skutsch 1985: 450.

that he embodies and, therefore, grants his powerful interlocutor the possibility of using this knowledge for his own benefit.[55]

While evoking the scenario informing Polybius' narrative, the list of qualities that Ennius attributes to the trusted and faithful companion finds at least one close parallel in the world of the Hellenistic rulers.[56] If Ennius was indeed thinking about that world, the passage suggests that he expressed his social subjectivity vis-à-vis the Roman elite by translating a character from a non-Roman context and by playing a game of projective identification in line with what we find in both Plautus and Livius Andronicus. In the economy of the *Annales,* however, this strategy can be defined as a variation on the theme of substitution that Ennius introduces at the beginning of the poem when he claims to be an incarnation of Homer. I would argue that Ennius' insistence on and exploration of this theme betrays in other ways the fact that the poets' relationship with the elite was becoming troubled and contested. To illustrate more pointedly how Ennius handled this issue, I find it useful to draw on our experiences with doubles in the cinematic medium.

In movies a double is adopted when the script requires the actor to do something physically or morally compromising. In action movies the actor is often replaced by a stuntman, while in movies that tease the erotic fantasies of the audience the actor may choose to have someone replace him or her in particularly sexual sequences. When a double comes into play, the audience is led to take the double as the actual actor through visible markers that recall the physical features of the actor substituted by the double (i.e., hairdo, height, bodily structure, clothes, and so on). As viewers, we play along and we can do so because the camera never comes so close as to fully reveal the trick of substitution. The character of the trusted and faithful companion can be seen to work in similar ways. He does not enter the audience's purview through visible markers as in the cinematic medium but the description of his behavior and the services that he provides to the Roman general immediately bestow on him the identity of a subordinate in line with Ennius' social inferiority. As opposed to what happens in movies, however, the identification is shrewdly delayed. In fact, Ennius, the reincarnated Homer, reveals the trick of substitution and invites the audience to identify the lesser epic character with himself only

---

55. In this sense, see now Hardie (2007: 132–39) with compelling observations on the resonance of this scene in Horace's satirical self-fashioning.

56. Skutsch 1968: 92–94; 1985: 449–51. In these contexts Skutsch points to a papyrus described by Page (1950 no.111) as "a fragment of an Hellenistic poem, praising an officer of the royal court of Alexandria."

when he hints at the knowledge that this character possesses (8.282–84 Sk). Accordingly, the moment of recognition is crafted in such a way as to keep Ennius, the social actor, at a distance from the world of the *Annales* and the achievements recounted but not so distant as to completely undercut the poet's chance to manipulate the gap between reality and fiction in order to insert a reflection on his own social subjectivity. Though pervasive, then, Ennius' presence is also significantly understated; as he insists towards the end of the fragment, the man fit for the job is cautious and is capable of measuring his speech acts (8.285 Sk).

The centrality of Ennius' strategy of delayed identification can be detected in the way critics do not hesitate to associate the anonymous friend with Ennius because of the *doctrina* that he is said to embody.[57] What generally goes unnoticed is that, although corrupted in some places, this subordinate person the text represents as someone who "contains" (*tenentem,* 8.283 Sk) knowledge. Accordingly, Ennius does make knowledge crucial to his self-identification with the lesser epic character, but he also encourages the audience of his poem to think of his cultural agency in bodily terms. As a reincarnated Homer, he first presents his selfhood as a vessel for the relocation of the primeval author of epic to Rome, afterwards, as a "body that matters" by containing knowledge from which the powerful can draw.

Considered together with Polybius' depiction of his own relationship with Aemilianus, the vignette incorporated in the *Annales* challenges the impression that individuals or groups are somehow stable identities and unchanging conduits of knowledge and memory. Constructed by 'others,' both scenes make visible how they dynamically tailored their own migratory subjectivities by capitalizing on the twofold attraction that the Roman ruling elite felt for them as objects over which to exercise their dominance and as subjects conveying knowledge. These snapshots suggest that some of these 'others' exercised a certain amount of control over their encounters with individual members of the ruling elite.[58] Even so, a long-term and felicitous relationship was still contingent upon their individual ability to call attention to the knowledge that they embodied and to act within the boundaries that defined their social subjectivity. In other words, by virtue of their bodily movements, speech acts, and silent withdrawals these 'others' can be seen to both absorb and manipulate into their creations the hierarchical schemes of perception that guided the actions and

---

57. E.g. Skutsch 1968: 92–94; Badian 1972: 180–82; Gruen 1990: 113; Gildenhard 2003a: 111.

58. In this sense, the anecdote about Scipio Nasica's visit to Ennius' house and his witty rejection is exemplary (see Cicero, *De Or.* 2.276).

behaviors of their social superiors. To valorize their knowledge and to hold out this knowledge at the right moment and in the right manner was a clear manifestation of this simultaneous process of adaptation and manipulation. Accordingly, an historian like Polybius and the Greek immigrants whom he mentions, poets like Livius Andronicus, Plautus, Naevius, and Ennius, were different products of the same history of displacement and their individual successes or failures were (and are) a visible sign of how they adjusted to this history. By the same token, their migration to Rome, their bodily expressions, their textual creations, and their speech acts were all mapped by Roman expansionistic practices and were all caught up in and ancillary to the individual and collective formation of Rome's body politic.

Ancestral Banquets and Elite Scenarios

In a much debated passage of the *Tusculan Disputations,* Cicero suggests that the acceptance of poets and poetry was both late and contested:

> Sero igitur a nostris poetae vel cogniti vel recepti. Quamquam est in Originibus solitos esse in epulis canere convivas ad tibicinem de clarorum hominum virtutibus; honorem tamen huic generi non fuisse declarat oratio Catonis in qua obiecit ut probrum M. Nobiliori quod is in provinciam poetas duxisset. Duxerat autem consul ille in Aetoliam, ut scimus, Ennium.[59]

> Therefore our people got to know or accept poets late. Although we find in the *Origines* the information that guests at banquets used to sing to the sound of the pipe about the manly deeds of distinguished men, a speech of Cato makes clear that there was no social prestige attached to this genre since he reproaches M. Nobilior for taking poets with him to his province. In fact, as we know, when consul, he had brought Ennius to Aetolia.

In all of its elliptical syntax, this passage encodes an abbreviated history of poetry in Rome. Implicated in this history is an allusion to the anxieties provoked by the encroachment of poets on the life of the Roman elite. Cicero hints at these anxieties by reporting that Cato the Censor delivered a speech in which he censured Fulvius Nobilior's decision to take poets on his military campaign and denied social value to poetry.[60] Somewhat

---

59. Cicero, *TD* 1.3.
60. It is generally assumed that the speech in question was delivered in 178 B.C.E., the year after Fulvius' censorship rather than on his contested claim to the triumph in 187 B.C.E. See Astin 1978: 110 note 22; Sblendorio Cugusi 1982: 294–96 (with reference to Cato's first-hand

unfortunately, the relationship between epic and the ancestral convivial practices invoked by Cato in the *Origines* and the specific object of Cato's attacks on Fulvius in the speech remain confused.⁶¹ Rather than simply rejecting their connection, I propose to reconstruct the scenario that informs Cato's positioning in relation to poetry by turning, first of all, to a much-cited fragment of his *carmen de moribus:*

> Poeticae artis honos non erat. Si quis in ea re studebat aut sese ad convivia adplicabat grassator vocabatur.⁶²

> There was no social prestige attached to poetic craftsmanship. If someone dedicated himself to it or applied himself to banquets he was called a 'mugger.'⁶³

In this fragment Cato measures the social worth of poetry and legitimates his negative judgment by invoking ancestral convivial practices. These two elements link the *carmen de moribus* to the speech which, according to Cicero, Cato delivered against Fulvius; even so, the *carmen de moribus* appears to have differed in focus. Whereas Cicero suggests that in the speech the invocation reinforced Cato's attack on Fulvius' decision to have poets take part in his military campaign, the *carmen* centers on the encroachment of nonelite practices and nonelite individuals on banquets. In turn, Cicero does not elucidate at all what linked war and banquets, but the scenario that Cato activates in the *Origines* clarifies it. In this scenario the ancestors sit at a banquet and sing about the manly deeds of distinguished men with the accompaniment of the pipe. In a later passage of the *Tusculan Disputations* Cicero turns once again to the *Origines* and unfolds a fuller version of Cato's invocation: those who sing are those who reclined and they did so by taking turns. The content of their songs included not only manly feats, but praise as well (*morem apud maiores hunc epularum fuisse, ut deinceps, qui accubarent, canerent ad tibiam*

---

experience as Fulvius' legate in Aetolia in 189 B.C.E. as evidenced from a fragment from another speech of Cato, namely, *orat.* 36.95 Sbl). Goldberg (2005: 26–27) situates the circulation of Ennius' *Annales* in the late 170s.

61. See Goldberg 2006.

62. Gellius 11.2.5 = Cato, *carmen de moribus* 2 C&Sbl. See also Festus 86L: Grassari antiqui ponebant pro adulari. grassari autem dicuntur latrones vias obsidentes; gradi siquidem ambulare est, unde tractum grassari, videlicet ab impetu gradiendi ("The ancients used *grassari* to mean "fawn upon" [*adulari*]. And *grassari* is used of thieves who lie in wait on the roads, since *gradi* means "walk" and *grassari* was derived from this—clearly, with reference to the violent force of the walking").

63. On the translation of *grassator* as "mugger," see further Sciarrino 2004a: 333–34.

clarorum virorum laudes atque virtutes, Cicero *TD* 4.3).

By and large, the scenario that Cato activates and anchors to the past in more than one place helps us gauge from yet another standpoint the constraints unsuccessfully challenged by Naevius and successfully negotiated by Ennius. In this scenario the battlefield and the banquet constitute some of the physical environments in which the sociopolitically dominant perform their social role. In war they command a group of armed men and compete for the benefits and privileges associated with a victorious outcome. At banquets, these same individuals measure new enterprises against previous ones, bestow praises on their authors in the form of songs, and nourish an exclusive repertoire of behavioral exempla transmitted in embodied form. Consequently, in Cato's convivial vignette the participants constitute a closed group of men worth being remembered in song for what they have been able to accomplish while performing their social role of community leaders. By the same token, the act of singing *laudes* and *virtutes* constitutes the means whereby the perceptual distinctiveness or *claritas* of these same men is constructed and their feats transformed into behavioral models for the reproduction of the group. Although the process requires for each *vir* to undergo the evaluative judgment of the other *viri,* the regulation of their singing acts is presented as conducive to the creation of a bond among the participants as well as between them and their successors.[64] Against this scenario, poetry is defined as a practice associated with the nonelite; as such, it is excluded from the war context *a priori.* In turn, this *a priori* exclusion sustains the evaluation of poetry in the *carmen de moribus* where Cato insists on its alienness to ancestral-like banquets.

It is generally assumed that Cato's *carmen de moribus* was not an original work of literature, but a collection of prescriptions drawn from other sources.[65] To keep focusing on Cato's lack of literary originality means to miss that these prescriptions derive their value from the fact that they are embedded in a composition that is defined as a *carmen.* Speaking somewhat generally, Thomas Habinek has emphasized that while relating to the musical aspect of a song at all times, the term *carmen* referred especially to a song that sought to establish or reinforce societal or cosmological hierarchies.[66] Following the same trajectory from a different point of departure,

---

64. For a discussion of *claritas* as perceptual distinctiveness either auditory or visual and its difference from *gloria* as related to the lessening of someone else, see Habinek 2000: 269–70.

65. See Astin 1978: 185–86; and most recently Goldberg 2005: 13.

66. Habinek 1998b. As for the specific model of Cato's own *carmen,* see also the so-called *carmen* of Appius Claudius Caecus (Cicero, *TD* 4.4, cf. Valerius Maximus 7.2.1). Citations from Appius' *carmen* can be found in FPL pp.11–13. This is rightly stressed by Goldberg 2005: 13 note 32.

Gildenhard has tapped on this important element, too, when he asserts that Ennius' rejection of the pre-poetic *carmen* was also a way of distancing himself from "speech-acts that make a difference, in religious, legal, or moral terms."[67] To my mind, the fact that Cato antagonizes poetry and poets in a composition identified as a *carmen* illustrates that at this stage the very notion of *carmen* stood in sharp opposition to poetry in both formal and social terms. At the same time, the content of the *carmen de moribus* makes clear that the poets and their practices were making a decisive entrance into the life of the Roman elite and confirms that in some quarters they were both perceived as disturbing factors in the regulation of intraelite relations. The fact that Cato addressed in more than one place the issue of poetry and poets is not at all surprising and is of a piece with his participation in ongoing disputes over conspicuous consumption, which I address below.[68]

In 195 B.C.E. Cato spoke against the abrogation of the *lex Oppia*, a law promulgated during wartime that limited expenditure on women's clothing and carriages.[69] As a censor in 184 B.C.E., he addressed the control of lavish expenditures,[70] the regulation of private habits and the illicit use of public resources,[71] and the improper display of war spoils in private houses.[72] Some of these issues made their way into the other prescriptions contained in the *carmen de moribus* as well. There, the subject of poetry and its practitioners' encroachment on elite banquets follows closely on a number of precepts concerning the regulation of extravagant clothes and the acquisition of "domestic personnel" for the preparation of food:

Vestiri in foro honeste mos erat, domi quod satis erat.
equos carius quam coquos emebant.[73]

It used to be the custom to dress becomingly in public and to wear the indispensable at home. They paid more for horses than for cooks.

Cato's anxieties over private expenditures in general and lavish banqueting in particular are also testified and elaborated by Polybius:

---

67. Gildenhard 2003a: 103–4.
68. This point is stressed by Goldberg 2005: 14–15, but for the purpose of denying that epic could have never been circulating in convivial contexts. For Cato's involvement in sumptuary legislations, see Astin 1978: 91–97; Gruen 1992: 69–72
69. All that remains of this specific speech is the elaborated version in Livy 34.2–4.
70. Cato, *orat.* 11.52 and 12.52–3 Sbl.
71. Cato, *orat.* 13.54–6, 14.57–8, 15.59–69, 20.73–9, 21.80 Sbl.
72. Cato, *orat.* 18.71, 19.72 Sbl.
73. Gellius 11.2.5 = *carmen de moribus* 1 C&Sbl. The relationship between poetry and cooking here is reflected in Ennius' translation of Archestratos' *Hedypatheia* where, simply put, Ennius presents himself as both a cook and a poet.

Some gave themselves up to affairs with boys, others to *hetairai*, and many to spectacles, drinking parties and the extravagance they involve (εἰς ἀκροάματα καὶ πότους καὶ τὴν ἐν τούτοις πολυτέλειαν), since in the course of the war with Perseus they had quickly become infected with Greek license in these things. In fact the incontinence that had broken out among the young men grew so great that many paid a talent for a favored boy and many paid three hundred drachmas for a jar of preserved fish from Pontus. Marcus Cato became so indignant at this that he said in a public speech that he recognized in these matters the surest sign of decline in the state when pretty boys are sold for more than fields and jars of preserved fish for more than plowmen.[74]

Following the depiction of his relationship with Aemilianus, Polybius' digression on the moral aftermath of the victory over Perseus is deeply implicated in his elucidation of Aemilianus' uprightness. As such, the depiction is both a song of praise addressed to Aemilianus for having remained untouched by new trends and an assertion of social superiority over those who provided entertainments at banquets. By cloaking himself under a vest of morality similar to that adopted by Cato, Polybius offers here a negative representation of his Greekness in line with elite representations of the impact of the expansion on the life of the Roman elite.[75] As we shall see in the next chapter, Cato's discursive strategies have less to do with narrow-minded conservatism, as is too often assumed, than with his promotion of self-sufficiency and cultural mastery.[76] Viewed under this light, Cato's attack on poetry and his invocation of specific convivial procedures aimed at nourishing exclusive practices and self-regulating relations within its upper crust. On the other hand, when considered side by side with Ennius' concerted effort to do something other than singing a *carmen,* Cato's activation of a convivial scenario bracketing out professional intrusions indicates that epic performances could well be bracketed under the spectacles (ἀκροάματα) that, according to Polybius, had "infected" the Roman youth after Pydna.

---

74. Polybius 31.25.5.
75. Goldberg 2005: 14.
76. For representations of Cato's 'narrow-mindedness' not only in relation to the poets but also Polybius, see, for example, Henrichs (1995: 254), where he asserts that Polybius, "a *Graecus captus* in the most literal sense, . . . captivated Aemilius Paullus, the victor of Pydna, and Scipio Africanus, the victor of Carthage, with his Greek *paideia* and converted the rustics of Republican Rome, including the likes of Cato, to Greek culture." Although arguing against this view, Gruen (1990: 116–17) tends to reduce Cato's positioning in relation to poetry as "purist posturing." Despite this, Gruen's discussion remains fundamental.

While we do not find explicit evidence suggesting that epic was performed at banquets, Cato's articulation of an exclusive convivial scenario points to the preexistence of convivial practices in Rome. In turn, the rules and behaviors that structure Cato's evocations are so markedly formulaic that one cannot fail to see the weight of innumerable repetitions.[77] With this, I find it important to stress that a scenario never stands in direct relationship with an historical reality because scenarios are constituted by cultural imaginings; nevertheless, they encompass an historical dimension in the measure that they guide discourses, behaviors, and practices. Moreover, scenarios do not remain the same through time; in fact, they tend to be adapted to changing conditions. In light of these considerations, a good way to go about the question of epic's relationship with banquet practices is to assess, first of all, the centrality of the convivial scenario by focusing on the formulaic features of the scenario promoted by Cato and to trace their emergence from one enactment to the other. As we shall see, these shape scenes and narratives in a variety of generically and chronologically disparate texts, suggesting that in Roman culture it was as central as (say) the scenario of discovery in the Americas, which made its first appearance in the summary of Colombus' journal put together by Bartolomé de las Casas in 1552. Although no original of the journal remains, nobody can deny that it was elaborated on historical events or that it continues to be reenacted to this very day even if in different media and guises.[78]

In Livy the exclusive banquet that sets the stage for the death of Lucretia can be indisputably subsumed under the rubric of "bad banquets" and seems to be part of an anti-Etruscan tradition recently discussed by Annapaola Zaccaria Ruggiu.[79] The war is lasting more than it should and the royal youths (*regii iuvenes*) are spending their time eating and drinking. During one of these parties, they begin to talk about wives. At that, "each man began to praise his own in admirable ways" (*suam quisque laudare miris modis,* Livy 1.57.6). The men enter into competition with one another until Collatinus asserts that words would not do to prove the preeminence of his wife, Lucretia.

Livy constructs his narrative by deploying some of the formulaic elements that we find in Cato and it is from them that his narrative draws its

---

77. This is, as Taylor (2003: 31) suggests, a typical feature of scenarios: "scenarios, by encapsulating both the set up and the action/behaviors, are formulaic structures . . . the frame is basically fixed and, as such, repeatable and transferable. Scenarios may consciously reference each other by the way they frame the situation and quote words and gestures."

78. Taylor 2003: 55–64.

79. Livy 1.57.4–7. Among the "bad banquets" a memorable one is Cicero, *In Cat.* 2.10. As for the anti-Etruscan trajectory, see Zaccaria Ruggiu 2003: 15–28.

cultural relevance. First of all, Livy's banquet features men belonging to the upper crust of society. Second, the male participants owe their social identity especially to their engagement in warlike activities. Third, banqueting is presented as a practice linked to time off from battles. Fourth, during the banquet the men evaluate each other by taking turns in praising.[80] Fifth, despite its disturbing outcome, the story takes for granted that reciprocal evaluation should culminate with an agreement over who should be granted the highest praise. Although singing is not mentioned, the relationship between banqueting and fighting, the exclusive character of the occasion, and the turn-taking rule that regulates the interaction are clearly detectable.[81] In turn, the episode narrated by Livy fits in the much larger historical picture that informs the earlier books of his work.

As Tim Cornell has recently stressed, in this section of Livy's work the definition of a group of young men as *iuvenes* is strongly associated with the term *sodalis*, which refers to a member of a band of warriors guided by a leader and a type of social bond that has left its traces on both material and epigraphic evidence.[82] While the convivial scene evoked by Cato is nowhere historical, it is not at all out of place to think that the scenario on which it is built bears the signs of the gentilician society of central Italy. In this sense, the appearance of the word *sodalis* in the so-called *Lapis Satricanus,* an inscription discovered in the foundations of a rebuilt temple dedicated to the Mater Matuta and dated to the late sixth or early fifth century B.C.E. is a case in point:

(?)IEI STETERAI POPLIOSIO VALESIOSIO
SVODALES MAMARTEI.[83]

The companions of Publius Valerius have erected this to Mars.

---

80. Note that the praise of each wife involves the individual doing the praise as well, since a wife is part of a man's assets. In the assessment of the wives' behaviors, morality and economy go hand in hand. As we learn later in the narrative, Lucretia will be found late at night spinning wool together with female slaves at home, whereas the other wives are off wasting resources in banqueting activities (Livy 1. 54.8–9). The behavior of Lucretia reflects on her husband in turn.

81. Although no explicit reference to singing can be detected, it is quite tempting to interpret the expression *miris modis* in musical terms.

82. Cornell 2003: 73–97, esp. 87–89 and 91–94. See also Torelli 1999: 17. See also the so called "Fucine Lake Inscription" (CIL I2 5) dated to the very late fourth century B.C.E. Here a form of *socii* (*allies*) appears and represents a votive inscription capturing a similar context of Italian raiding and warfare pursued around condottieri that we find in the *Lapis Satricanus.* For a linguistic discussion and recent reconstruction, see Clackson and Horrocks 2007: 112–14.

83. This reading is just one among many, see Stibbe 1980; Cornell 2003: 89. For a brief summary of interpretations, see Baldi 1999: 204–6.

First, the *sodales* mentioned in the text are associated with Mars, the god of war; second, the inscription works as a dedication made by these *sodales* to Poplios Valesios, identified as the legendary Publius Valerius; third, the grammatical constituents of the text inscribed are organized in a colometric structure that looks to the saturnian.[84] In other words, the inscription encapsulates some of the paradigmatic features inherent in the convivial scenario activated by Cato and it is the same scenario with which the early poets had to deal in the process of translating and domesticating epic in Rome.

It might seem like a mere stretch of the imagination, but the same scenario looms over Horace's approach to his own poetry as well. As is often pointed out, Horace adopted the fiction of pure singing (*canere*) in order to inscribe himself in the performance tradition of Greek lyric and articulate his *recusatio* to compose epic.[85] In relation to Roman cultural history, however, Horace leaned towards pure singing and rejected epic primarily because his main object was to resurrect for himself the pre-poetic figure of the *vates*. Indeed, it is in view of this resurrection that Horace looks down upon the recitation of texts (*recitare*) or singing practices outside exclusive banquets and sacred festivals (*cantare*).[86] At the same time, by following the precedent of the early poets Horace aggrandizes and invigorates his project by translating Greek literature and, specifically, an area of this literature strictly connected with the performance setting of the symposium. Though phrased in terms of aesthetic decorum, Horace's strategy for devaluing *recitare* and *cantare* was part of a more encompassing effort to invest his own poetry with an aura of authority drawn from the past. Accordingly, Horace constructs the superiority of his poetic project in part on the exclusive features and the unmediated nature of the singing that characterizes the ancestral scenario.

The higher cultural value bestowed on *canere* as pure singing can also be detected in Quintilian. Sure enough, he too substantiates this value by drawing on the convivial scenario:

Quamvis autem satis iam ex ipsis, quibus sum modo usus, exemplis credam esse manifestum, quae mihi et quatenus musice placeat: apertius

---

84. Coarelli 1995: 209. This is rightly stressed by Habinek 2005a: 38–40.

85. Markus 2000: 152; Lowrie 1997: 64–65; Lefèvre 1993. For Horace's self-presentation as a *poeta/vates/sacerdos,* see also Bowditch 2001.

86. As Markus (2000: 142) points out, Horace uses *cantare* in a derogatory manner (i.e., *Sat.* 1.10.17–19) except when this act is circumscribed within the realm of the sacred (i.e., *Odes* 3.1.4). Note that *cantare,* in its derogatory sense, encompasses stage performances as well, since they had lost much of their sacral dimension at this stage of Roman cultural history (i.e., *Epist.* 1.19.41–4).

tamen profitendum puto, non hanc a me praecipi, quaque nunc in scenis effeminata et impudicis modis fracta non ex parte minima, si quid in nobis virilis roboris manebat, excidit; sed qua laudes fortium canebantur, quaque ipsi fortes canebant.[87]

Although I believe that from the examples I have just used it is clear what type of music I prefer and to what extent this type should be used, nevertheless I think that I should be clearer about it. What I prescribe is not that contemporary type which, effeminized on the stage and mollified by lascivious melodies, has to no small extent destroyed whatever manly vigor was remaining in us; rather, it is the music once used to sing the praises of the brave and that the brave themselves used to sing.

In this passage Quinitilian constructs his precepts on a binary opposition between modern and ancient customs that, as we can see in Cato, is typical of authoritative speaking. In turn, this binary is gendered so that contemporary stage performances are presented as woman-like and soft and are opposed to the masculine ways in which the brave of old used to sing praises. Not surprisingly, Quintilian associates this manly practice with epic. In fact, in a previous passage he had already granted the first place to Homer and Virgil, and had prescribed the ways in which poetry should be read:

Sit autem in primis lectio virilis et cum suavitate [*Radermacher,* sanctitate *Winterbottom*] quadam gravis, et non quidem prosa similes, quia et carmen est et se poetae canere testantur, non tamen in canticum dissolute nec plasmate, ut nunc a plerisque fit, effeminate; de quo genere optime C. Caesarem praetextatum adhuc accepimus dixisse: Si cantas, male cantas; si legis cantas.[88]

But above all the reading must be manly and combined with a certain dignified charm and certainly different from prose, because it is song and the poets claim to be singing, not however, in the way of stage-like performance, effeminate and lascivious as it happens nowadays. About this genre, we learn that Caesar while still a boy said: if you sing in that way, you do it badly; if you read, you sing in that way.

---

87. Quintilian 1.10.31. Markus (2000: 142–43) has compellingly highlighted this passage and the following. However, my reading undermines her proposition that epic lacked "birth defects" (141).

88. Quintilian 1.8.2.

In this passage Quintilian strives to draw a line between *canere* and *cantare*. On the one hand, he builds upon the poets that claimed for their songs the status of *carmen* and *canere*; on the other, he invokes the authority of Caesar who spoke a *dictum* on the subject of *cantare*. Quintilian's distinction remains powerful as long as one accepts the poets' claim to *canere* and the association of *cantare* with stage performances. But once the attention is turned away from where Quintilian directs it, what stands out is that his definition of "good song" is based on a flawed equation and a self-serving interpretation of Caesar's words. In fact, Quintilian capitalizes on the overlap between the poetic and the convivial even while invoking the convivial scenario activated where the people doing the singing were the brave. Moreover, he distracts us from Caesar's fundamental association between *legere* and *cantare* in order to prescribe only a certain type of reading practice. What we should not forget, however, is that poetry in Rome was a type of song heavily dependent on reading and that the poets were definitely not the brave whom we find in the convivial scenario. In other words, Quintilian summons the convivial scenario, which pointed to the lesser value of scripted songs; at the same time, he stretches the categories of *carmen* and *canere* by relying on poetic claims in order to encompass what some members of the ruling elite in the second century B.C.E. had definitely bracketed out of those categories. The point that I should like to stress, then, is that Cato's activation of the convivial scenario maintained its power well into the first century C.E.; however, at that stage its reactivation suggests that some of its features had changed to allow for the higher social value that poetry had accrued over time.

Overall, the cultural framework revealed in just these few examples makes manifest the centrality of the socialized body and the interaction of this body within the highly structured environment of an elite *convivium* or exclusive social settings mapped on its features. Such environments were not constructed in texts; rather, they were the product of a mnemonic system that preceded the texts. These spaces, that is to say, were hedged about by rules that were part of larger taxonomic paradigms; these existed and were transmitted in embodied form. By activating the convivial scenario, Cato did not aim to recover or even bear witness to past practices; rather, he responded to contemporary trends and tried to define a space of social interaction that envisioned the exclusive participation of individuals involved in military or equally authority-building activities. The physicality of this environment is made clear by the ways in which the participants are required to act. In the scene elicited by Cato they recline on couches and take turns in producing songs; formulaic in nature, these patterns of behaviors served Cato's purpose to minimize the impact of poetry on elite life. In spite of Cato, however, poetry and its practitioners became integral to convivial-like events. Indeed, one may even go so far as to say that Cato activated his version of the convivial scenario precisely because these had already taken hold.

The Roman Elite Goes 'Other'

According to Suetonius, Publius Terentius Afer was born in Carthage in 185 B.C.E. and came to Rome as a slave of Terentius Lucanus, who gave him an education first and his freedom later on account of his beauty and intelligence. Soon enough, Terence attracted the interest of Scipio Aemilianus and his friend, Gaius Laelius. This interest led to the slanderous insinuations that his powerful friends were the actual authors of his plays. Suetonius comments that the poet never contested the rumors and by citing the prologue to the *Adelphoe* he remarks that Terence helped them spread around:

> Nam quod isti dicunt malivoli, homines nobilis
> Hunc adiutare adsidueque una scribere:
> Quod illi maledictum vehemens esse existumant,
> Eam laudem hic ducit maxumam, quom illis placet,
> Qui vobis univorsis et populo placent,
> Quorum opera in bello, in otio, in negotio
> Suo quisque tempore usust sine superbia.[89]

> As to the spiteful accusation that eminent persons assist him and often write them together, his accusers may reckon it a grave imputation; however, he takes it as an utmost compliment since he is pleasing to those who find favor with all of you and with the general public, men whose services in war, in peace, and in your affairs are given at the right moment, without haughtiness, to each of you.

In this passage, the character of the *prologus* turns the allegations concerning the authorship of Terence's plays to the poet's advantage: his connections with eminent aristocrats prove his appeal and the merit of his literary skills; in turn, their recognition is an expression of the services that these men lavish on the community. Plagiarism, however, is not the only allegation that the poet appears to have confronted. A few lines before, the

---

89. Terence, *Ad.* 15–21; Suetonius, *Ter.* 1–4.

prologus alludes also to criticisms directed to the way Terence had gone about translating and argues in his favor by pointing out that in the process of assembling the *Commorientes,* Plautus had exercised the freedom to excise a scene belonging to the beginning of his Greek 'original' (6–11). Terence had extracted (*extulit,* 11) that scene and went about translating it "word by word" (*verbum de verbo expressum,* 11). The same allegation emerges in the prologue to the *Andria.* This time the *prologus* explains that Terence had used two plays by Menander, the *Andria* and the *Perinthia,* by extrapolating scenes from the latter in order to assemble his Latin rendition of the former (9–14). A few lines later he adds that, in doing so, Terence had followed the precedent of Naevius, Plautus, and Ennius (18–19). In the prologue to the *Heauton Timorumenos,* the issue of authorship crops up again (24) alongside renewed allegations concerning Terence's translation practices (16–21). Here reference is explicitly made to a rival poet later identified by Gellius (2.23) as Luscius Lanuvinus and the use of more than one Greek 'original' for assembling one Latin play, which is defined as an act of "pollution" (*contaminare,* 17). Once again, the poet's proxy takes as a line of defense the example of previous authors (*bonorum exemplum,* 20). Finally, in the *Eunuch*'s prologue the poet's proxy goes so far as to conjure up the scene of accusation: during a rehearsal before the aediles, Terence's rival had interrupted the performance by claiming that the play had not been composed by a poet but by a thief who had ripped off the character of the sponger and the soldier from the *Colax* of Naevius and Plautus (22–26).

Some two decades ago, Sander Goldberg remarked that the charges of *contaminatio* lodged against Terence had less to do with an aesthetic issue as modern critics from Leo onwards have assumed than with the practical fact that, by making many plays into a few, the poet was unfairly reducing the store of Greek 'originals' available to the poets operating in Rome.[90] In another way, however, it could be argued that the charges call attention to the fact that Greek 'originals' had risen in value in a way that was tantamount to the depreciation of the other cultural materials that until then had been employed to assemble dramatic scripts. In this view, the allegations of Terence's rivals reveal a view of Greek 'originals' as resources that the poets could no longer freely pillage and transform. Indeed, they would suggest that, once a part of the 'original' had been translated, this became the individual possession of the translating poet and could no longer be

---

90. Goldberg 1986: 95. For the more generalized understanding that the question of *contaminatio* reveals a heightened literary awareness among the audience see, for example, Martin [1976] 2001: 6–10.

retranslated by others. If so, Terence's prologues would indicate that new rules of engagement with Greek 'originals' were articulated from within the poetic ranks; the enforcement of these rules, on the other hand, would reveal that the poets were losing control over their circulation. On this score, the charges of plagiarism directed to Terence point to a heightened elite familiarity with both 'originals' and 'translations,' an outcome that is generally read as the development of an increasingly Hellenized taste.

Terence's reply that his rival had dared interrupting a performance before the aediles implies, to some extent, that the poets trusted the aediles' ability to establish right or wrong by way of comparing texts. How the magistrate in question would have acquired the skills to judge a case of *contaminatio* is impossible to know. A better case can perhaps be made from the insinuations concerning the authorship of Terence's plays in the *Adelphoe* and the circumstances that led to its production. While acknowledging that the play was performed in 160 B.C.E. at the funeral of Aemilius Paullus, Goldberg rejects the association of the *nobiles* mentioned with Aemilianus and Laelius as a later construction on the ground that the former was too young, even though he had distinguished himself at Pydna at the age of seventeen.[91] Regardless, it is hard to deny that the production of this specific play may have looked to the library of King Perseus that Paullus had shipped to Rome and that Polybius may have had in mind as the scene of his earliest encounters with the young Aemilianus. Moreover, in light of the shortage of 'originals' hypothesized by Goldberg and an evidently heightened competition among poets, it seems likely that for Terence to enjoy the patronage of the Scipios constituted a double asset. On the one hand, it allowed him to exploit his connections in order to claim literary prestige against his competitors; on the other, it gave him the chance to get his hands on Greek 'originals' in the very city of Rome. If so, the attacks on the authorship of Terence's plays could well be viewed as both an expression of corporate in-fights and a criticism on his patrons' involvement in poetic practices.

If we focus on the poets, these attacks bespeak the intersection between the increasing importance of elite support in poetic success and a progressive change of cultural ownership from the poets to their elite patrons. If we focus on the elite, these same attacks point to the domestication of poetry and its practitioners in the ludic sphere of the Roman aristocracy as

---

91. Goldberg 1986: 8–15, see especially 9; Gruen 1992: 200. The suggestion that Terence's plays were written by Laelius is found also in Cicero, *Ad Att.* 7.3.10, whereas Quintilian (10.1.99) makes Aemilianus the rumored author. In Cicero's *De Amicitia* 24.89 the character of Laelius speaks about Terence as his *familiaris*.

exchangeable goods that helped reinforce bonds between elite males. In this sense, David Konstan has recently proposed that the insinuations that we read in Terence's prologues had more to do with a slur against aristocrats who stooped to writing poetry than with the literary incompetence of their protégé.[92] Konstan's interpretation makes a great deal of sense especially if considered in light of Cato's reaction to poetic encroachments on elite life. If we do so, the charges of plagiarism directed to Terence alert us to at least two sets of anxieties. The first relates to the surplus value generated from the physical ownership of Greek 'originals'; the second to the contamination of manly formation by a dependency on cultural practices associated with social subordinates. For this reason, the representation of Terence's relationship with young aristocrats in erotic terms deserves to be taken seriously at least for what it reveals about social formations at the time.

As I mentioned above, in Suetonius' biography of Terence the question of authorship is bound up with allegations about his erotic involvement with Scipio Aemilianus and Gaius Laelius. Suetonius' very effort to offer the contrasting opinions of the first century B.C.E. antiquarian Fenestella and the late second century B.C.E. poet Porcius Licinius makes the intersection particularly conspicuous.[93] Fenestella argued against these insinuations by suggesting that the poet was considerably older than both men; but by citing Porcius, Suetonius makes them exponentially more central and surely more compelling:

> Dum lasciviam nobilium et laudes fucosas petit,
> Dum Africani vocem divinam inhiat avidis auribus,
> Dum ad Philum se cenitare et Laelium pulchrum putat,
> Dum in Albanum crebro rapitur ob florem aetatis suae:
> Suis post latis rebus ad summam inopiam redactus est.
> Itaque ex conspectu omnium abit in Graeciam terram ultumam.
> Mortuos Stymphalist Arcadieae oppido. Nil Publius
> Scipio profuit, nil illi Laelius, nil Furius,
> Tres per id tempus qui agitabant nobiles facillume.
> Eorum ille opera ne domum quidem habuit conducticiam,
> Saltem ut esset quo referret obitum dominum servolus.[94]

In the meantime he [i.e., Terence] courted the drone-like nobility and their pretended admiration, drank in the godlike voice of Africanus with greedy

---

92. Konstan 2005: 349.
93. Suetonius, *Ter.* 1–2.
94. Suetonius, *Ter.* 1.

ears, thought it fine to dine regularly with Philus, found Laelius pretty, and was often snatched to the Alban property on account of his youthful charms; later on, he was stripped of his possessions and was reduced to dire poverty. So he fled from men's sight to a remote part of Greece and died at Stymphalus, a town in Arcadia. Thus he gained nothing from Scipio, nothing from Laelius and Furius, the three noble men who were most affluent at the time. They did not help him even with a rented house, which he could at least use as a place for a slave to announce his master's death.

In these few lines, Porcius Licinius dramatizes in tragic terms the difficulties encountered by Terence during his short poetic career. Terence's tragedy takes as a point of departure his inability to resist the aura of nobility emanating from Aemilianus and his failure to exercise some control over his engagement with the young aristocrat. While the poet covets the attention of his patron, this never demeans the legitimacy of his status as self-possessed proprietor of the poet's knowledge. As such, the blindness with which Terence devotes himself to Aemilianus and his friend dovetails with a change of cultural ownership that satisfies the possessive desires of the young aristocrats and reinforces their power over him. Constructed on the same scenario presented by Polybius and Ennius, Porcius Licinius articulates in explicitly sexual terms the transfer of knowledge that the more intimate relationship between the elite and their 'others' ultimately achieved. I would argue that the shift in tone and outcome points to an important cultural and historical watershed.[95]

While it is right to think that Porcius Licinius is historically unreliable, I would say that his erotization of Terence's relationship with his patrons brings to center-stage the poet's body as the site where the limits and excesses of second century B.C.E. elite masculinity are articulated and defined. In turn, through the homology between the poet's body and his poetry Porcius dramatizes the instrumental role that poetry itself had begun to play in elite male relations and ludic practices. On the other hand, Porcius' resentful tone towards the behavior of Terence's patrons reveals a set of anxieties that we see emerging from within the poetic ranks around the same time.

---

95. Such shifts can be seen, for example, in slasher-movies. Though the scenario has stayed the same, after the eighties the female victim is no longer rescued at the end of the movie by the male savior; as a matter of fact, he is often ridiculed or undermined by the female character who ends up taking care of the slasher without male support. As Clover (1987: 218–21) suggests, this shift is informed by the changing role of women in society.

Valerius Maximus (3.7.11) reports that when one day Caesar Strabo visited the *collegium poetarum* housed in the Temple of Hercules and the Muses, the poet Accius did not stand up to greet him. Valerius Maximus explains that Accius refrained from showing him respect not because he was unaware of Strabo's aristocratic status but because he was Strabo's superior in the poetic pursuit. If read together with Porcius Licinius's life of Terence, the anecdote suggests that when Roman aristocrats began to engage poetic practices, the poets attempted to guard their corporate interests and contested the encroachments on their profession of those who were supposed to act as their patrons. In this sense, the association of Terence's body with his poetic production draws further power and meaning: the poet's efforts to incite and sustain the interest of the elite bespeak the inescapable relationship between poetry and patronage, while the sexual attraction elicited by the poet's physical beauty comes to stand for the irresistible charm that poetry exercised on the elite. In this picture, the sexual violation of the poet and the poet's diminished capacity to live and survive in Rome thematizes a drastic change of cultural ownership of both 'originals' and 'translations.'[96] Not only did the Roman aristocrats now have 'originals' in their own homes, they had also managed to steal from their 'others' the knowledge and skills that they needed in order to directly manipulate these 'originals' for their own individual and corporate purposes.

Later on in his biography, Suetonius provides further details about Terence's short career and the issue of authorship crops up again:

> ... causa vitandae opinionis qua videbatur aliena pro suis edere, seu percipiendi Graecorum instituta moresque quos non perinde exprimeret in scriptis.[97]

> ... to get away from the rumor that he was passing off other people's work as his own, or to study the institutions and customs of the Greeks which he had not always represented accurately in his scripts.

In this passage Suetonius offers a view on the end of Terence's life that obliquely points to a reduction in the poets' possibilities to capitalize on their migratory subjectivity. The ability to move across linguistic, cultural, and social divides in which the poets had initially reveled is now redefined

---

96. For the classic treatment of homosocial relations played over a "beloved third," see Kosofsky Sedgwick [1985] 1993.
97. Suetonius, *Ter.* 4.

in terms of cultural theft and hybridism. The poets are now stealing from their patrons and are polluting the cultural flow from Greece. On this score, the additional testimony of Cosconius reported by Suetonius, about Terence's premature death at sea on his return to Rome with new translations of Menander, rephrases the ultimate dream of the Roman male elite that we find in Livy's account of the origins of drama.[98] In this dream, the 'others' convey new cultural goods and disappear somewhere at the margin of the world, leaving Roman aristocrats free from the labor-intensive effort to define and redefine their own cultural mastery.

In the late nineteenth century the alleged 'erotic triangle' involving Terence as an object of exchange was used as a building block in the construction of the powerful mythology of a broadminded intellectual milieu known as the 'Scipionic circle.'[99] Other members of this circle would have been Polybius and Panaetius of Rhodes after the latter moved to Rome in 145 B.C.E. At the time of its formation, this mythology drew force from the practices of intellectual circles such as the one that Madame de Staël had initiated in the early nineteenth century.[100] Yet the scenario that this mythology produced can still be traced in the late 1960s. In the introduction to a still popular translation of Terence's comedies, Betty Radice questions the historical reliability of Suetonius' biography; even so, she comments on Terence's connection with Aemilianus and Laelius in the following way:[101]

> one can imagine these young men more ready to make a friend of someone of different race and social class. . . . And it seems from the plays that Terence was more in sympathy with the civilizing influence of the new Hellenism than with the strict discipline and conservatism preached by the elder Cato, or the robust humour of Italian rural life.[102]

In this passage, Radice recycles the scenario of the intellectual circle and constructs the relationship of Aemilianus and Laelius with a man of lower status and African origins as a signal expression of their open-mindedness. In doing so, she was looking more to developments contemporary to the

---

98. Suetonius, *Ter.* 5.
99. The idea of such a circle made its first appearance in Bernhardy 1850. Cf. Brown 1934.
100. In 1816 Madame de Staël published in the *Biblioteca italiana* an article entitled "Sull'utilità della traduzione" that supported the spread of the then-cutting edge Romantic movement in Italy. Not only did she surround herself with German intellectuals such as Goethe and Schlegel, but she also kindled a broader discussion over the opposition between romanticism and classicism.
101. Radice 1967: 12.
102. Radice 1967: 14.

time of her translation than to the cultural dynamics at play in mid-second-century B.C.E. Rome.

The general consensus nowadays is that the mythology of the 'Scipionic circle' is a pure fantasy that emerges from Cicero's retrospective reading of Aemilianus' friendship with Laelius.[103] Likewise, the allegations concerning Terence's questionable ties with the two young *nobiles* are now considered nothing more than gossip fabricated by the poet Porcius Licinius.[104] Although convincing, these assessments have had the negative effect of blinding us to the cultural framework that informs Suetonius' biography of Terence. Far from contradicting each other, the varied opinions that Suetonius reports are nothing more than variations on the more intimate commerce between the Roman upper class and its 'others' that we find articulated in Polybius and Ennius. In other words, even if the notion of a 'Scipionic circle' is untenable, Suetonius' narrative remains central for at least two reasons. First, it gives bodily facticity to the possessive love that Roman elite males felt towards their 'others' and the pivotal role that these 'others' played in their homosocial relations. Second, it sheds light on the predicaments that loomed over poetic practices and, specifically, on their indissoluble bond with written objects which, by being liable to be appropriated by others, rendered poetic authorship both volatile and vulnerable.

---

103. For the dismantling of the "Scipionic circle" see Hartung 2004: 71 note 21; Goldberg 1986: 8–15; Zetzel 1972; Astin 1967: 294–96. As for Cicero, Aemilianus and Laelius appear in the *De Senectute* and on their friendship Cicero plots a philosophical inquiry in *De Amicitia*. In the *De Republica* the two come into play again, this time in the company of Furius Philus, and in the *De Oratore* (2.6.22) Cicero portrays the two young men gathering shells on the beach.

104. Gruen 1992: 200.

Chapter 4

Inventing Latin Prose

Cato the Censor and the Formation of a New Aristocracy

While the macro-system of economic and migratory circulation underwent changes as a consequence of military expansion, Rome earned the stature of a capital in part through the massive concentration of cultural commodities in the hands of its most affluent and powerful citizens. As we have seen in the previous chapters, this phenomenon took several shapes at the same time. First, the city witnessed the development of a performance tradition based on Greek dramatic scripts translated by professional immigrants called *poetae*. This tradition sustained the conspicuous display of the ruling elite and mediated new encounters among different social groups in the ever-shifting human landscape of the city. Second, the intensified circulation of poets and other nonelite and alien cultural agents in the highest spheres led to the structuring of a closed system of cultural circulation along with the formation of new social subjectivities. Whereas these cultural agents turned into objects of desire trafficked among the powerful few, being at the top of the social ladder meant being involved in this traffic in one way or the other. The ultimate consequence of this multifaceted phenomenon is that the Roman elite acquired the skills necessary to take hold of the cultural resources of their 'others' and began to flaunt a new type of cultural mastery. My aim in this chapter is to investigate in detail the nature and the dynamics that characterized this further outcome and how, in turn, this outcome expressed itself in the establishment of a prose tradition in Latin.

Although our focus is once again on texts, the cultural mastery that the early second century B.C.E. Roman elite sought to acquire and exhibit had little to do with the construction of texts per se. As a signal expression of social authority, expertise in new cultural expressions or practices was attained and displayed in embodied form. Once again, we need to search for the body in the text. Once again, the textual material available for investigation is scanty. Despite these limitations, the obsessive concern with social behaviors and cultural activities that characterizes our material reveals an underlying anxiety over the redefinition of aristocracy. Attention to the formalities and modalities in which such an anxiety is expressed and redressed grants us the possibility to account for the formation of Latin prose and its impact on the Roman aristocracy at the same time.

Ancestorship and Aristocratic Status

For the members of any given society the attribution of qualities and values to things and people determines the identity and the position of these things and people in the ordering and functioning of that society. While the perpetuation of a societal structure requires for such qualities and values to be continuously defined and legitimated, competition and manipulation most often express the maneuvering of power and authority played out by individuals operating in the highest echelons. Like everything and everybody these individuals undergo a process of quality and value attribution; as opposed to the rest of the community, however, they are accorded 'aristocratic' status and, therefore, distinguish themselves from the rest of the community by being identified as qualitatively distinct beings.

The most widely recognized quality attributed to aristocrats is their adherence to archetypes situated in a not readily accessible location associated with the past. This quality is evinced by the insistence on ancestors and ancestorship that typifies discourses about aristocrats and aristocratic practices. Located in the 'back then,' the ancestors are invariably characterized as entities responsible for the creation and maintenance of the social order. As Mary Helms points out, it is precisely by virtue of their link with these outer entities that aristocrats are believed to be "imbued with ancestral qualities and to be distinguished as a social collectivity by a *living* ancestorship that places them in a qualitatively different state or condition of being relative to commoners."[1] In other words, aristocrats are generally considered living embodiments of the ancestors and their qualities.

---

1. Helms 1998: 6.

From our standpoint, the relationship between aristocrats and ancestors in the context of early second century B.C.E. Rome emerges most clearly from Polybius' description of the funeral ceremony:[2]

> For whenever one of the distinguished men among them dies, when the funeral has been arranged, the body is carried with the rest of the adornment to the place called the ship's prows (rostra) in the forum. There, it is usually propped up for all to see, it is laid out only rarely. (2) If a grown-up son is left behind and happens to be present, he steps onto the rostra with all the people standing around. If not, another member of the family that is available speaks about the virtues of the dead man and what he has accomplished during his lifetime. . . . (4) After that, they bury the body and perform the customary rites. Then they place an image of the dead person in the most public part of the house, keeping it in a small wooden shrine. . . . (6) They reveal these masks during public sacrifices and compete in decorating them. And whenever a leading member of the family dies, they introduce them into the funeral procession, putting them on men who most resemble the deceased in height and in general appearance. . . . (8) These men now ride on wagons, and the rods and axes and the other customary equipment of those in power accompany them according to the dignity of the rank and station achieved by each man in politics during his life. (9) When they reach the rostra, they all sit in order on ivory stools. It is not easy for an ambitious and high-minded man to see a finer spectacle than this. (10) For who would not be won over at the sight of all the masks together of those men who had been extolled for virtue as if they were alive and breathing? (54.1) None except the man who is speaking over the one who is about to be buried; who, when he has finished his eulogy, starts praising the others who are present beginning with the oldest, and recounts the successes and the achievements of each. . . . (3) But the greatest result is that young men are encouraged to undergo anything for the sake of the commonwealth in the hope of gaining the renown that attends the great deeds of men.[3]
> (trans. Paton)

As evidenced by this passage, the funeral ceremony impressed the Greek Polybius for the way it helped establish a connection between aristocrats and ancestors. This connection was achieved and exhibited in several

---

2. For the Roman funerary ritual at large, see Scheid 1984; for useful remarks, see Feldherr 2000.
3. Polybius 6.53.1–4

ways. First, the clan's ancestors (*maiores*) were paraded through the city when living individuals wore the wax masks of dead members of the clan and accompanied the newly dead to the rostra in the forum. In this context, the wax masks played a fundamental role. They materialized the extraordinary achievements of the ancestors whose features the masks reproduced beyond the decay of the physical body; at the same time, they made conspicuous before the community the link between the living members of the clan and an energizing past.[4] In turn, the attending community assisted the transformation of the newly dead into an ancestor and legitimated the attribution of ancestral qualities to the living members of the clan by virtue of its spectatorship. Second, when delivering his eulogy from the rostra, the chosen young male unfolded in speech the achievements of his predecessors up to the newly dead and made explicit the qualities attached to these achievements. Moreover, he pledged before the ancestors made 'alive' through the wearing of the wax masks and the attending community to replicate or outshine his predecessors and, therefore, to become a living ancestor himself. Finally, Polybius lingers on the effects of the ceremony on the audience. In particular, he focuses on the young men and suggests that, by watching the spectacle, they were fired with the desire to risk everything for the community and to win the immortality and the renown epitomized by the ceremony in its entirety.

By and large, Polybius' description of the Roman aristocratic funeral suggests that the notion of aristocracy held a centripetal as well as a centrifugal social force. The identification of aristocrats as living ancestors elicited by the wax masks and their association with outstanding deeds put a limit on the expansion of the aristocracy as a group. Produced only when an individual had reached the curule rank, the wax masks were jealously guarded by a small number of office-holding households.[5] Similarly, the funeral oration fashioned a new ancestor out of the newly dead and expressed the promise that the excellence unfolded throughout the ceremony would be embodied once again within a particular clan. This emphasis on the exclusive continuity of ancestral qualities through familial lines can be detected elsewhere. For example, in exemplary discourses models of imitation and patterns of behavior (either to espouse or to reject) are often said or felt to be staple features of a single clan. Accordingly, three generations of Decii Mures are said to have died in

---

4. On the social weight of ancestral masks in Roman society and for a convenient survey of sources, see the appendix in Flower 1996.

5. For the so-called *ius imaginum,* see Cicero, *Verr.* 5.14.36; for the terms of the discussion relating to it, see Flower 1996: 53–59.

battles as consuls and two sacrifice themselves in similar acts of *devotio;* M. Iunius Brutus, the assassin of Caesar, seems to have felt the pressure to act against tyranny by virtue of his ancestor's example, L. Iunius Brutus, founder of the Republic.[6]

This centripetal social force was clearly countered by a centrifugal one. Because aristocratic status was linked to socially significant actions like achievement of office and victory in battle, any free male citizen performing these actions had, at least virtually, the possibility of being counted among the aristocrats independent of the clan to which he belonged. This is what underlies Polybius' reference to the generic group of young male spectators inspired by the ceremony; the enthusiasm that, according to Polybius, they expressed takes for granted that any male citizen could, at least in theory, measure himself against the achievements remembered and, therefore, be granted ancestral qualities. Intriguingly, this option stemmed from the very display of the exclusive connections with the past that permeated the ceremony in general and the oration in particular. The paraphernalia paraded throughout made conspicuous familial deeds and ancestral qualities, but the words pronounced during the laudation typified social standards and unfolded them to those outside the gentilician group. Thus, those who belonged to households with an established record of achievements and approved patterns of behavior were more easily granted entrance into the closer circle of legitimate leaders (*nobiles*); however, the focus on achievements in the largest sense and their continuous standardization made it possible for new men (*homines novi*) to enter that circle as well.[7]

The testimony of Pliny the Elder about the laudation of Q. Caecilius Metellus (cos. 206 B.C.E.) delivered for his father Lucius (cos. 251 and 247 B.C.E.) in 221 B.C.E. can serve as an illustration of how these two-directional social forces worked:

> Q. Metellus in ea oratione quam habuit supremis laudibus patris sui L. Metelli pontificis, bis consulis, dictatoris, magistri equitum, XVuiri agris dandis, qui primus elephantos ex primo Punico bello duxit in triumphum scriptum reliquit decem maximas res optimasque in quibus quaerendis

---

6. For the Decii Mures, see Cicero, *TD* 1.89, *De Fin.* 2.61; Dio Cass. *Apud Zonar.* 8.5; for M. Iunius Brutus, see Cicero, *Phil* 2.26; Dio Cass. 44.12; Appian 2.112. I owe these references to Roller 2004: 24–25 and note 57; on this issue, see also Blösel 2000: 46–53 and Treggiari 2003.

7. On the concepts of *nobilitas* and *novitas* Gelzer 1969 and Burckhardt 1990 are key. See also Hölkeskamp 2004, especially 169–98. On the ideology of *novitas* with attention to the case of Cicero, see Wiseman 1971: 107–16 and Dugan 2005: 7–15.

sapientes aetatem exigerent, consumasse eum. voluisse enim primarium bellatorem esse, optimum oratorem, fortissimum imperatorem, auspicio suo maximas res geri, maximo honore uti, summa sapientia esse, summum senatorem haberi, pecuniam magnam bono modo invenire, multos liberos relinquere et clarissimum in civitate esse. haec contigisse ei nec ulli alii post Romam conditam.[8]

Q. Metellus in that oration which he delivered with the highest praises of his father Lucius Metellus, pontifex, twice consul, dictator, master of the horse, one of the fifteen men who looked over the distribution of land, who was the first to lead elephants in triumph in the first Punic war, left written that he devoted himself to achieving the ten greatest and best things in which wise men spend their life: to be a leading warrior, the best orator, the bravest commander, to achieve the greatest deeds under his auspices, to hold the highest office, to be of the highest shrewdness, to be held the highest senator, to acquire great fortune in an honorable way, to leave many children behind, and to be the most distinguished man of the city. He achieved all of this as no other man since the foundation of Rome.

Pliny here appears to be citing from the final portion of Metellus' eulogy, the part dedicated to the dead father. The first section encompasses a list of offices and feats performed by the eulogized; the second comprises a standardized catalogue of qualities.[9] Although repetitious and unexciting, the catalogue shape and the use of superlatives can be seen to construct the supernormal status of the newly dead. To be sure, it is precisely by means of these formalities that the life of the eulogized is reduced to discrete actions and the eulogized projected into a competition for prestige and recognition that extended beyond the 'here and now' and into the past. In this sense, the speaker's work was to measure the dead man's achievements against absolute and timeless norms of excellence and augment his distance from the lived world of the attending audience to its maximum. The final sentence elucidates precisely that: "he achieved all of this as no other man since the foundation of Rome."

Distanciation, however, was beset by the necessity to transform the supernormal qualities associated with the eulogized into positive energy

---

8. Pliny, *NH* 7.139. According to Flower (1996: 137–38), he is the consul featuring in the anecdote about Naevius and his infelicitous representation of the Metellis' achievements.

9. To give a number to the different standardized qualities is typical. See, for example, Gellius 1.13.10 about P. Licinius Crassus Mucianus (cos. 113 B.C.E.) and Pliny, *NH* 7.100 about Cato the Censor (cos. 195 B.C.E.).

for the living society at large. In our example the eulogizer can be seen to bridge that expanse when, in laying out the standards of excellence, he refers to what we may term 'a judging community.' The ten criteria articulated by Q. Caecilius Metellus noticeably include "to be held the highest senator" (*summum senatorem haberi*) and "to be considered the most distinguished man in the city" (*clarissimum in civitate esse*). These criteria presuppose that ancestral qualities and, therefore, aristocratic standing could only be attained through a direct involvement in communal affairs and only after undergoing an evaluation performed by a group external to the clan. This process of evaluation was so pervasively important for the notion of aristocracy that it is a staple feature even in compositions textually preserved in less public contexts (family tombs) such as the Scipionic *elogia* and the *elogium* of Atilius Calatinus. Accordingly, those who belonged to the inner elite circle by familial affiliation had to actively regain and reaffirm the ancestral qualities that they inherited before their peers and the Roman people.[10] By same token, those who did not come from a clan sustained by an ancestry of accomplishments had the chance to compete for legitimate leadership and authority by emulating the achievements and qualities laid out by aristocrats. Even so, their success was equally contingent upon their ability to incarnate ancestral qualities and to establish a connection with ancestral archetypes that would meet, if not the consensus, at least the acknowledgment of a judging community. The successful case of Cato the Censor is in this sense exemplary.

In the Roman historical memory Cato is famous for having built an outstanding political career by challenging the notion that aristocratic authority was the exclusive possession of a few clans even while affirming the aristocratic commitment to the replication or reperformance of ancestral practices and behaviors.[11] Contradictory to all appearances, Cato's twofold attitude pertains both to his entrance into the close aristocratic circle as a *homo novus* and the socially sanctioned weight granted to the *maiores*. By aspiring to move (and indeed moving) into the center of power where legitimate leadership was located, Cato had no choice but to establish a socially approved link with the ancestral realm. Because he lacked the support of a familial past, Cato exploited the centrality of

---

10. Reaffirming inherited ancestral qualities could be a source of great anxiety. See, for example, the case of young Scipio Aemilianus as described in Polybius 31.24, discussed in chapter 3.

11. For his contrasts with the traditional aristocracy, see especially Livy 37.57–58; 39.40.9. With special reference to his censorship, see Livy 39.40–41 *passim;* 39.42.5 and 7; Nepos, *Cato* 2.3; Plutarch, *Cato Mai.* 16. For a recent assessment of Cato's relationship with aristocratic ideology, see Blösel 2000: 53–59.

action implicit in the notion of *nobilitas*. Thus, he strove to measure single actions (his own and those of others) against behavioral models that he locates in an ancestrally constructed past; at the same time, he emptied this ancestral past of any familial specificity. In the process, Cato articulated an aristocratic code of speaking and behaving that allowed the Roman elite to culturally subjugate their 'others' and to redefine themselves as an aristocracy ruling over an ever expanding world.

Oratory and the Socio-cosmological Order

Current works on the oratorical texts attributed to Cato the Censor tend to emphasize his extensive use of paratactical constructions, lexical parallelisms, and phonetic repetitions.[12] These features are generally viewed as the mark of an underdeveloped phase of literary development and are unanimously connected with the Italic *carmen*. Under this rubric have been grouped cultural expressions as diverse as prayers, magic formulas, laws, treaties, accounts, dedications, vows, *elogia,* and sententious speech. Their common denominator is not to be found in the use of a strictly defined rhythmical pattern, even though compositions in Saturnians—as we have seen—were bracketed under the category of *carmen;* nor can these forms be classified within a neat system of literary genres, even though they are preserved in inscriptional and literary materials.[13] From a purely formal point of view, the *carmen* was loosely marked in three ways: by juxtaposing a long compositional segment before a shorter one, by deploying a range of figures of sound, and by aligning two or three words and/or phrases.[14] From a socially-oriented perspective, a *carmen* can also be described as a speech act that seeks to establish or confirm socio-cosmological hierarchies.[15] Although anyone could produce speech bearing *carmen*-like features, its ultimate effect on both the social positioning of the performer and the socio-cosmological order depended upon a number of other variables. These included the context of performance, the performer's positioning in the larger scheme of social relations, and the acknowledgment of a judging audience.

---

12. See especially Sblendorio Cugusi 1971; Courtney 1999: 41–43.

13. For a recent discussion on the relationship between *carmen* and *tabulae,* see Meyer 2004: 44–72.

14. For discussions of the *carmen* and its stylistic features, see Norden 1986: 172–73; Palmer 1961: 346–57; Timpanaro 1988: 257–61; von Albrecht 1989: 9–20; Courtney 1999: 1–11. For the history of these discussions especially in relation to the definition of prose, see Luiselli 1969.

15. Habinek 1998b and 2005a *passim.*

As we have seen in the previous chapter, the relationship between formally marked speech and the socio-cosmological universe inherent in the notion of *carmen* underlies the contested establishment of an epic tradition in Rome. Livius Andronicus and Naevius turned to the *carmen* as a model of song for the construction of their epic artifacts. To these imitative attempts, the ruling elite responded in two ways. Whereas some looked to expand their individual authority through representations crafted by the poets, the narratives that we read around Naevius suggest that others viewed this type of mediation as a disturbing encroachment on the socially demarcating practices of the ruling elite. Cato articulated the latter position and on a number of occasions spelled out a convivial scenario that excluded nonelite interferences. In the face of this resistance, Ennius turned away from the *carmen* and established for himself a model of scripted song redeployed from the Greek tradition.

Cato's involvement in the elite controversies sparked by the popularity of poetry invites us to investigate the triangular relationship of his oratorical style with the *carmen,* on the one hand, and poetry, on the other. Indeed, attention to the strategies of formalization adopted by Cato in his oratory allows us to do two things at once: to gauge how he maximized his invocations of authoritative precedents located in the ancestral past to sustain his positioning within the ruling aristocracy; and to explore the paradigm of cultural domination over nonelite cultural forms that he proposed to his peers through his oratorical performances.

The earliest oratorical fragments attributed to Cato belong to a speech delivered in Spain during his 195 B.C.E. consulship. Perhaps a *suasio* addressed to the knights in their military function, the speech aimed to stimulate their valor.[16] The first fragment consists of a very elaborate *sententia* about the long-lasting benefits that derive from hard work and honorable deeds:

> Cogitate cum animis vestris; si quid vos per laborem recte feceritis, labor ille a vobis cito recedet, bene factum a vobis dum vivitis non abscedet; sed si qua per voluptatem nequiter feceritis, voluptas cito abibit, nequiter factum illud apud vos semper manebit.[17]

> Reflect very carefully in your own mind; if by working hard you do right, the fatigue will withdraw fast and the good deed will not leave you as long

---

16. Sblendorio Cugusi 1982: 131–32.
17. Cato, *orat.* 1.1 Sbl.

as you live; but if by obeying pleasure you do wrong, pleasure will soon leave and the evil deed will always remain with you.

Formally this *sententia* is organized around syntactical parallelisms (*si quid . . . feceritis* picked up by *si qua . . . feceritis, labor . . . cito recedet* duplicated by *voluptas cito abibit, bene factum . . . non abscedet* corresponding to *nequiter factum . . . manebit*) and figures of sound (adnominatio in *recedet . . . discedet* and homoioteleuton in the triads *feceritis- recedet- abscedet* and *feceritis- abibit- manebit*).[18] Parallel phrases and exploitation of the phonetic layer of the language are typical of the *carmen*. Rather than stressing their primitivism and uncouthness, it is best to conceptualize these formal devices as integral components of an actual performance. In so doing, we can observe that Cato used these formalities to establish a secure connection between his oratorical performance and the socio-cosmological order that these formalities invoked. Moreover, in order to strengthen his authoritative position as consul in relation to the attending knights, he gives ancestral substance to his overall intervention by explicitly calling on the ancestors and enumerating the material tokens of honors established by them:

> maiores seorsum atque divorsum pretium paravere bonis atque strenuis, decurionatus, optionatus, hastas donaticas aliosque honores.[19]

> The ancestors established separate and differentiated prizes to the good and the courageous, the office of decurion, that of helpmate, honorific javelins and other honors.

Significantly, the ancestors that Cato invokes here are not identified as his direct progenitors; they constitute a generic group of beings located in the past and responsible for the existing and widely recognized system of rewards. Such a generic invocation allows Cato to transform the aristocratic notion of ancestorship into an asset to be shared by the elite in its entirety and helps him validate his sententious proposition whereby action is what defines the social quality of an individual. Not surprisingly, he achieves all of this by organizing his speech in *carmen*-like parallelisms and by exploiting the phonetic layer of the language once again.

The formal aspect of Cato's oratory in these instances suggests that

---

18. These features are noted in Sblendorio Cugusi 1982: 133–36.
19. Cato, *orat.* 1.2 Sbl.

authority could be expressed through the deft use of formalized speech and the appropriation of behavioral patterns that looked back to the ancestral past as the fountainhead of *auctoritas* itself. But Cato's formal allegiance to the *carmen*-style allowed him to achieve more than just projecting his performance beyond the ordinary everyday and into an ancestral past. It also helped him naturalize alien cultural forms into his assertions of authority and, therefore, to expand the socio-cosmological dimensions of his interventions. Cato achieved this expansion by enmeshing into the *carmen*-like organization of his speeches quantitative devices foreign to the Roman song tradition. In relation to this early speech, Antonio Traglia has pointed out that Cato's *sententia* in the first fragment presents a double trochee at the end of the period (*semper manebit*) that looks back to self-conscious trochaic variations located at the end of colon and comma.[20] It could be (and it has been) argued that Cato's adoption of metrical clausulae is to be linked to his exposure to Greek rhetorical teaching.[21] It may be so; however, with its pervasive reliance on quantitative structures and its performance appeal, poetry must have stood out as a much more alluring resource than Greek rhetoric to draw upon.[22]

Ancestral invocations, attention to social behavior, and exploitation of diverse cultural traditions come to play a pervasive role in what remains of a speech delivered by Cato in 190 B.C.E. against Q. Minucius Thermus known as *De Falsis Pugnis*. After obtaining the right of a triumph in 196 B.C.E. for his campaign against the Iberians, Q. Minucius Thermus had asked for a second one in recognition of his military engagements against the Ligurians, but was denied the triumph perhaps because of Cato's very involvement.[23] What remains suggests that the overall speech pivoted

---

20. Traglia 1985: 354. These would have been located at the end of colon (*non abscedet* [spondee + trochee]) and at the end of comma (*recte feceritis* [spondee + cretic]) and *cito recedet* [tribrach + trochee] in the first half of the *sententia* and *nequiter feceritis* [spondee + cretic] as well as *voluptas cito abibit* [dactyl + trochee] in the second half).

21. Much has been said on the influence of Greek rhetoric on Cato's oratory, but no definite answers have been reached. Most important contributions to the debate are Clarke 1966: 38–42; Kennedy 1994: 110–11; Leeman 1963: 43–49; Astin 1978: 147–56; von Albrecht 1989: 11–20; Cavarzere 2000: 47–56; Calboli 2003: 11–35. For a review of this debate, see Sciarrino 2007: 57–58. Interestingly, Traglia (1985: 350–51) turns to the rhetorical tradition of southern Italy and hypothesizes that this had an impact on Ennius, but does not develop his argument all the way. For the influence of rhetoric on poetry, see Barsby 2007. The edict of 161 B.C.E. testifies to the encroaching presence of Greek rhetoricians, but their influence on the oratory of the time is much less detectable. For a recent discussion of this edict, see Stroup 2007.

22. On the influence of poetry on Latin prose in general and oratory in particular, see Habinek 1985: 188–89; Oberhelman 2003: 236–42.

23. Livy 25.21.7–8; 36.38.1–3; 37.46.1–2. See also discussion of the circumstances and bibliography in Sblendorio Cugusi 1982: 193–95 and Cugusi and Sblendorio Cugusi 2001: 278–80.

around a parallelism between Thermus' feigned military successes and his administrative shortcomings.[24] If so, the surviving fragment would have referred to the latter argument and would have focused on the public beating of local magistrates that Thermus had orchestrated in the provinces:

> Dixit a decemviris parum bene sibi cibaria curata esse. iussit vestimenta detrahi atque flagro caedi. decemviros Bruttiani verberavere, videre multi mortales. quis hanc contumeliam, quis hoc imperium, quis hanc servitutem ferre potest? nemo hoc rex ausus est facere: eane fieri bonis, bono genere gnatis, boni consultis! ubi societas? ubi fides maiorum? insignitas iniurias, plagas, verbera, vibices, eos dolores atque carnificinas per dedecus atque maximam contumeliam, inspectantibus popularibus suis atque multis mortalibus, te facere ausum esse! set quantum luctum, quantum gemitum, quid lacrimarum, quantum fletum factum audivi! servi iniurias nimis aegre ferunt: quid illos, bonos genere gnatos, magna virtute praeditos, opinamini animi habuisse atque habituros, dum vivent?[25]

> He asserted that the local *decemviri* had neglected to arrange well the food provisions allocated to him. He ordered them to be stripped and whipped severely. The Bruttiani scourged the *decemviri* and many men stood there to watch. Who could tolerate such an offense, this abuse of power, this imposition of servitude? No king ever dared commit such a crime: now these crimes are inflicted on honorable men, men born from honorable stock, men held to be honorable! What happened to the respect of the allies? What happened to the allegiance to the ancestors? How did you dare to inflict atrocious offences, beatings, thrashings, wounds, those torments and tortures in addition to dishonor and most despicable insults, before the eyes of fellow citizens and many other mortals! And yet, how much affliction, how much groaning, how many tears I heard that were provoked! Most painfully slaves endure offenses: what do you think that they, born from honorable stock and equipped by great virtue, felt and will feel as long as they live?

As testified by a great variety of sources, beating had a peculiarly performative force in making distinctions of status. The *fasces* that accompanied the magistrates with *imperium* and the association of *libertas* with immunity from bodily violations made the divide between citizens and noncitizens, enfranchised and disenfranchised, ideologically clear.[26] In practice, the

---
24. Sblendorio Cugusi 1982: 194–95 and Cugusi and Sblendorio Cugusi 2001: 278.
25. Cato, *orat.* 6.42 Sbl.
26. For a useful discussion of all these points, see Saller 1994: 133–42.

divide was much more blurred, especially when beating and being beaten involved citizens living outside Rome. As the fragment suggests, when a magistrate decided to exercise his authority in physical terms, a citizen's immunity from beating was breached. Within the city, the offended citizen could resort to the *lex Valeria de provocatione* which was traditionally dated back to the foundation of the Republic and granted male citizens the right of appeal (*provocatio*). Outside of Rome, however, he was not equally protected so that, around the time of this speech, the law was being updated with the promulgation of the so-called *leges Porciae*. The details of these new laws are not clear, but they must have had something to do with the prohibition of public scourging of citizens living in the provinces.[27] To what degree Cato was involved in the promulgation of one or more of these laws is debated.[28] Whatever the case, in 184 B.C.E., in a speech known as the *Si se M. Caelius tribunus plebis appellasset* (22.87 Sblendorio), Cato mentions his contribution to the protection of "the shoulders of citizens" and in the fragment above he can be seen to take advantage of the contemporary legal debate to sustain his attack on Thermus.[29]

Rather than offer a detailed account of Thermus' offense, Cato conjures up a scene focused on the effects of beating on all involved: the consul, the executioners, the *decemviri,* and the spectators. In this scene, the action moves quickly from the consul's commands to their performance by the executioners. Whereas the consul's assertion of authority is associated with kingly practices and is, therefore, figured as uprooting the standing social order, the executioners become both an extension and a mirror of the consul. Their ethnic identification would have recalled disloyalty since during the Punic war the Bruttians had defected to Hannibal. In turn, their performance of beating would have underscored the disgrace that Thermus had allowed by having slaves whipping Roman magistrates whom, as a punishment for their disloyalty, the Bruttians were supposed to serve.[30] When the focus moves to the victims, Cato invokes the ancestral rules that regulated the interaction with the allies. Through this invocation, he heightens the ignominy of the entire episode and the shame suffered by the local *decemviri*. Finally, Cato uses the same ploy that we find in funeral orations and other textualized aristocratic compositions when he calls attention to the attending spectators. Here, however, the spectators

---

27. Astin 1978: 21 note 23. For a general discussion, see Lintott 1999: 97–99.

28. On the debate over Cato's involvement in the promulgation of the *leges Porciae* and his position vis-à-vis the popular cause, see Astin 1978: 22–23; 326–28.

29. On the wording *pro scapulis* used in the *Si se M. Caelius tribunus plebis appellasset* to refer to the law, see Cugusi and Sblendorio Cugusi 2001: 309; Sblendorio Cugusi 1982: 270–71.

30. About the Bruttiani, see Gellius 10.3.18–19; Festus 28.19L.

are drawn into the frame to become actors in the scene. In the economy of the speech, their bodily responses (tears, groaning, and mourning) have the effect of giving material facticity to Thermus' inadequacies as a member of Rome's body politic and reconstitute his actions as a sociocosmologically disruptive event.

If being alert to the narrative details preserved in this fragment can help us grasp Cato's representational maneuvers, even more can be gained from paying attention to his strategies of formalization. From a purely stylistic viewpoint, the speech act preserved in writing presents a thick array of features typical of the *carmen*. Indeed, it tends to pivot around two or three lexical elements strung together in such a way as to achieve a climactic effect. Embedded in two or three parallel syntactical units, these lexical elements are underscored by the *anaphora* of interrogatives (as in *quis hanc contumeliam / quis hoc imperium / quis hanc servitutem* and *ubi societas / ubi fides*) or intensified by alliterative polyptoton (as in *boni / bono genere gnatis / boni consultis*). Similarly, the triad *luctum-gemitum-fletum* is introduced by the repetition of *quantum*, while the reiteration of the final phoneme–*um* creates a rhyme that virtually extends to *fact(um)*, a lexical unit tightly linked to *fletum* by the duplication of the initial consonant. Furthermore, Cato's juxtaposition of the socially antithetical terms, *decemviros Bruttiani* and his decision to embed the last term in a construction characterized by a *chiasmus, Bruttiani* (A) *verberavere* (B), *videre* (B) *multi* (A) is outstanding since the two internal terms, tied together by homoioteleuton, emphasize the focal actions: beating and seeing.[31] The *adnominatio* in *opinamini animi* and the strategy of accumulating synonyms are also striking. The latter are either hurried by *asyndeton* as in *iniurias, plagas, verbera, vibices* or delayed by the conjunction *atque* as in *dolores atque carnificinas* and *per dedecus atque maximam contumeliam*. Finally, the colometric analysis of the final period (*servi iniurias nimis aegre ferunt / quid illos, bonos genere gnatos / magna virtute praeditos / opinamini animi habuisse atque habituros / dum vivent?*) would point to Cato's predilection for ending a syntactical structure with a short and unemphatic colon. Mapped on the long-short sequence of cola that characterizes the Saturnian and other textualized samples of *carmen*, this device is generally identified as "appositional style."[32]

So pervasively linked to the *carmen* tradition through form, this

---

31. It has been argued that, far from being stylistically refined, the *chiasmus* is the natural untutored way of combining two pairs, more natural than *abab*. See Leeman 1963: 22; Courtney 1999: 6–7; Barsby 2007: 43.

32. von Albrecht 1989: 4–5, 18, 20; Habinek 1985: 175–81.

speech was particularly loved by the later archaizing author Aulus Gellius, who cites this passage to illustrate highly emotional oratory.[33] But in the senatorial context in which the speech was originally performed, Cato's pervasive exploitation of the *carmen*-style had an effect that went beyond the mere arousal of indignation from his peers.[34] It constituted the very means whereby he was able to construct his oratorical performance and the reenacted social drama as happenings of extraordinary caliber. Indeed, syntactical parallelisms and phonetic reiterations would have helped Cato recreate the public beating suffered by the local magistrates in such a way as to characterize himself as the ultimate custodian of the sociocosmological order and Thermus as its ultimate violator. What is more, the *carmen*-like repetitions that pervade the syntactical and phonetic layer of this fragment are reinforced by metrical patterns.

Double spondees can be detected in at least two places: in the closing phrase *multi mortales* where the metrical structure is interlaced with an alliterative nexus already used as a second colon of a Saturnian by Naevius in his *Bellum Poenicum*, and in the sequence *boni consultis, fac(tum) audivi, habituros dum vivent*.[35] A hypodochmiac ($-\cup-\cup$ x) frames once an initial colon (*quis hanc contumeliam*) and twice a mid colon (*atque maximam contumeliam* and *magna virtute praeditos*). Furthermore, trochees veering towards the spondaic rhythm stress the phonetic, lexical, and syntactical *carmen*-like repetitions that mark the reaction of those watching the appalling spectacle: *quantum luctum / quantum gemitum/ quid lacrimarum / quantum fletum fact(um) audivi*. As pointed out by Thomas Habinek, these metrical patterns are among those used in Plautus' comedies to draw to a close a *canticum* characterized by diverse but similar meters.[36]

In this particular context Cato's choice to turn to comedy could be explained by the fact that this poetic form expressed a special interest in beating through persistent references to the signs of the whip left on the slave's back and exuberant elaborations on the vocabulary and the sound of whipping.[37] Although Cato does not linger at all on the beaten body

---

33. Gellius (10.3.15–16) compared this fragment with Gaius Gracchus, *De Legibus promulgatis* (48 Malcovati[4]) and Cicero, *Verr.* 2.5.161–3. Cf. also 13.25 (24). 12.

34. For the senatorial context of the speech, see Slendorio Cugusi 1982: 194.

35. M. Barchiesi 1962: 360–61: *eorum sectam sequuntur multi mortales / multi alii e Troia strenui viri / u<r>bi foras cum auro illic exibant*.

36. Habinek 1985: 191–92. For the importance of his contribution for the interpretation of pre-ciceronian oratory more generally, see Sciarrino 2007: 60.

37. References to beating in comedy have long been central to the interpretation of comedy's social effects. See especially Segal 1987; Parker 1989; Fitzgerald 2000: 32–41. For the exploration of beating at the phonetic level of the language, especially in the form of onomatopoeia, see Traina 1977: 164.

132 • Chapter 4

of the magistrates, his metrical gestures to comedy would have certainly sustained its evocation. In an oratorical performance, however, such an evocation would not have produced laughter; rather, it would have conjured up a rather horrifying mental picture. Then again, Cato persevered in rhythmically echoing drama in other circumstances as well. A most outstanding case is the opening of the *Pro Rhodiensibus*.

Cato delivered this speech in 167 B.C.E. Later on its written version was inserted into the *Origines*.[38] The speech consisted of a senatorial intervention in the debate over the fate of the Rhodians after the end of the third Macedonic war. During the hostilities they had shown sympathy to Perseus and had tried to mediate between the two sides. After the end of the war, the arrival in Rome of a Rhodian embassy meant to clarify the position of Rhodes in the new East sparked a heated discussion over the procedures to follow. With his intervention, Cato argued in favor of the Rhodians and sustained their forgiveness.[39] In a letter to Quintus Axius, Tiro, the faithful freedman and secretary of Cicero, used the text of the *Pro Rhodiensibus* to draw a comparison between the oratorical styles of Cato and Cicero. In that context, he criticized the former for not following the proper rhetorical procedure in structuring his discourse. In the second century C.E. Aulus Gellius cites the letter and refutes Tiro's criticism by quoting and commenting on seven long passages.[40]

Gellius' interest in measuring this speech against a Greek rhetorical framework is very much linked to the centrality that Greek rhetoric was soon to acquire among the Roman elite. Rather than giving credit to Gellius' frame of reference, I propose giving attention to the formal components of this speech within their own milieu. By so doing, we can see that Cato went so far as to organize the opening of his intervention into a string of syntactic cola structured like Plautus' cretic cola:[41]

Scio solere pleribusque hominibus
rebus secundis – ᴗ – x

---

38. The speech is preserved in large part by Gellius 6.3 = Cato, *Orig.* 5.100–106 C&Sbl. The bibliography on this speech is particularly vast. See conveniently the updated edition of the speech by Calboli (2003: 99–224).
39. Polybius 30.4–5; Livy 45.20–25.
40. Gellius 6 (7). 3.
41. Habinek 1985: 193–94; Traglia (1985: 353–54) identifies similar structures in other fragments of this speech used as clausulae at the end of colon and period. Calboli (2003: 395–96) has extended Habinek's metrical analysis to the entire fragment, corroborating the presence of cretics in last position even while remaining hesitant before Cicero's testimony about the lack of *numerus* in Cato (*Brut.* 68).

```
atque prolixis    – ∪ – – x
atque prosperis   – ∪ – ∪ x
animum excellere  ∪∪ – – ∪ x
atque superbiam   – ∪∪ – ∪ x
atque ferocia     – ∪∪ – ∪ x
augescere atque crescere[42]  – ∪ – ∪ x
```

I know that most people, when things evolve favorably, fortunately, and prosperously, become overconfident and their arrogance and cruelty augment and grow.

The content of this fragment suggests that Cato began his senatorial intervention by reaffirming his legitimacy as a speaker. He did so by challenging his audience to acknowledge his practical wisdom and his oratorical virtuosity at the same time. Cato launched his challenge with a strong assertion of the self by placing *scio*, "I know," in initial position and by pronouncing a generalizing *sententia* about human nature immediately after.[43] Tiro picks up the challenging tone when he condemns Cato's opening statement as too arrogant, harsh, and reproachful since, in his opinion, it would have implied that the senators were unable to think the matter through because of their successes.[44] What he fails to observe is that Cato would have also staked out his cultural deftness by using a poetic meter as the structuring principle for organizing the *carmen*-like tricolon, the accumulation of synonyms, and the phonetic reiterations that, on other occasions, constituted the backbone of his speech. Some have suggested that one of Cato's aims was to undermine the success that the speech by the head of the Rhodian embassy, Astimedes, had attracted.[45] If so, his desire to display his cultural mastery regardless of any other particular purpose becomes even more notable.

On the whole, the formal link between Cato's oratory and the *carmen*

---

42. 32.118 Sbl.

43. Cato's choice to begin his intervention with *scio* is not limited to the *Pro Rhodiensibus*, see Sblendorio Cugusi 1982: 320; 42–43 (with references to *Rhet. Her.*1.8). The other instance, however, has to do with what appears to be a defense speech rather than a senatorial intervention (23.90 Sbl).

44. Gellius 6 (7).3.12.

45. Cugusi and Sblendorio Cugusi 2001: 331–32. The two editors rely on Polybius (30.4.6) who asserts that the speech by Astimedes was also circulated in written form. Moreover, by drawing on Gellius (6 (7). 3.7), who refers to *Pro Rhodiensibus* as a text and as a component of the *Origines*, they elaborate on the impact of the speech on a reading public rather than as a performance. For speculations about the circulation of this speech together or separately from the *Origines*, see Calboli 2003: 5–11.

prompts us to conceptualize oratory as a song, that is, as an embodied practice marked by formalized speech acts and bodily movements.[46] Understanding oratory in this way has its methodological advantages, for it allows us to focus on the sociocultural aspects that made it similar to and yet distinct from other types of public song. Formalization (the repetition of certain verbal and bodily acts) and periodization (the repetition of these acts at certain times) suggest that oratory was homologous to other public songs performed in the cityscape of Rome, including poetic drama. As opposed to these other songs, oratory was privileged in its significance and consequences because access to the contexts in which it was practiced (the Senate house, the rostra in the forum, and the law courts) was limited exclusively to those who belonged to the highest echelons of society.

From these restricted contexts Cato capitalized on actions as factors determining the social quality of individuals and appealed to patterned behaviors situated in the past in order to sustain his relocation into the center of power. Among these patterned behaviors are the strategies of formalization generally associated with the *carmen*. It is precisely by exploiting these strategies that Cato contributed to the invention of Latin prose, acting very much along the lines suggested by Eric Hobsbwam, that is, by appropriating elements that were closely related to the past and values associated with it.[47] In the *Brutus* Cicero argues that oratory existed long before Cato by pointing to Brutus, the founder of the Republic, and proposing that he must have had a certain degree of oratorical skills because he had been able to interpret an oracle correctly and had established offices, laws, and courts.[48] Interestingly, Cicero constructs his argument by drawing on a scenario organized around the triangular relationship between *carmen*-related rituals, embodied authority, and the socio-cosmological order that Cato had exploited in his oratorical performances. In the same vein, Cicero mentions that while performing a public sacrifice as a *flamen carmentalis* Marcus Popilius was forced to hurry to the assembly and by his authority and speech he was able to allay a riot.[49] By bringing into view the same cultural framework that Cato had exploited some generations before, Cicero makes evident that this framework was informed by a highly articulated system of embodied schemes. In the context of second-century B.C.E. Rome Cato's self-serving incorporation of these schemes went hand in hand with the unfolding of practical

---

46. See Habinek 1998b; 2005a *passim.*
47. Hobsbawm 1983: 280.
48. Cicero, *Brut.* 53.
49. Cicero, *Brut.* 56–57.

strategies for keeping under control the challenges posed by an expanding empire on the ruling elite as a whole.

The metrical echoes that we detect in Cato's speeches emerge as a variation on the same practices of communal and individual expansion that had guided the employment of poets and other cultural mediators in the first place. Through Cato we can see that the embodied appropriation and display of alien and nonelite cultural forms within the restricted contexts of oratory helped intensify the performer's presence within and mastery of the socio-cosmological order. But as we shall see next, in the economy of in-group relations these mimetic acts produced an additional space on which battles over cultural ownership, political power, and social values were fought.

Differential Imitations
Slavish Replications versus Empowered Appropriations

I have already pointed out how the *Pro Rhodiensibus* reveals Cato's intent to show off his cultural mastery before his peers from the very start. His desire of self-display makes absolute sense in light of the competitive nature of Roman intraelite relations and went hand in hand with other gambits meant to enhance his honor and decrease that of his competitors. These included shaming the appropriative moves adopted by his peers and proposing a self-sufficient pattern of cultural mastery.

Perhaps delivered in 184 B.C.E., the so-called speech *Si se M. Caelius tribunus plebis appellasset* is generally interpreted as a preemptive defense of his censorship centered on ridiculing the oratorical performances of M. Caelius, an otherwise unknown tribune of the plebs.[50] Cato's narrow focus on his opponent's use of the body has long been read as a sign of his resistance to a modernist style that overvalued *actio*.[51] Resting upon the retrospective projection of the later opposition between Asianism and Atticism, this reading fails to view Cato's oratorical strategies in their immediate purview.[52] What remains of this speech sheds important light on some of the features that, for Cato, distinguished slavish imitations of nonelite and alien cultural expressions from the empowered appropriations in which he engaged.

---

50. For a discussion of dating, structure, and content of this speech, see Sblendorio Cugusi 1982: 259–61. For the identification of M. Caelius, see Niccolini 1934: 116–18.
51. Sblendorio Cugusi 1982: 260; Cugusi and Sblendorio Cugusi 2001: 305.
52. For a critique of this type of retrospective projections, see Sciarrino 2007: 58.

One of the longest surviving fragments from the *Si se M. Caelius tribunus plebis appellasset* reads as follows:

> Numquam tacet, quem morbus tenet loquendi tamquam veternosum bibendi atque dormiendi. Quod si non conveniatis cum convocari iubet, ita cupidus orationis conducat qui auscultet. Itaque auditis, non auscultatis, tamquam pharmacopolam: nam eius verba audiuntur, vero se nemo committit si aeger est.[53]

> He never shuts up, the malady of speaking holds him just like that of eating and sleeping holds the hydropic. If you do not gather when he calls upon an assembly, he is so eager to hold a speech that he would hire listeners. So you hear him but don't listen, just as you do with someone who sells medicines on the street: his words are heard, but no one indeed entrusts oneself to him if sick.

Caelius' exercise of oratory is here debased to the pathological incontinence that plagues someone suffering from dropsy. His manner of calling upon a popular assembly is equated to what a street performer does when hiring a claque to boost the number of listeners. Drawn into the frame, these listeners are also said to pay heed to him as they would to a street hawker of alien extraction selling unreliable cures. Accordingly, Cato constructs an image of Caelius in speech by measuring his opponent's oratorical performances against culturally-specific schemes linking embodied practices to social types. By doing so, he figures Caelius as someone missing even the most intuitive understanding of and control over the associations elicited by the body in action. In the economy of Cato's speech, this representation serves to nullify his right to take up the role of plaintiff and delegitimizes his authority as a magistrate.[54]

Three other fragments attributed to the same speech expand on Caelius' misuse of the body:

> Quid ego cum illo dissertem amplius, quem ego denique credo in pompa vectitatum ire ludis pro citeria, atque cum spectatoribus sermocinaturum?[55]

> Why should I keep debating with that man, who—I believe—is willing to

---

53. Cato, *orat.* 22.81 Sbl.
54. Sblendorio Cugusi (1982: 259) points out that the speech presupposes an attack on Cato's censorship initiated exclusively by a magistrate.
55. Cato, *orat.* 22.83 Sbl.

go to festival processions exhibited in place of a caricature-like statue and to interact with the spectators?

Descendit de cantherio, inde staticulos dare, riducularia fundere.[56]

He comes down from the workhorse, then moves softly around, and engages in mocking acts.

Praeterea cantat ubi collibuit, interdum Graecos versus agit, iocos dicit, voces demutat, staticulos dat.[57]

Moreover he sings when it pleases him, from time to time he performs Greek verses, tells jokes, changes the pitch of his voice, and moves softly around.

If we weed out the scorn that Cato heaps on Caelius, what we are left with is the image of an elite individual striving to enhance his authoritative assertions by mimicking nonelite practices. This image confirms that Cato's vested interest in taking up poetic forms was part of a much larger elite phenomenon of self-aggrandizement through cultural appropriations pursued by embodied means. But precisely because Caelius is represented as acting upon the same social imperatives that guide Cato's mimetic moves, the target of Cato's contempt cannot be identified simply with Caelius' adoption of Hellenizing or modernist customs, as is often argued.[58] It also needs to be related to his attempt to characterize Caelius as incapable of anchoring his cultural appropriations to ancestral archetypes. Accordingly, Caelius' failure is represented as a submission to alien and unbecoming impulses having the misfired effect of transforming the oratorical space into a moving stage hosting a hodgepodge of histrionic acts. In other words, Cato typifies Caelius as someone inept at producing an independent song according to the constraints dictated by the embodied tradition of authoritative speaking. Accordingly, the only thing that Caelius would have achieved was nothing more than reenacting foreign compositions and making an unchecked use of his voice and body. For our purposes, Cato's representation of Caelius' mimetic acts are a convenient foil for understanding the cultural disowning that, on the one hand, accompanied Cato's appropriation of socially secondary cultural forms

---

56. Cato, *orat.* 22.84 Sbl.
57. Cato, *orat.* 22.85 Sbl.
58. Sblendorio Cugusi 1982: 260–61; Cugusi and Sblendorio Cugusi 2001: 305–9 *passim*.

and, on the other, supported his activation of ancestral schemes. Other speeches allow us to explore further Cato's strategies of self-possessed appropriation.

Commentators have long noted that a fragment derived from the *Dierum Dictarum de Consulatu Suo,* a defense speech delivered by Cato in 191–190 B.C.E., is poetic in diction and hexametrical in form:[59]

Deinde postquam Massiliam praeterimus, inde omnem classem ventus Auster lenis fert; mare velis florere videres.[60] (– – – ‿‿ – x)

Hence, after we passed Marseille, then a gentle south wind carried the entire fleet; you could have seen the sea blooming with sails.

Hexametrical forms are to be found in Plautus' *cantica* in the form of heroic clausulae and are more fully deployed in other more or less contemporary nonelite expressions;[61] however, the extension of the hexametrical rhythm one foot beyond the clausula and its framing of a poetic image in what is obviously a narrative section points to Ennius and his *Annales* as Cato's source of imitation.[62] Later authors suggest that Cato sponsored Ennius' arrival to Rome in 204 B.C.E. and that the two enjoyed close familiar ties.[63] If so, the insertion of an Ennian-like phrase during an oratorical performance that seems to have taken place before the completion of the *Annales* makes a great deal of sense.[64] Indeed, it would indicate that Cato's engagement with Ennius had less to do with what the poet could do for him than with his interest in taking hold of the poet's imports and putting on them his mark of ownership. After all, Cornelius Nepos obliquely points to Cato's proprietorial attitude when he describes his initiative to take Ennius to Rome as his "Sardinian triumph."[65]

In 191 B.C.E., during the campaign led by M'. Acilius Glabrio against Antioch III, Cato spoke as a military tribune before the Athenian assembly.[66] Very little remains of the speech that he pronounced, but what does

---

59. On the structure of the entire speech, see Sblendorio Cugusi 1980. On this fragment, see also Cugusi and Sblendorio Cugusi 2001: 266–67; Sblendorio Cugusi 1982: 163–64; Till 1968: 41–42; Sblendorio Cugusi 1971: 31; Habinek 1985: 188–89.

60. Cato, *orat.* 4.17 Sbl.

61. Questa 1967: 248; 257–58; 265; for their presence in other nonelite cultural expressions, see the case of the epitaph for the mime Protogenes discussed by Massaro 2001.

62. Norden 1986: 180; Habinek 1985: 188 and note 30.

63. Nepos, *Cato* 1.4; Cicero, *De Sen.* 10.

64. For dating, see Goldberg 2005: 11.

65. Nepos, *Cato* 1.4.

66. Sources on this episode of Cato's life are Livy 35.50.4; Plut. *Cato Mai.* 12.4 and,

remain has attracted a great deal of attention:

> Epistulis bellum gerit (– – – ⏑⏑)
> Calamo et atramento militat⁶⁷ (– – – ⏑⏑)
>
> He wages war by means of epistles and fights with pen and ink.

Organized in parallel cola joined by asyndeton in a manner typical of the *carmen*, this fragment reveals Cato's employment of heroic clausulae and an obvious gesture to Demosthenes' *Philippics* 1.30.[68] In the face of the Macedonian threat, Demosthenes had mentioned sophisms and epistle-writing to criticize the Athenians' passivity; in his speech, Cato exploits the textually transmitted oration of Demosthenes to attack Antioch and convince the Athenians to turn their attention to Rome. Accordingly, this fragment indicates not only that Cato was familiar with the Demosthenic text, but also that he had acquired the skills necessary to translate it in such a way as to make it an integral part of his own oratorical performance. In other words, Cato can be seen to exploit a Greek text in a manner similar to the poets and to employ his acquired skill in the more socially valuable contexts of oratory. But there is more. In his *Life of Cato* Plutarch reports that Cato delivered this speech in Latin by choice and left the task of conveying the message in Greek to an interpreter.[69]

Together with the fragment from the Athenian speech, Plutarch's report has been used to suggest that Cato employed Greek culture as a foil for articulating a Roman national character and for cultivating in his fellow countrymen a sense of cultural self-esteem. According to this view, Cato would have refused to address the Athenian assembly in Greek in order to exhibit Roman ascendancy in matters political and cultural through linguistic means.[70] While calling attention to the intersection between military and cultural expansion, this reading goes amiss by assuming that the Romans suffered from a complex of cultural inferiority and that this complex kindled in them a desire to construct a seamless national identity. When our attention is turned to the intercultural exchanges that shape our testimonies, a more complicated picture is bound to emerge.

---

perhaps, 12.5. For the cultural importance of this speech, see Cugusi and Sblendorio Cugusi 2001: 258–59; Sblendorio Cugusi 1982: 131–32; Astin 1978: 56–57.

67. Cato, orat. 3.4 Sbl.
68. Fraenkel 1968: 130; Della Corte 1969: 263; Till 1968: 47; Letta 1984: 9.
69. Plut. *Cato mai.* 12.4–5.
70. Gruen 1992: 52–83. On the issue of Cato's (anti-)hellenism, see also Astin 1978: 156–81.

First of all, our sources make clear that the concentration of cultural wealth in Rome and in the highest social spheres had less to do with a disembodied conception of national identity than with an embodied process of cultural expansion. Once we take as a fact that Cato's address to the Athenians testifies to an environment in which learning Greek and reading Greek literature was becoming a routine elite practice, his employment of an interpreter suggests that the use of linguistic skills and literary knowledge as means to gain authority was a contested matter. In Athens Cato would have asserted himself as a Roman ruler not only by addressing the local audience in Latin, but also, and more especially, by having his speech translated into Greek. By viewing the scene conjured up by Plutarch from a performance-oriented perspective, it is impossible to disregard that the interpreter's voice would have amplified Cato's oratorical address. In this sense, one should not underestimate the fact that, in the process of translating, the interpreter would have retranslated Cato's translation from Demosthenes embedded in his speech. As such, Cato would have impressed his Athenian listeners by presenting himself not only as a political leader but also as a self-sufficient and self-confident proprietor of their cultural patrimony.

Another episode recounted by Plutarch provides us with further clues. According to Plutarch, in 155 B.C.E. the philosopher Carneades arrived in Rome on a diplomatic mission and delays in the senatorial hearing gave him the chance to lecture before an enthralled audience. Cato sped up Carneades' departure and reproached the senator C. Acilius for showing too much eagerness in offering himself as an interpreter.[71] It is customary to simply note that in Cato's eyes Acilius had cheapened his senatorial status by acting as a subaltern.[72] But if we read this episode by taking into account Cato's own use of an interpreter in Athens, what we realize is that he also viewed Acilius' loss of authority as directly proportional to the one gained by Carneades. For what Acilius had done was not to exploit his linguistic competence to produce an independent song, but to make himself instrumental to the performance of the Greek philosopher. Consequently, the episode dramatizes a crucial difference between acts of translation. It is one thing to remain attached to the source and perform a simple transposition across linguistic boundaries; it is quite another to draw freely from the source and leave an imprint on it by making it one's own.[73] The political dimension associated with Cato's understanding of cultural mastery as a form of authority is well illustrated by Polybius in his account of Cato's reaction to the history in Greek composed by another Roman senator, Postumius Albinus.

---

71. Plutarch, *Cato Mai.* 12.7; see also Pliny, *NH* 29.14
72. E.g., Gruen 1992: 73.
73. On interpreters vis-à-vis Cicero's theorization of translation, see McElduff 2009

According to Polybius, in the preface to his work Postumius had asked his readers to excuse him if, being Roman, he was not fully competent in the Greek language and methods of inquiry.[74] To this, he adds:

> In my opinion Marcus Porcius answered him [i.e., Postumius Albinus] very fittingly. For he stated that he wondered about the reasons that pushed him to apologize. If the Amphictyonic assembly had ordered him to write a history, perhaps it would have been necessary to write so and make excuses; but to write of his own will and under no compulsion and then again to ask for forgiveness if he should produce barbarisms made no sense at all, and was just as useless as if a man who had entered his name at the games for the boxing or the pancration, once in the stadium, when the time to fight arrived should beg the spectators to excuse him if he should not be capable of enduring the effort or the blows.[75]
> (trans. Paton—modified)

This passage could not make more conspicuous the extent to which for Cato cultural mastery and political supremacy were entwined both conceptually and practically. First, Postumius' apology for his linguistic and cultural shortcomings is represented as a failure to meet the demands that went along with his senatorial role and as a denial of Rome's ascendency over Greece. Second, the invocation of boxing and pancration for exemplary purposes gives substance to a conceptualization of cultural mastery and political supremacy in bodily and competitive terms. Third, the allusion to a spectatorship reaffirms scrutiny by a judging audience as an essential process for the acquisition of authority. In this respect, the passage as a whole suggests that for Cato the audience that mattered the most was the Roman ruling elite to which both he and Postumius belonged.

Good Authoritative Habits Are Learned at Home

Generally acclaimed as the first work of Latin prose that survives in its entirety, the *De Agricultura* is a text divided into 162 chapters. These chapters are introduced by titles most probably added by later editors. Despite the implicit order that the chapter organization may suggest, scholars have

---

74. Cf. also Plutarch, *Cato Mai.* 12.5 and Gellius 11.8. Gellius states that at the start of his work Postumius stated his Roman and Latin origins as well as his unfamiliarity with Greek ("nam sum," inquit, "homo Romanus natus in Latio, Graeca oratio a nobis alienissima est"). Gellius' version of Cato's response deviates from Polybius' and is drawn from Nepos, *Vir. Ill.* 13.

75. Polybius 39.1.1–9.

long been struggling with its seemingly irreducible inconsistencies. First of all, the Preface does not appear to be well integrated with what follows. While in the opening section Cato supports agricultural practices against usury and commerce, the remainder takes the form of a series of instructions that range from agricultural topics to medical, dietary, legal, and religious prescriptions. To be precise, the first twenty-two chapters deal with the themes of purchasing, locating, managing, and expanding an existing farm. The next thirty chapters or so (chapters 23–53) are organized around farm operations starting with the grape-harvest and ending with a variety of summer operations, while the third part (69–130) includes medical and veterinary recipes as well as instructions for making bread and cakes. The final part is composed of miscellaneous materials including instructions on rituals, contract templates, suggestions on where to buy equipment, more instructions to be given to the overseer, and other recipes.

The assemblage of haphazard materials and the piling up of instructions on different topics can be described as the main features of this text, but repetitions and associations hinging on particular objects or practices add up to the impression of an overarching lack of organization. For example, instructions on the layering of trees are given in chapter 51 and 52, and then duplicated in 133. On the other hand, the *amurca* or the dregs that remain after the pressing of olives link together instructions on the construction of the threshing-floor, a cure for a sterile olive tree, a mixture meant to keep caterpillars off vines, a solution for scabies in sheep, and, finally, a number of suggestions on how to preserve myrtle and twigs bearing berries (chapters 91–101).[76]

In an important monograph published in the late nineteen-seventies, Alan Astin suggested that "the fundamental explanation for the lack of system and the lack of disciplined thought in the *De Agricultura* is to be found precisely in Cato's role as the virtual founder of Latin prose literature, a role which is invariably recognized but the implications of which are easily overlooked. . . . Cato did not live in an environment which constantly inculcated ideals [of relevance, consistency, clarity] and techniques of composition, and had little previous experience of constructing books and equally little opportunity to benefit from the experience of others."[77] In recent years, the preoccupation over Cato's failure to compose a well-wrought piece of literature has been superseded by a more fruitful effort to view the *De Agricultura* within its own cultural horizon.

---

76. Astin 1978: 197–98.
77. Astin 1978: 198.

Building upon Thomas Habinek's reevaluation of the *De Agricultura*, Brendon Reay has brilliantly explored Cato's most recognized strategy of self-promotion, the presentation of himself as the modern embodiment of former farmer-statesmen like Manlius Curius Dentatus (consul in 290, 284, 275, 274 B.C.E. and censor in 272 B.C.E.) and Lucius Quinctius Cincinnatus (consul in 460 B.C. and dictator in 458 B.C.E. and 439 B.C.E.). In a speech pronounced after his censorship, perhaps in 183 B.C.E., Cato defends his services and turns to his agricultural roots. The move implies that, just like those figures of old, his hands-on labor in the fields has been the source of his frugality, austerity, and industry and had prepared him to be equally ready to act on behalf of the State:

> Ego iam a principio in parsimonia atque in duritia atque industria omnem adulescentiam meam abstinui agro colendo, saxis Sabinis, silicibus repastinandis atque conserendis.[78]

> From the very beginning I confined my entire youth in thrift and austerity and industry by farming, by clearing away Sabine rocks and stones again and again, and planting.

According to Reay, Cato's agricultural biography in this fragment needs to be understood as a strategy of aristocratic self-fashioning that finds its most articulate expression in the Preface to the *De Agricultura:*

> Est<o> interdum praestare mercaturis rem quaerere, nisi tam periculosum sit, et item fenerari, si tam honestum sit. maiores nostri sic habuerunt et ita in legibus posiverunt, furem dupli condemnari, feneratorem quadrupli. quanto peiorem civem existimarint feneratorem quam furem, hinc licet existimare. et virum bonum quom laudabant, ita laudabant, bonum agricolam bonumque colonum. amplissime laudari existimabatur qui ita laudabatur. mercatorem autem strenuum studiosumque rei quaerendae existimo, verum ut supra dixi, periculosum et calamitosum. at ex agricolis et viri fortissimi et milites strenuissimi gignuntur, maximeque pius quaestus stabilissimusque consequitur minimeque invidiosus, minimeque male cogitantes sunt qui in eo studio occupati sunt.[79]

> Let us grant that at times it is better to make money by trading, were it not

---

78. Cato, *orat.* 24.93 Sbl. For dating and other issues, see Sblendorio Cugusi 1982: 277–78.
79. Sblendorio Cugusi 2001. See also Courtney 1999: 43, 50–52 and for possible emendations, Gratwick 2002.

so hazardous, and likewise to loan money at interest, if it were as honorable. Our ancestors thought so and established in their laws that a thief should be punished twofold, a usurer fourfold. How much worse a citizen they reckoned a usurer than a thief, one can reckon from this. And when they praised a good man, they praised him thus: "good farmer and good cultivator." A man who was praised in this way was reckoned to have been praised to the fullest. Now I reckon a trader to be energetic and zealous in his pursuit of profit but, as I said above, he is liable to danger and disaster. But from farmers come both the bravest men and the most energetic soldiers, and, as a consequence, their livelihood is especially respected, most secure and least susceptible to hostility from others, and those who are engaged in this occupation are least likely to be malcontents.
(trans. Reay—slightly adapted)

By evoking the ancestors as a generic group in the same way as he does in his speeches, Cato stakes out here the claim that agriculture and its practitioners hold the highest place in the Roman social and ethical hierarchy. To put it in Reay's words, his argument "unfolds historically, with Cato carrying forward into the present the evaluative process (*existimo*) and conclusion (farmers are superior) established by the ancients (*existimarint, amplissime laudari existimabatur qui ita* [*bonum agricolam bonumque colonum*] *laudabatur*). The conspicuous repetition of forms of the verb *existimare* dramatizes the superiority of agriculture over and against other occupations, and, at the same time, characterizes this superiority as traditional, for the origin of agriculture's lofty social valuation is ascribed to the anonymous (and therefore unimpeachable) *maiores*."[80] What is more, Cato's movement from the past to the present coincides with a shift into the first person (*existimo*).[81] The shift has the effect of making the evaluative opinion of the ancestors his own, constructing the possibility of presenting himself as an incarnated ancestor. Through such a ploy, Cato sets the stage for what follows, a catalogue-like string of advice about the care of the land expressed in the imperative mood or in the hortatory subjunctive.

For the most part, Cato's advice is addressed to an anonymous (would-be) master/head of the household, a *dominus/pater familias* that stands in a synecdochal relation with the Latin-speaking elite addressees of the entire work. His advice centers on the management of an estate that has little to do with the small plot figured in his evocation of earlier farming practices.

---

80. Reay 2005: 338.
81. Cf. Habinek 1998a: 47–48.

In fact, his precepts relate to the acquisition, equipment, organization, and administration of a villa-based estate powered by slave and hired labor where the day-to-day operation is the responsibility of an overseer (*vilicus*), probably a slave acting on behalf of his largely absent owner (*dominus/pater familias*).[82] As Reay once again notes, Cato is able to bridge the gap between the past figured in the Preface and the present that informs the remainder by relying on a cultural tenet typical of traditional aristocracies: the extension of the master's body through servile prostheses with which the master accomplishes various tasks and transactions. The pervasive use of the second person expresses this tenet by effacing the distinction between the work of the (would-be) *dominus/pater familias* and the labor of his subalterns. This effacement feeds the illusion that the *dominus/pater familias* is doing the same agricultural work as in the past; nowhere, however, does the confusion between master and slave entail that the former is supposed to get his hands dirty. In the same sense, the commands that are now and then directed to the *vilicus* do not imply that Cato counted the *vilici* among his readers; on the contrary, they represent the kind of commands that his elite addressees are invited to use when dealing with their own *vilici*.

Reay's interpretation draws heavily on the pivotal role that the *De Agricultura* has long enjoyed in the interpretation of the socioeconomic transformations that took place in Italy after the Second Punic War. In recent years, however, the nature and impact of the war against Hannibal on agricultural practices in central Italy and the population growth in Rome has been undergoing a major reappraisal.[83] If this were not enough, archaeologists are undermining the documentary value of the *De Agricultura* altogether. For Nicola Terrenato, the presence of large villas in both central Italy and Rome before Cato's time is at odds with his invocation of hands-on farming that we find in the Preface; his prescriptions for wine presses call for sizes and capacity that are not even equaled two hundred years later, when wine was produced on a much larger scale. Also, Cato's unawareness of the vitally important amphora system needed to trade wine and oil (which in his time was just starting at some sites in southern Italy) casts serious doubt on his understanding of the realities of the new trade.[84] For my purposes, the rift between reality and representation that Terrenato has identified counters the unquestioned definition of the *De Agricultura* as a handbook and corroborates the necessity of rethinking its nature and scope.

---

82. See Treggiari 1969: 106–10 and Brunt 1971: 122 note 2.
83. See especially, Cornell 1996: 97–117 and Jongman 2003.
84. Terrenato forthcoming.

One way to do so is to acknowledge the centrality of the body. Reay's attention to how Cato exploits the prosthetic function of slaves to reenact the past draws attention to the participation of the body in the transmission of knowledge and memory. If viewed in terms of scenario, the mythology of the farmer-statesmen makes evident that Cato relies on embodied frameworks within which shared memories are localized and individual bodies act in very specific ways. In the older scenario the farmer-statesman lives in the country and his body is single-handedly engaged in agricultural work. When the State calls, he moves out of that space and returns to it only after fulfilling his duty. Cato's imperatives presuppose the older scenario and build onto it by bringing to center stage the *dominus/pater familias,* the master/head of the household. He is seldom present at the farm and acts in the agricultural setting through the work performed by those whom he commands. Since the new scenario is legitimated by reference to an older scenario linking agricultural and political activities, the change in the way the body acts signals much more than just Cato's vested interest in his own aristocratic self-fashioning. At one level, the shift may be informed by the problems of ruling without being physically present that Rome's military successes had intensified. If so, the imperatives that structure the *De Agricultura* have the performative force of creating the slave-powered farm as the setting in which (would-be) *domini/patres familias* can learn the skill of extending their bodies through the bodies of others. At another level, the older scenario promotes a view of self-sufficiency that obscures the longstanding gentilician reliance on subordinates and promotes self-mastery as the springboard for an effective aggrandizement of the self. Attention to how Cato constructs the environment of his farm and the characters that act within it reveals the scope of Cato's prose from yet another perspective.

It is generally assumed that, when composing the *De Agricultura,* Cato had his own farm in mind and that its location should be identified somewhere between southern Latium and northern Campania.[85] At 8.2 Cato speaks about the organization of vegetable gardens outside Rome; Venafrum and Casinum are mentioned at 136 in relation to variations on tenancy agreement; Suessa is indicated as the place in which an olive crushing mill can be bought (22.3); finally, at 135 he gives a list of places for the purchase of clothes and tools and refers to Cales, Minturnae, Lucania, Trebla Alba, Pompeii, Rufrium, Capua, and Nola. In her recent book, *Romulus' Asylum,* Emma Dench relies on these references in order to problematize our understanding of Romanization as the one-way appro-

---

85. Astin 1978: 243 and note 9.

priation of Roman cultural and political motifs on the part of the Italians and to propose in its stead a more nuanced model of imperialism. Her model takes into account not only the subjugation of people but also the transformation of land on a large scale. Interestingly, she locates the seeds of this practice in the fourth century B.C.E. and in the traditions relating to the conquest of Sabinum by Curius Dentatus, one of the farmer-statesman inherent in the scenario evoked by Cato in the Preface. Finally, she brings into relief the proprietorial behavior displayed by the Romans in general; at the same time, she stresses the multiple focal points revealed by the notion of specialties associated with individual locations.[86]

The link between the reconfiguration of conquered land and the fourth-century B.C.E. figure of Curius Dentatus uncovered by Dench helps us see that Cato's imperatives construct the farm environment on a territory perceived as already conquered and reorganized. This underlying perception, in turn, sustains Cato's overall proprietorial stance, a stance that encompasses the local specialties that he mentions and the knowledge embodied by those who are commanded to do the actual work. To be sure, there is not a single sentence in the *De Agricultura* that does not project Cato's expertise over the practical techniques or material instruments that the *vilicus,* the slaves, or the hired workers are to adopt in performing their job. Indeed, Cato is so in control of the subordinate characters who populate the *De Agricultura* that in chapter 2.2 he is even able to anticipate the actions as well as the words of the *vilicus:*

> Si ei opus non apparet,
> Dicit vilicus sedulo se fecisse,
> Servos non valuisse,
> Tempestates malas fuisse,
> Servos aufugisse,
> Opus publicum effecisse.

> If the work seems wanting,
> The overseer says that he has done his best,
> That slaves were sick,
> That the weather was bad,
> That the slaves ran away,
> That they were involved in public work.

---

86. Dench 2005: 162–73.

Writing in the early fifties and commenting on the dialogic nature of this passage, Antonio Mazzarino pointed out that by structuring the *vilicus'* justifications into cola marked by assonances and rhyming, Cato parades a feeling of self-satisfaction for knowing what the *vilicus* will say.[87] Although not stated as follows, Mazzarino's impression derives from two elements: one, the words attributed to the *vilicus* are of Cato's own making and, two, their *carmen*-style structuring communicates that for him the *vilicus'* excuses are a trite and timeless reality. As I have pointed out earlier, the remains of Cato's speeches suggest that he used the *carmen*-style in order to enhance his authoritative presence. In this instance, he puts similarly formalized speech of his own making into the mouth of the *vilicus* not only to display his grasp of the ways of the world, but also to construct this character's lesser status. This fact becomes particularly conspicuous once we look at the list of replies that Cato proposes to the *dominus/pater familias* as responses to the *vilicus'* justifications:

> Cum tempestates pluviae fuerint, quae operae per imbrem fieri potuerint: dolia lavari, picari, villam purgari, frumentum transferri, stercus foras efferri, stercilium fieri, semen purgari, funes sarciri, novos fieri, centones, cuculiones familiam oportuisse sibi sarcire. Per ferias potuisse fossas veteres tergeri, viam publicam muniri, vepres recidi, hortum fodiri, pratum purgari, virgas vinciri, spinas eruncari, expinsi far, munditias fieri; cum servi aegrotarint, cibaria tanta dari non oportuisse.[88]

> If the weather has been bad, this is the work that could have been done while it rained: washing and pitching vats, cleaning the farm, moving grain, shoveling dung outside, making a dung-heap, cleaning the seed, mending ropes, making new ones, the slaves could have been mending their cloaks and hoods. During the holidays, the old ditches could have been cleaned, the public road redone, the hedges cut, the vegetable patch dug, the meadow cleared, the vines tied up, the thorny plants cut back, the grain husked, a general clean-up done; when the slaves have been sick, not too much food should have been given.
> (trans. Dalby—slightly adapted)

From a structural point of view, this list is composed of periods consisting of small units made up, for the most part, of a noun and a passive infinitive.

---

87. Mazzarino 1952: 130–31.
88. Cato, *De Agr.* 2.3–4.

In turn, each unit is linked through rather weak assonances created by the infinitival endings. When compared to the list of excuses attributed to the *vilicus,* this new list features Cato holding back from imposing a tight pattern of speech on the *dominus/pater familias*. He does not structure the list of replies into clear cola and appears to simply outline the kind of answers that the *dominus/pater familias* may choose to use in order to respond to a subordinate. In this sense, Mazzarino was right when he said that it is a great mistake to intervene in the manuscript tradition and modify the list to match the *vilicus*'s excuses.[89] Certainly, by leaving the passage as is we observe that degrees of formalization and imposition of speech serve to mark a character's relative standing.

The connection between formal constraints, imposition of speech, and construction of characters displayed in these two passages calls attention to the social dimension inherent in the way later Romans referred to prose as *verba soluta* (loosened, unrestrained words). Indeed, it makes clear that prose emerged from within the tradition of the *carmen* and presented itself as speech acts attached to individuals involved in authority-building activities and free from formal restrictions enforced by others. On the other hand, the instructional dimension that informs Cato's interplay with the anonymous *dominus/pater familias* inside the world of the *De Agricultura* and, by synecdoche, with the addressees of his work qualifies the link between the emergence of prose and the social formation of a new aristocracy. In order to clarify this twofold outcome, I find it useful to return to the *carmen* by plumbing more deeply recent insights into the understanding of ritual and ritualization.

While it is often stated that the *carmen*-style finds its roots in marked social events such as religious rites and juridical actions, less attention has been paid to the link between language and body that this statement implies.[90] This lack of attention derives mostly from the fact that in ritual contexts formalized speech plays a key role by enabling the effectiveness of the accompanying actions. But formalized speech is itself a component of embodied schemes and these schemes structure a social actor's experience of the world through endless oppositions and homologies. Deployed through the body understood in all of its dimensions, these oppositions and homologies privilege one activity over others and generate hierarchical schemes that are perceived as ordering the world. In this view, formalized

---

89. Mazzarino 1952: 131.

90. Some have also proposed that the extension to the juridical sphere belongs to a later stage, see Luiselli 1969: 123–71; De Meo 1986: 116 and *passim.* Cf. also Frankel 1964: 69–70, 223.

speech, body postures, periodicity, and invocation of divine beings are among the strategies that sustain the differentiation of certain activities from others. Ritualization refers precisely to this process of privileging. To put it in Catherine Bell's words, "ritualization is fundamentally a way of doing things to trigger the impression that these practices are distinct and the associations that they engender are special. A great deal of strategy is employed simply in the degree to which some activities are ritualized and therein differentiated from other acts."[91] In the same vein, Bell reminds us that the goal of ritualization does not relate to the resolution of conflict or to social solidarity as such, but rather to the re-production of ritualized agents, people who are able to act on the instinctual knowledge of the schemes of hierarchization in such a way as to appropriate and mold a whole range of experiences in an empowered manner.[92] Accordingly, she defines ritual mastery as the "ability—not equally shared, desired or recognized—to (1) take and remake schemes from the shared culture that strategically nuance, privilege, or transform, (2) deploy them in the formulation of a privileged ritual experience, which in turn (3) impresses them in a new form upon agents able to deploy them in a variety of circumstances beyond the circumference of the rite itself."[93]

The so-called Prayer to Mars that we find in chapter 141.2–4 of the *De Agricultura* is considered one of the earliest examples of *carmen;* as such, next to the Preface it is the passage that has received most of the scholarly attention.[94] The Prayer to Mars, however, is not the only instance of *carmen* that we encounter in the *De Agricultura*.[95] And even in this case, the highly structured context created by the shorter prayers and the formally marked instructions that precede them should not be disregarded. Closer attention to the entire section will serve to bring into focus Cato's ability to impress upon his elite addressees a new form of shared schemes of doing and speaking stemming from the *carmen;* what in other words we identify as Latin prose and the Romans as *verba soluta:*

> 139. Lucum conlucare romano more sic oportet: porco piaculo facito, sic verba concipito:

---

91. Bell 1992: 220.
92. Bell 1992: 221 and *passim.*
93. Bell 1992: 116.
94. See recently, Courtney 1999: 62–67, De Meo 1986: 133–69. For more strictly linguistic analysis and comparative observations, see Watkins 1995: 197–225; for a renewed view of this prayer via the Saturnian, see Mercado 2006.
95. See also chapters 83, 131, 132, 134; as far as I know, Dalby (1998: 21) is the only one to clearly acknowledge that there is more to look at than just the Prayer to Mars.

"Si deus, si dea es quoium illud sacrum est, uti tibi ius est porco piaculo facere illiusce sacri coercendi ergo harumque rerum ergo, sive ego sive quis iussu meo fecerit, uti id recte factum siet, eius rei ergo te hoc porco piaculo immolando bonas preces precor uti sies volens propitius mihi, domo familiaeque meae liberisque meis; harumce rerum ergo macte hoc porco piaculo immolando esto."

140. Si fodere velis, altero piaculo eodem modo facito, hoc amplius dicito: "Operis faciundi causa"; dum opus, cotidie per partes facito; si intermiseris aut feriae publicae aut familiares intercesserint, altero piaculo facito.

141. Agrum lustrare sic oportet: impera suovitaurilia circumagi:

"Cum divis volentibus quodque bene eveniat, mando tibi, Mani, uti illace suovitaurilia fundum, agrum, terramque meam quota ex parte sive circumagi sive circumferenda censeas, uti cures lustrare."

2. Ianum Iovemque vino praefamino, sic dicito:

"Mars pater, te precor quaesoque uti sies volens propitius mihi, domo, familiaeque nostrae: quoius rei ergo agrum, terram, fundumque meum suovitaurilia circumagi iussi, uti tu morbos visos invisosque, viduertatem vastitudinemque, calamitates intemperiasque prohibessis, defendas, averruncesque, utique tu fruges, frumenta, vineta, virgultaque grandire beneque evenire siris, 3. pastores pecuaque salva servassis duisque bonam salutem valetudinemque mihi, domo, familiaeque nostrae; harumce rerum ergo, fundi, terrae, agrique mei lustrandi lustrique faciendi ergo, sicuti dixi, macte hisce suovitaurilibus lactentibus immolandis esto; Mars pater, eiusdem rei ergo macte hisce suovitaurilibus lactentibus esto"; item.

4. Cultro facito; struem et fertum uti adsiet, inde obmoueto. Ubi porcum immolabis, agnum vitulumque, sic oportet:

"Eiusque rei ergo macte suovitaurilibus immolandis esto"; nominare vetat Martem neque agnum vitulumque.

Si minus in omnis litabit, sic verba concipito:

"Mars pater, si quid tibi in illisce suovitaurilibus lactentibus neque satisfactum est, te hisce suovitaurilibus piaculo";

si uno duobusve dubitabit, sic verba concipito:

"Mars pater, quod tibi illoc porco neque satisfactum est, te hoc porco piaculo."[96]

139. To open up a clearing, you must use the Roman rite, as follows. Do sacrifice of an expiation piglet, and say it thus:

"Whatever god, whatever goddess you may be to whom this place is

---

96. Cato, *De Agr.* 139–41.

sacred, since it is proper to sacrifice the expiation swine for the taking of this sacred place, therefore, may what I do or what another by my order does be rightly done. Therefore in slaughtering for you this expiation swine I pray with good prayers that you be willing and favorable to me, to my house and household and to my children; wherefore, accept the slaughter of this expiatory piglet."

140. If you want to dig there, do another Expiation. Say explicitly "for the purpose of working the land." Then do some of the work on each consecutive day till all is done. If you interrupt it, or public or household holidays intervene, you must do another Expiation.

141. You must consecrate the field as follows. Instruct Pig, Sheep and Ox to be driven all around:

"So that all may turn out well with the gods on our side, I entrust to you, Mr. X, to consecrate by your care my farm, my field, and my land; driving or drawing around Pig, Sheep, and Ox wherever you may determine." First invoke Janus and Jove with wine, and say:

"Father Mars, I ask and pray that you be ready and favorable to me, our house and household. Wherefore I have ordered Pig, Sheep and Ox to be driven all around my field, land and farm, so that you will prevent, ward off and avert sicknesses seen and unseen, childlessness and fruitlessness, disaster and storm; so that you will permit fruits, grains, vines and saplings to flourish and come to fruition; so that you will keep safe shepherds and flocks and give good heart and health to me, our house and household. Therefore, for the consecration and making sacred of my farm, field and land as aforesaid, accept the slaughter of this suckling Pig, Sheep and Ox." Repeat:

" . . . therefore, Father Mars, accept the slaughter of this suckling Pig, Sheep and Ox."

Do it with a knife. Have *strues* and *fertum* at hand. Offer immediately. As you slaughter the piglet, lamb and calf, then:

" . . . therefore accept the slaughter of Pig, Sheep and Ox."

Mars must not be named, nor must one say "lamb" or "calf." If all the offerings are unpromising, say it thus: " . . . Father Mars, if anything dissatisfies you in that suckling Pig, Sheep and Ox, I offer you this Pig, Sheep and Ox in expiation."

If only one or two are doubtful, say it thus: " . . . Father Mars, since you were dissatisfied with that piglet, I offer you this piglet in expiation."
(Trans. Dalby—slightly modified)

Following the arrangement that we find in the text, we first have the sacrifice of a piglet. According to Cato, this is to be done while clearing a new piece of land and must be accompanied by a general prayer for the safeguarding of the entire household. Cato's injunctions are expressed by two clauses dominated by future imperatives and joined by asyndeton: *porco piaculo facito, sic verba concipito* ("you ought to perform the sacrifice of an expiation piglet, you ought to pronounce words conceived along these lines," 139). In the next chapter, Cato states that the same prayer is to be performed in case of actual ploughing: *si fodere velis, altero piaculo eodem modo facito, hoc amplius dicito* ("if you want to dig there, you ought to do another expiation following the same method and say this explicitly," 140). Once again, we find the use of two clauses featuring future imperatives joined by asyndeton; this time, however, the two clauses follow a more legalistic pattern, being preceded by a future-less-vivid hypothetical clause that sets up the condition of the action directed by the imperatives.[97] Finally, in chapter 141, Cato gives instructions about the actual lustration of the field. The act is divided into two movements: first, the *dominus/pater familias* is instructed to order the herdsman to drive the animals around by adopting a specific formula; afterwards, the *dominus/pater familias* is urged to pronounce the prayer to Mars. For the first act, he says: *agrum lustrare sic oportet: impera suovitaurilia circumagi* ("it is necessary to lustrate the field in this way: order that the pig, sheep, and ox be driven all around"). Accordingly, he states the necessity of the lustration and instructs the *dominus/pater familias* in the present imperative to command a subaltern to perform an action. Afterwards, but before finally unfolding the Prayer to Mars, Cato instructs the *dominus/pater familias* to establish a relationship with the divine world through libation and prayer: *Ianum Iouemque uino praefamino, sic dicito* ("you ought to invoke first of all Janus and Juppiter with wine and say in this way").

In all of these instances, we see the prevalence of future imperatives directed to the *dominus/pater familias;* some are also joined by asyndeton in such a way as to stress the simultaneity of doing and saying.[98] In legal contexts, the future imperative—known also as the imperative of instruction—is standard in main clauses and is used for instructions to be carried out whenever required or after some condition has been fulfilled.[99] Conversely, the present imperative tends to be used for commands to be carried out immediately. In the above scene, the only instance of present

---

97. Meyer 2004: 49 and *passim.*
98. The prevalence of future imperatives coincides with what we find in the *De Agricultura* as a whole. Vairel-Carron (1975: 287–88) counts 976 instances of the second person future imperative, and only 31 of the present imperative.
99. Crawford 1996: ii.571; De Meo 1986: 102–3; Powell 2005: 127.

imperative (141) serves to advise the *dominus/pater familias* to command the execution of an action. What follows, however, is not simply a command; it is a speech act that, on the one hand, draws its performativity from the ritual actions outlined in chapters 139–41 and, on the other, marks the *dominus/pater familias'* act of bestowing on a generic underling (*Manius*) the power of consecrating his property on his behalf.

Bearing formalities drawn from the *carmen* such as figura etymologica (*preces precor*), asyndetical synonyms (*volens propitius*), archaicisms (*quoium, siet*), and *uti*-clauses (*uti sies*), the opening prayer appeases the local divinity and solicits his or her assistance in the endeavor of transforming a piece of uncultivated land into an agriculturally productive field. But the plea and the sacrifice that the *dominus/pater familias* is supposed to perform also unfold the relations of power working within the household by explicitly invoking its structure in all of its spatial and human dimensions (cf. *mihi, domo familiaeque meae liberisque meis*, "for me, my house, my household, and my children," 139). Thus, the sequence of actions that occupies chapters 139 can be taken as a ritual act that is so thanks to the innumerable oppositions and homologies that are both spoken out and acted upon. The most conspicuous include binaries like divine/human, cultivated/uncultivated, speaking/not speaking, everyday speech/formalized speech, doing/not doing, commanding/executing. Basic to the understanding of the entire event, however, is these binaries' relationship with classifications that homologize the act of clearing and ploughing a new field in the context of a farm to the *sulcus primigenius* that marked the foundation of cities and colonies.[100] Moreover, in these classifications Cato's experience with censorial practices plays a pivotal role. Indeed, it is hard to miss that the *suovitaurilia* that he projects in the context of the farm is a redeployed form of the rite that the censors performed during the taking of the census.[101] In light of this, the activities unfolded in the *De Agricultura* have less to do with the performance of routine agricultural practices than with Cato's manipulation of traditions and conventions filtered through his own perception and experience of reality. By taking this passage as a working sample, I propose to analyze more pointedly how Cato deploys the *carmen* tradition in his instructional addresses to the *dominus/pater familias*.

As I have noted above, Cato puts into the *vilicus'* mouth formalized speech of his own making in order to construct this character's lesser

---

100. See Gargola 1995: 72–75.
101. See Gargola 1995: 77. It is generally taken for granted that the civic and the private rites of lustration are related without taking into account that this relationship may have been Cato's invention.

standing and display his hold on power relations. Conversely, the looser formal organization that marks the list of replies proposed to the *dominus/ pater familias* calls attention to the equivalence between freedom from externally imposed speech and social authority. This scheme can be seen to guide Cato elsewhere.

For example, when he articulates the first and foundational advice to the *dominus/pater familias* for inaugurating the cultivation of a new field, Cato adopts the verb *concipere* in the future imperative (139); later on, he anticipates the addenda to the prayer to Mars with the same verbal form (140.4). In the sphere of law and religion the Romans distinguished between *concepta verba* and *certa verba:* the former phrase refers to words that have undergone some type of adjustment either in pattern or form; the latter, to words that are fixed and unchangeable in pattern or form.[102] In chapter 83 Cato prescribes the making of offerings for the health of the cattle without mentioning any particular prayer and concludes: *hoc votum in annos singulos, si voles, licebit vovere* ("you may make this offering every single year if you are willing to do so"). The same liberty characterizes the prescription of a spring offering for the oxen in chapter 132: *Vestae, si voles, dato* ("you do that for Vesta if you like"). If we look outside the rituals and at the contracts that we find in chapters 136–37 and 144–50, we see that these do not set out the main points of the agreement; rather, they tend to focus on potentially problematic clauses. Since they are not complete, these contracts cannot be considered texts to be rehearsed verbatim in the first place. As Britta Ager rightly points out, if it makes sense that the details of the contracts needed to be modified by the reader, the same conclusion should be applied to the rituals that are, in fact, found alongside the contracts. Like the contracts, so too the rituals appear to be providing frameworks within which some variation is anticipated. After all, a noticeable link between the two spheres is the use of generic names. In the sequence of actions surrounding the Prayer to Mars the subordinate who is supposed to lead the three animals is called Manius; in the contract templates in chapter 144 (contract for hiring olive harvesters) and 145 (contract for the milling of olives) this is L. Manlius, with the prenomen alluding to the different standing of the person involved in the figured transaction.[103]

Taken together, these passages suggest that Cato does not bind the *dominus/pater familias* to repeat his exact words in the exact same way;

---

102. Meyer 2004: 61–62.
103. Ager 2009.

on the contrary, he imposes on him the choice of varying and modulating the model of speech and behavior that he proposes. After all, Cato does the same when redeploying expressions from one instance of prayer to the other. For example, the phrase *uti sies volens propitius mihi, domo, familiaeque nostrae* that we find in the opening prayer to the *suovitaurilia* (139) is integral to the Prayer to Mars that concludes the sequence of structured activities. The longer version, *bonas preces precor uti sies volens propitius mihi, domo familiaeque meae liberisque meis* embedded in the prayer to Mars features also in the prayers to Ianus and Juppiter pronounced during the sacrifice of a sow before the harvest (134.2 and 3). Thus, what stands out from such strategies is that Cato addresses the *dominus/pater familias* by commanding him to both master and freely manipulate patterns of speech and behavior that, by deferring back to a super-ordinary reality, guarantee the order of things. In other words, Cato relates to the *dominus/pater familias* as a Roman father would to his son.

That Cato was particularly concerned about the education of his children is well known. In this respect, it is customary to point to Plutarch, who states that Cato took in his hands the upbringing of his son and did not allow him to be taught by Chilon, a Greek slave and *grammatistes* living in his household.[104] Fortunately for us, Cato's educational choices also find expression in a number of fragments hortatory in tone and generally considered to be part of a larger work known as the *Ad Filium*.

The study of these fragments is characterized by a generalized tendency to fit what remains into some coherent Greek literary precedent and into books organized by subjects. This tendency tends to override the tradition of father-to-son teaching that underlies Cato's strategic choices in the first place.[105] The near contemporary parody of an exchange between father and son that we find in Plautus' *Trinummus* (276–390), so pervasively filled with maxims, could be effective only if the embodied schemes that sustained the parody were well entrenched. Together with the often-cited agricultural precept, *hiberno pulvere, verno luto, grandia*

---

104. Plutarch, *Cato mai.* 20.4–5), Cato's ideas about education are often discussed in relation to his attitude towards the Greeks. E.g., Astin 1978: 341–42; Gruen 1992: 67; Leigh 2004: 158–91.

105. Exemplary in this sense are Astin's comments (1978: 339–40). The division into topics is still followed by Cugusi and Sblendorio Cugusi in their 2001 edition of the fragments. Cf. also Sblendorio Cugusi and Cugusi 1996: 193 and the introduction to their edition (2001:75–76). And yet, already in the early nineteen-fifties Mazzarino had unfolded a sound philological argument against seeing in the *Ad Filium* an encyclopedic project and had brought into the foreground their nonliterary model as well as their oracular tone.

farra, Camille, metes (" Camillus, you will reap abundant spelt in the dust of winter and the mud of spring," Festus, 82.18–22L), the *Trinumnus* is a crucial pointer to the understanding of intergenerational instruction as a ritualized practice that looks to the *carmen* tradition.

At a formal level, the inclusion of father-to-son teaching under the rubric of *carmen* is warranted by the bipartite structure and the two-line length that characterize most of the surviving *sententiae*. While contextual details are hard to discern, it is clear that, generally speaking, a *sententia* objectified shared schemes of perception and action through the body of the social actor who articulated it. During the interaction, this same social actor communicated an empowered and empowering understanding of the cosmos.[106] Seen in this light, *sententiae* associated with intergenerational relations emerge as a subgenre characterized by the interpellation of the younger party by name.[107] This form of interpellation appeals emotionally and persuasively to the younger listener by prompting him to act according to the framework that the older speaker makes explicit and, therefore, to extend generationally the knowledge embodied by the older speaker. That this extensibility was a 'bodily matter' strictly entangled with the greater authority enjoyed by the speaker can, perhaps, be more easily observed if we use other instances of interpellation by name as a foil. One such instance, as I note above, is to be found in the lustration scene of the *De Agricultura* where the *dominus/pater familias* is asked to call by name the herdsman upon whom he bestows the power to drive the animals on his behalf during the rite (141). Whereas the herdsman acts simply as a prosthesis to the master's physical body, *sententiae* involving a generationally lopsided relationship call into play embodied knowledge as well. In the tradition of juridical *responsa* the act of summoning by name located the hierarchical relationship between speaker and listener in a chain of homologies and oppositions that looked to a legitimating and superordinary reality. On this score, Aldo Schiavone has recently pointed out that in the archaic period the *responsum* constituted an authoritative manifestation of the recondite knowledge of the *pontifices* and had a structuring and regulatory impact on the ways the *patres* related to one another. For Schiavone, the fact that the *responsa* often contain the name of the consulting person underscores the practical nature of *ius* and its intricate

---

106. Some useful remarks on proverbs and similar types of speech acts are in Bourdieu 1990: 107–11. For a view on *sententiae* in relation to the system of *sapientia,* see Habinek 2006.
107. Note that Cicero acts upon the same cultural framework in his *De Officiis* (1.1).

relationship with a shifting but always exclusive social network.[108] The *Ad Filium* needs to be viewed under this light.

Interpellation by name marks only three fragments grouped under the heading of *Ad Filium,* but the didactic tone of the remaining ones suggests that we are dealing with the same father-to-son relationship.[109] In some cases, this impression is philologically confirmed by the reference "*Ad Filium*" that precedes the quotation or is implied by an imperative prescribing a behavior, a practice, or an action that is clearly associated with the elite.[110] Accordingly, sometimes the son is explicitly called upon, as in *orator est, Marce fili, uir bonus dicendi peritus* ("An orator, my son Marcus, is an honorable man skilled in speaking," *Ad Filium* fr.*18 C&Sbl); other times the topic gives a clue, as in the famous case, *rem tene verba sequentur* ("Hold the subject matter, the words will follow," *Ad Filium* fr. 19* C&Sbl). Focused on authoritative speaking, these two precepts follow the bipartite structure that we find in other samples of maxims. In turn, the expanded and modified version of the first of the two precepts just mentioned, *vir bonus est, Marce fili, colendi peritus cuius ferramenta splendent* ("an honorable man, my son Marcus, is skilled in cultivating and his instruments shine," *Ad Filium,* fr. 7 C&Sbl) undermine modern attempts to impose encyclopedic headings on this material and reveals once again Cato's tendency to expand received schemes. In fact, we are not dealing here with two separate precepts, one about oratory and another about agriculture. Critics have long pointed out that the latter expresses the same preoccupation with the definition of the *vir bonus* that we find in the Preface to the *De Agricultura;* what has gone unnoticed is that agricultural and oratorical themes belong to the same sphere of activities.[111] As the *De Agricultura* teaches us, speaking authoritatively is the same as caring for one's farm since what the latter ultimately means is to exercise one's control over the weave of constraints and possibilities that inform power relations.

Just as with the case of structural expansion, topical dilation is to be

---

108. Schiavone 2005: 66–69; 144–45. It would appear that the *responsum* concluded with a maxim as well. I should also like to point out that Cato and his son are central to the scholarly discussion of *ius*. Indeed, the *De Agricultura* bears a clear sign of his juridical expertise in the contracts inserted into it; as I mention above, these too feature a generic name to be replaced by the *pater familias* adopting Cato's templates. For further bibliography and discussion, see Cugusi and Sblendorio Cugusi 2001: 2.234–47.

109. The interpellation by name appears in Cato, *Ad Filium* fr. *1; 7; *18 C&Sbl. I should also add that the material that Cugusi and Sblendorio Cugusi (2001: 2. 422–39) collect under this title is organized as if it were conceived as a book divided into specific topics.

110. For the philological argument, see Astin 1978: 338.

111. See, Mazzarino 1952: 53–54 and Calboli 2003: 20–22.

understood as an expression of Cato's mastery of received traditions. In this sense, the longest fragment attributed to the *Ad Filium* (Pliny *NH* 29.14 = *Ad Filium* 1 C&Sbl) so focused on alien cultural practices like Greek literature and medicine is rather outstanding. In fact, it pushes the boundaries of precept-oriented father-to-son instruction in length and topicality so much that Cato can be seen to rein in his intervention by incorporating a direct address to his son, an explicit invocation of the pre-poetic figure of the *vates,* and a strong concluding imperative. What is crucial for our purposes is to recognize that by acting in such a self-possessed way Cato displays his holistic understanding of reality and impresses on his son a new tangible orientation to an unchanging cosmos. Not surprisingly, later commentators describe Cato's precepts as oracular in manner and pitch.[112] Accordingly, Cato's precepts to his son should not be approached by adopting a strictly literary framework; however, this does not imply that we discard philological analyses since these provide us with a venue for grasping more firmly the *Ad Filium*'s relationship with the *De Agricultura.*

In the mid-nineteen-fifties Antonio Mazzarino constructed a rather inspiring editorial history for the *De Agricultura* that took into serious account the precepts transmitted under the title of *Ad Filium.* From the comments that Pliny the Elder attaches to the piece on Greek literature and medicine, Mazzarino inferred that Cato had also made reference to a private *commentarius.* This would have contained medical recipes gathered over time which Cato would have used in order to care for his extended household. From such a *commentarius,* Cato would have derived a series of precepts addressed to the son without any particular order and focused on a great variety of topics (agriculture, medicine, and rhetoric). Finally, Cato would have gone on to compose the *De Agricultura,* a text left unfinished that included some of the previous material. That he intended to circulate this outside of his household would find confirmation in the suppression of the son's interpellation. I will return to the specifics of Cato's use of the writing medium in the following chapter; for the moment, I find it important to go back to two of Mazzarino's points.

Clearly, in his philological reconstruction Mazzarino adopted an editorial model that has more to do with modern literary drafting than is warranted.[113] Even so, by positing that the *De Agricultura* grew out of the *Ad Filium* he obliquely pointed to Cato's tendency to modify and stretch

---

112. Most notably, Pliny, *NH* 29.14, 7.17; Seneca, *Controv.* 1, Praef. 9. Astin (1978: 338) downsizes the importance of this later reception.

113. Mazzarino 1952: 38–39; 53.

inherited schemes. In his speeches Cato displays this tendency when he inserts alien and nonelite expressions into traditional and authoritative forms drawn from the *carmen;* in the *De Agricultura* when he intervenes in the intergenerational tradition of father-to-son instruction by structurally and topically expanding it. On this score, the conspicuous suppression of the son's address constitutes a further expression of the same overall attitude. This suppression finds different resolutions in the Preface and the body of the *De Agricultura:* in the Preface it sustains his language of praise and evaluation;[114] in the remainder it serves him to construct the *dominus/pater familias* as the character with whom his addressees are invited to identify and to whom he relates on a man-to-man relationship.[115] Finally, if a performance-oriented approach to the *Ad Filium* allows us to see that Cato's interpellation to his son was guided by the aim of preparing him for a great variety of authoritative roles, by the same token the *De Agricultura* reveals that every single (would-be) estate owner who turned to the *De Agricultura* would have figured himself as Cato's metaphorical son. Accordingly, while displaying Cato's self-possessed grasp of the socio-cosmological order, the *De Agricultura* encoded forms and themes that secured its exclusivity and contributed to the socialization of a very small sector of Roman society.

---

114. Habinek 1998a: 46–50.
115. A feature stressed by Gratwick 2002: 70.

Chapter 5

Power Differentials in Writing

Texts and Authority

In the *Brutus* Cicero contends that oratory in Rome was late in its origin and development. Although he infers from episodes of the far past that certain men had achieved brilliant results thanks to their speaking abilities, Cicero remarks that he had never read that any of them was considered an orator or that eloquence offered any prize.[1] With this allusion to reading, Cicero sets the stage for his claim that Roman oratory effectively emerged in the early second century B.C.E., when the Roman elite learned to write their speeches. Through a number of convoluted analogies and chronological assessments Cicero argues that Cato the Censor was the first to produce oratorical texts worth reading and defines oratory as an art comparable to sculpture and poetry: just like these arts, oratory had followed an evolutionary path towards stylistic perfection.[2] Later in the dialogue he proposes that this perfection was reached a generation before him, with Marcus Antonius and L. Licinius Crassus.[3] But when Atticus, a friend of Cicero and one of the characters in the *Brutus,* finally intervenes, this suggestion is replaced by another: it is Cicero the orator who makes everybody else before him look obsolete and unrefined.[4]

As recently remarked, the *Brutus* was very much the product of Cice-

---

1. Cicero, *Brut.* 56.
2. Cicero, *Brut.* 60–76.
3. Cicero, *Brut.* 143.
4. Cicero, *Brut.* 292–96.

ro's own circumstances.⁵ After Caesar's victory at Thapsus in 46 B.C.E., he had obtained the pardon of the new leader, but his political position remained very uncertain. If this were not enough, he had not been present on the oratorical scene for a while and his oratorical reputation had been thwarted by the attacks of those who found his style fundamentally decadent. As a way to redress the situation, Cicero turns to the past or, rather, to texts of speeches left behind by his predecessors with the object of canonizing their oratorical style and his own. In the process he produced a historically based theoretical framework in order to sustain his transformation of Roman oratory into a primarily written practice and into an object amenable to textual scrutiny.⁶ According to Emanuele Narducci, Cicero could push such an outcome because it was only at this time that a book market had started to develop and a public opinion made up of elite readers had began to exist in Rome and the rest of Italy.⁷ John Dugan has recently added to the picture by charting how Cicero's promotion of textuality was part of a larger and multifaceted strategy of self-fashioning. Particularly enlightening in this sense is his analysis of the *Orator*. For Dugan, the bodily-figured discourse that informs Cicero's theorization of textual polish betrays an attempt to endow his oratorical texts with a bodily integrity that would enable them to live apart from him and yet embody his *ingenium*. Finally, Dugan has shown that Cicero's relationship with writing shifted over time. Whereas in his earlier career it helped him advance his political goals and aims, in the last years of his life writing became a substitute for direct political involvement and an alternative route to restore his loss of *dignitas*.⁸ For our purposes, the recent upsurge of Ciceronian studies alerts us to the pitfalls of generalizing Cicero's *modus operandi* and his aesthetic benchmarks.⁹ In what follows I take Cicero's representation of second century B.C.E. oratorical writing in the *Brutus* as a point of departure for engaging more directly with the frameworks that guided Cato's own approach to texts and writing.

Resisting Cicero

One of the most compelling moments of the *Brutus* pivots around the

---

5. Stroup 2003.
6. Narducci 1997: 157–73.
7. Narducci 1997: 158.
8. Dugan 2005; for the *Orator*, see especially 267–88.
9. Recent contributions to the renaissance of Ciceronian studies include Gildenhard 2007a; Connolly 2007; Powell and Paterson 2004; Steel 2001; Krostenko 2001.

portrayal of Servius Sulpicius Galba, a contemporary of Cato. In *Brutus* 87 Cicero reports an anecdote allegedly heard from Rutilius Rufus. In the anecdote Galba is conjured up during the preparatory moments leading up to the pleading of a case. Closed away from everybody, he is portrayed as hard at work preparing an outline (*commentarius*) by frenetically dictating different things to different scribes. Fired up by this exercise, Cicero concludes that Galba offered a brilliant performance.[10] In a later passage, Cicero speaks in more detail about Galba's merits as a speaker. At a certain point, Brutus interrupts him and asks why nothing of Galba's performance skills can be detected in the written speeches that he left behind, something that—Brutus points out—cannot be tested in the case of those who did not write at all. Brutus' interruption allows Cicero to clarify that *dicere* and *scribere* are distinct practices; as such, they require the development of different skills. Focusing on the latter, he explains that *scribere* is an activity that takes place at home, after the oratorical performance. But while some are unwilling to undertake the extra labor, others do not write at all as a choice, while still others speak better than they write. When dealing with the second group, Cicero is obviously in some difficulty. He begins by saying that they have no desire to improve their speaking skills and emphasizes that this is what writing is for; subsequently, he goes on to stress that those who do not commit their oratory to writing are unwilling to preserve the memory of their *ingenium* for the benefit of future generations because they think that more *gloria* is drawn from the act of *dicere* if their texts do not come under the scrutiny of others.[11]

The scholarly discussion over the relationship between the oratorical performance and its textualization dramatized in Cicero's portrayal of Galba has long centered on establishing the degree of accuracy of the text as a record of the speech.[12] What continues to remain unanswered is why the Roman elite avoided composing scripts before their oratorical performances and textualized them only afterwards and only in some cases. Catherine Steel has recently touched on the matter by proposing that, as opposed to what we find in Athens, the job of the *patronus* in Rome was not to provide the text of a speech for someone else to deliver but rather to deliver a speech himself. Thus, she concludes that "the transition from spoken to written was not an essential part of the legal process at Rome in the way that it had been in Athens, and a Roman orator was always faced

---

10. Cicero, *Brut.* 87.
11. Cicero, *Brut.* 91–92. See discussion of this passage in Dugan (2005: 292–300), which includes a survey of Cicero's judgements on the transcripts of other orators.
12. Humbert (1925: 23–97) is still central, but see also the convenient summary of the problem in Steel 2006: 26–27.

with a *choice* of whether or not to produce a written version which could then be disseminated."[13] Steel's remarks foreground some of the most fundamental differences that set the Roman experience of public speaking apart from its Greek counterpart; in light of these differences, I propose to consider the social hierarchies that informed the elite relationship with writing 'before Cicero' by reading Cicero against the grain.

The fact that Cicero does not explicitly discuss the possibility that oratorical writing has anything to do with scripting a speech confirms that scripting was perceived as a socially secondary activity in the first place. Moreover, against the very picture that he constructs Cicero is an exception: not only did he transcribe speeches that he had actually performed, he also produced texts of speeches never delivered and in some places discusses them as if he actually had.[14] Thus, although Cicero never engaged in oratorical scripting per se, it is clear that he self-consciously attempted to blur the boundaries that set an oratorical text apart from its poetic or rhetorical counterparts by capitalizing on the fact that, at the reception end, approaching a scripted speech had become not at all dissimilar from approaching a transcribed speech.[15] Historically this is not at all surprising. By Cicero's time, to rehearse from poetically and rhetorically constructed texts had become practices deeply entangled in the ludic life of the Roman elite, the first as a leisure-oriented activity and the latter as a means for developing new tactics of speech-making. For this reason, Cicero's labor-intensive transcription practices and his construction of oratorical texts disengaged from actual performances can be said to bespeak his subjectivity as *homo novus* and his political failures at the same time. In this respect, the nervousness that he manifests in the *Brutus* when commenting on those who invested everything in the oratorical event reveals the larger perception of oratorical writing as preparatory or secondary to the exercise of *auctoritas* through the body-in-action.[16] Cicero strenuously resisted this twofold perception in theory and practice in order to open up for himself new possibilities of self-fashioning and survival, as Dugan suggests. Accordingly, I would argue that his writings both disclose and conceal a deeply fraught and variegated history of elite writing.

In the economy of our inquiry into the beginnings of Latin prose, Cicero's representation of Galba is crucial. If the Roman elite learned to

---

13. Steel 2006: 29–30. Emphasis in the original.
14. Narducci 1997: 161–62 with reference to Cicero, *Orat.* 103–4 where he points to the seven books of the *Verrines*. See also Riggsby 1999: 178–84.
15. This fact is mentioned but not fully discussed by Narducci 1997: 163–64.
16. Dugan 2005: 84 and *passim;* Habinek 1998a: 103.

write their speeches only in the second century B.C.E., it is also clear that they did not write scripts beforehand in the manner of the poets or, to a much lesser extent, the rhetoricians who were progressively making their way into the life of the elite. And if they did decide to take up the stylus through their slaves' hand, they did it only to prepare an outline before the performance and to produce a transcription afterward.[17] Equally crucial to our investigation is Cicero's claim that Cato was the first to produce textual samples worth reading. Like Galba's, so too Cato's characterization looks forward to the proclamation of Cicero's own superiority later in the dialogue;[18] unlike in Galba's case, however, Cicero's treatment of Cato's oratory pivots on a close stylistic assessment that draws force from his flaunted familiarity with more than 150 speeches.[19] From a methodological point of view, the sheer number of textualized speeches known by Cicero and his silence over the specifics of Cato's own relationship with writing encourages us to take for granted that their writing activities were guided by the same practical principles.[20] Although it is right to think that Cato's penchant for writing, like Cicero's, is somewhat linked to his *novitas*, nevertheless one ought not forget that he lived at a different cultural and historical juncture and that his political career was a very successful one.[21]

Tacitly or unconsciously relying on the historical coincidence promoted in the *Brutus* between Cato, the beginning of oratory, and the establishment of poetry, some critics justify Cato's writing bent by invoking Greek prose precedents, while others are happy with the explanation that the emergence of prose writing was, at that point of Rome's cultural history, inevitable.[22] But when our attention is turned to Cato's invocation of writing and writings in his oratorical fragments and beyond, the picture that emerges is both peculiar and illuminating. Cato did not look to the scripting activities of the poets or to Greek models to develop his own; rather, he established the practice of transcribing by redeploying forms of writing entangled with rituals connected with the performance of his political duties as a

---

17. For generalized discussions about reading with a special focus on later and more documented periods, see Starr 1991; Small 1997: 177–88; Johnson 2000; Johnson and Parker 2009.
18. Cicero, *Brut.* 60. Cf. Cicero, *Brut.* 292–96 with comments by Hinds 1998: 67.
19. Cicero, *Brut.* 63, 65, 68.
20. This *assumptio ex silentio* guides, for example, Steel 2001: 31.
21. In relation to the pre-Catonian period, the relationship between writing and *novitas* established by Cato follows the same trajectory that Schiavone (2005: 97–101) and Costa (2000: 46–58) see in the contraposition between secret knowledge and revealing writing in the narratives concerning the development of *ius* and the encroachment of new social agents (generally identified as plebeians) in its exercise.
22. Astin 1978: 206–10.

magistrate. Within its immediate sociocultural purview, the paradigm that Cato proposed constituted yet another strategic ploy meant to counter the increasing elite reliance on alien professionals and their scripted writings. Yet this same paradigm served as a counterplay to those who, like Scipio Africanus, enjoyed such an unimpeachable aristocratic pedigree and could count on such military successes that they found it unnecessary to leave self-produced writings encoding their outstanding achievements. My analysis of Cato's self-positioning vis-à-vis Scipio Africanus corroborates an existing perception of writing as a threat to *auctoritas* understood as traditionally located in the body; at the same time, it allows us to define Cato's articulation of prose writing as transcription.

Plunging into the World of *Tabulae*

Performed in 159 or 154 B.C.E., what remains of the speech known as *De Sumptu Suo* conjures up Cato himself dealing with the handling of an oratorical text:

> Iussi caudicem proferri ubi mea oratio scripta erat de ea re quod sponsionem feceram cum M. Cornelio; tabulae prolatae. maiorum bene facta perlecta; deinde quae ego pro re publica fecissem leguntur. ubi id utrumque perlectum est, deinde scriptum erat in oratione: "numquam ego pecuniam neque meam neque sociorum per ambitionem largitus sum." "Attat noli, noli <s>cribere [recitare, *Query*]," "inquam," istud: nolunt audire." deinde recitavit: "numqua*m* <ego> praefectos per sociorum vestrum oppida imposivi, qui eorum bona liberos deriperent." istud quoque dele, nolunt audire; recita porro. "numquam ego praedam neque quod de hostibus captum esset neque manubias inter paucolos amicos meos divisi, ut illis eriperem qui cepissent." istuc quoque dele: nihil <e>o minus volunt dici; non opus est recitato. "numquam ego evectionem datavi, quo amici mei per symbolos pecunias magnas caperent." perge istuc quoque uti cum maxime delere. "Numquam <ego> argentum pro vino congiario inter apparitores atque amicos meos disdidi neque eos malo publico divites feci." "enimvero usque istuc ad lignum dele. vide sis quo loco re<s> publica siet, uti quod rei publicae bene fecissem, unde gratiam capiebam, nunc idem illud memorare non audeo ne invidiae siet. ita inductum est male facere inpoene, bene facere non inpoene licere."[23]

---

23. Cato, *orat.* 51.169 Sbl.

I ordered the tablets to be brought out on which my speech concerning the judicial wager with Marcus Cornelius had been written. The tablets were fetched: the services of my ancestors were read out; then those that I had done for the state were read. When the reading out of both of these was finished, the speech went on as follows: "Never have I lavished my money or that of the allies in order to win favors." "Oh no!" I said "Don't, don't write that: they don't want to hear it." Then he read out, "Never have I imposed prefects on the towns of your allies, to plunder their property and their children." "Delete that too; they don't want to hear that. Read further." "Never have I divided booty taken from the enemy or prize money among the small circle of my friends and therefore snatch it away from those who had captured it." "Erase as far as that too: there is nothing they want said less than that. It is not necessary, read on." "Never have I granted travel-passes so that my friends could gain large sums by means of the warrants." "Go on and delete up to there too, immediately." "The money intended for the wine distribution I have never shared out among my attendants and friends nor have I made them rich to the detriment of the state." "Most certainly erase that, right down to the wood. See, if you please, in what condition the state is, when for fear that it could cause anxieties I dare not recall the good services that I performed for the state, from which I used to gain gratitude. Thus it has become normal practice to do ill with impunity, but not to be allowed to do well without impunity."

Most critics agree that in this speech Cato portrays himself tampering with the text of a previously textualized speech with the help of a literary slave while planning a new speech, one that, albeit in fragments, we can still read today. Yet, the scene as a whole has also raised the possibility that Cato did not produce a *commentarius* in the way illustrated by Cicero's anecdote about Galba; rather, he went so far as to elaborate an actual script for the performance to come, giving up oral improvisation and moving towards the art of reenacting a prepared text.[24] A minority of scholars, however, contends that the scene does not relate to the pre-performance phase but, rather, to an in-performance charade played around the official reading of his textualized *sponsio cum M. Cornelio*.[25]

---

24. Cavarzere 2000: 44, 46–47; Kennedy 1994:107–8; Sblendorio Cugusi 1982: 413; Astin 1978: 135–36.

25. Courtney 1999: 89–90; Meyer 2004: 89. The reading of documents by a lector during trials is well attested by Cicero. Cf. Cicero, *De Orat.* 2.223, *Pro Clu.* 51; *Pro Q. Rosc.* 7. See also discussion in Butler 2002. For a discussion of the *sponsio* as an extrajudicial procedure, see Crook 1976: 132–38.

Rather than opting for one interpretation to the exclusion of the other, it is worth highlighting the elements that make Cato's self-depiction so compelling by taking into account the two points of view expressed. The scene frozen in the fragment confirms that writing and reading were activities generally performed by the elite through slaves. But to sustain that Cato went so far as to compose a script beforehand is not made explicit here or elsewhere in the Catonian corpus. Moreover, if it had been so, Cicero would have certainly spent a word or two on the oddity and would have used Cato's precedent to sustain his own transformation of oratory into a textual affair leaning towards poetry and rhetoric. If we turn to the fragment, the use of past tenses starting from the verb *iussi* (I ordered) may indicate that during his performance Cato went out of his way to report how he had prepared for his ongoing speech. In this sense, the in-performance interpretation has on its side the advantage of bringing to light Cato's eagerness to publicize and valorize his writing habits. If so, to sustain his argument Cato did not rely so much on the *praeteritio*, a rhetorical figure of speech; rather, he would have argued through his body in action that the attacks launched against his respectability were leading him to physically tamper with a speech transcribed on *tabulae* and bundled up in a *caudex*. On this score, his in-performance display of a previously transcribed speech would have driven home the message that the damage provoked by these attacks were going to be redressed thanks to his transcribing habits. For if the speech concerning the wager with Marcus Cornelius had been transcribed after its performance, the transcription of his tampering—which constitutes the text of *De Sumptu Suo*—would have guaranteed the integrity of those previously textualized words together with his own morality. By and large, then, what remains of the *De Sumptu Suo* calls attention to post-performance writing practices centered on the *tabula,* a specific writing material, rectangular in shape, often made of smoothed-out wood coated with wax onto which words were inscribed with a stylus.

In her study on *tabulae* in the Roman world, Elizabeth Meyer uses the fragment of the *De Sumptu Suo* as one of the many testimonies that attest to their pivotal sociocultural significance.[26] By relying on her finds, she resists the association between *tabulae* and elementary instruction that is generally assumed on the basis of their erasability and the numerous depictions of schoolboys handling them. Likewise, she opposes the widespread impression that they were meant for rough drafting only because

---

26. Meyer 2004: 89.

they often feature in the hands of scribes and poets. In turn, Meyer argues that in the Roman world *tabulae* were connected "with acts that order the state and the household; they observe no clear distinction between public and private; they are not temporary jottings, but authoritative and final embodiments of the new reality that they help to create."[27] Accordingly, she turns to the role played by this writing medium in the creation of *templa,* areas marked off and rendered sacred for the performance of the augurs' activities; she also notes that on them treaties, laws, and plebiscites were recorded as well as public contracts, expenses, and income. Surveyors' maps were drawn on *tabulae* as well and they were also central to the taking of the census and the compilation of censorial lists. And just as land, people, and official decisions were reported on *tabulae,* so too political achievements and noteworthy events were written on them by the *pontifex maximus*. But, as Meyer remarks, *tabulae* were not only bound to the public and religious sphere; they also extended into the private, blurring the divide between the civic and the domestic. Not only did magistrates keep *tabulae* relating to their offices in a special area of the house called the *tablinium,* but financial matters concerning the management of the household were also recorded on them by private citizens.

Though ranging over a wide period of time, the evidence compiled by Meyer clarifies that writing and reading activities revolving around *tabulae* were integrated in sociocosmologically loaded actions performed on behalf of the State and during religious events from a fairly ancient time. The *carmen*-like organization that typifies the words inscribed on them gives further substance to the fact that writing on and reading from *tabulae* were ritualized activities.[28] But because *tabulae* were redeployed beyond specific rites, they also impacted on everyday life and social subjectivities by providing a general model of action and by defining respectable Roman citizens.[29]

Although Nepos asserts that Cato began to put together (*confecit*) speeches in his adolescence, the oldest surviving oratorical fragment attributed to Cato goes back to 195 B.C.E., the year of his consulship.[30] This fact does not necessarily mean that he had not developed an interest in writing before then, but it may indicate that it was during this time that he began to textualize his speeches more systematically. If so, Cato perceived his oratorical performances as one of the ways in which he exer-

---

27. Meyer 2004: 22.
28. For a discussion of ritualized reading, see Valette-Cagnac 1997.
29. Meyer 2004: 21–72 for discussion and evidence.
30. Nepos, *Cato* 3.2.

cised his political prerogatives and responsibilities; at the same time, he understood their written objectifications as a means for drawing on them the same "aura" of authority that characterized other types of officially recorded business. Accordingly, Cato acted on the lived prestige order that he shared with his aristocratic peers and benefited from a keen sense of his place within the structure of power relations: lacking the support of a familial history of high political achievements, he transcribed his speeches to maximize his embodied assertions of *auctoritas*. What this mean is that he looked to publication as well. Critics have dealt with this matter by perusing later testimonies.[31] I believe that more can be gained from plumbing the specific frameworks that Cato deployed and the path of reception that he envisioned for his writings by following up on the link between social performance and transcription on *tabulae* conjured up in the *De Sumptu Suo*.

The Censorial Scenario and Its Impact on Cato's Understanding of Prose Writing

In his *Politics of Latin Literature,* Habinek argues that the shift from *laudare* to *existimare* that takes place in the Preface to the *De Agricultura* evokes evaluative songs performed at elite *convivia* and supplants them with a form of assessment that draws on the sphere of economics.[32] Though highly fragmentary, what remains of the Preface to the *Origines* adds to the economic meaning of *existimare* and provides some important clues about the relationship between Cato's prose writing and the ancestral convivial scenario that in the Preface to the *De Agricultura* is only indirectly evoked.

In the last few decades the Preface to the *Origines* has undergone a major philological makeover. In 1988 Luca Cardinali went back to its opening fragment and argued that *homines* is a gloss, which, added by later grammarians, was meant to explain the rare and archaic form of *ques*. Thus, he elided the word and called attention to the presence of a spondaic hexameter:

---

31. In the *De Senectute* 38 Cicero suggests that in the latter years of his life, Cato worked intensively on putting his speeches together (*conficere*) with, perhaps, the implied aim of publishing them. The *De Sumptu Suo* indicates that he did not wait that long and that he kept his transcriptions for the use and consumption of those who lived in his house. If so, he would have followed the example briefly mentioned (and scorned) by Cicero in *Brutus* 62 relating to the preservation of the funeral orations. For a compelling discussion of these testimonies, see Calboli 2003: 6–7 and note 5.

32. Habinek 1998a: 46–50.

Sí ques [homines] súnt quos délectát populí Románi gesta discribere.³³

If there are men for whom to describe the deeds of the Roman people is pleasing.

While unearthing the fountainhead of those idiosyncratic hexameters that we find in the opening of later historiographical works, Cardinali's intervention has also opened up new interpretative possibilities.³⁴ In a way, we can say that the line alludes in form to Ennius' *Annales* and pits historiography against epic by focusing on the "deeds of the Roman people" rather than those of its leaders.³⁵ But if we take into account the different social constraints and possibilities that loomed over Cato and Ennius with regard to their ability to exercise agency, the object of this allusion is to supersede Ennius' epic and preclude poetic meddling in the construction of elite memories. The musical and sociopolitical meanings covered by *discribere* make this move conspicuous and allow us to grapple with the specificity of Cato's approach to writing.³⁶

Within the musical sphere *discribere* denotes the act of matching words to a musical scale;³⁷ within the sociopolitical sphere this verb relates to the act of hierarchically organizing people, land, and the like performed by a person enjoying *auctoritas*.³⁸ In two other fragments of the Preface

---

33. Pompeius, *Ad Donatum GL* 5.208, 13 ff = Cato, *Orig.* 1.1 C&Sbl.

34. Sallust, *Iug. 5 (bellum scripturus sum quod populus Romanus)*; Livy, 1.1 (*facturusne operae pretium sim*); Tacitus, *Ann.* 1.1 (*Urbem Romam a principio reges habuere*). Cugusi (1994: 265–66), Sblendorio Cugusi and Cugusi (1996: 146–70) reject Cardinali's reading by claiming that the presence of *homines* in other places of the Catonian corpus supports its retention in this context. Though seemingly circular (whereby we would be reading our experience of later historians back into Cato), Cardinali's argument is reinforced by examples of *si ques* or *si quis* closer in time to Cato (see, the *Senatus consultum de Bacchanalibus* in the phrase *sei ques esent qui sibi deicerent necese ese Bacanal habere* and in proemial contexts in Terence, *Phorm.* 12 and *Eun.* 4). See also discussion in Churchill (1995).

35. This is the line of interpretation taken by Conte (1986: 78–79) when considering hexametrical patterns in the prose of later historians (Tacitus especially). For the shift in focus from Ennius' epic, see Goldberg 1995: 28.

36. For a detailed analysis of *discribere* in the *Origines* and its manifestation at the level of structure, see Sciarrino 2004a.

37. In *Tusculan Disputations* 4.3 Cicero corrects the belief concerning Numa's encounter with Pythagoras by comparing the Pythagorean and the Roman song traditions. As he takes for granted the exclusivity of both, he also stresses the musical nature of the *convivium* by reporting Cato's invocation of ancestral practices in the *Origines*. Finally, he draws the conclusion that both *cantus* and *carmina* were produced in tune to a musical scale. To denote the act of matching words to a musical scale, he adopts the verb *discribere*. In his famous discussion about the beginning of Roman drama, Livy (7.2.7) uses the verb *discribere* in the same manner, and he does so to indicate the production of verbal utterances matched to the sound of the flute.

38. See Nicolet 1991: 174; for narratives about the census featuring *discribere*, see Livy 1.43; Cicero, *De Rep.* 2.39; Florus 1.6.3.

Cato builds upon each of these meanings. The first has been recently returned to the Preface and reads as follows:

> gravissimus auctor in Originibus dixit Cato morem apud maiores hunc epularum fuisse, ut deinceps, qui accubarent, canerent ad tibiam clarorum virorum laudes atque virtutes.[39]

> That most sober author Cato said in the *Origines* that there was the following custom during banquets among the ancestors: those who were reclining would sing in turn to the sound of the pipe the praises and the manly deeds of famous men.

In this fragment we find Cato invoking the convivial scenario in order to construct a particular scene. First, this scene features a select group of people associated with the ancestral realm; second, these people gather at a *convivium;* third, they recline and sing taking turns; fourth, their songs are about the praises and manly deeds of *clari viri*. Through this scene, Cato builds upon the musical meaning of *discribere* by defining a type of song that reinforces in-group relations and asserts the singers' independence from the materiality of texts or the skills of 'others.' Moreover, this scene allows Cato to illustrate that perceptual distinctiveness or *claritas* is derived from individual achievements.[40] Objectified in song, these achievements undergo an evaluation process that fosters in-group cohesion. In another fragment, Cato adds to it by elaborating on the sociopolitical meaning of *discribere:*

> Etenim M. Catonis illud quod in principio scripsit Originum suarum, semper magnificum et praeclarum putavi, clarorum hominum atque magnorum non minus otii quam negotii rationem exstare oportet.[41]

> Indeed I always deemed magnificent and outstanding what Cato wrote at the beginning of his *Origines,* that no less an account of leisure time than of work time of famous and great men ought to remain.

---

39. Cicero, *TD*. 4.3 = Cato, *Orig.* 1.4 C&Sbl.
40. For a discussion of *claritas* as perceptual distinctiveness either auditory or visual and its difference from *gloria* as related to the lessening of someone else, see Habinek 2000: 269–70. For an account of Cicero's understanding of *gloria,* see Mazzoli 2004.
41. Cicero, *Pro Planc.* 66 = Cato, *Orig.* 1.2 C&Sbl. Imitated with variations by Cicero, *Ad Att.* 5.20.9; Symmachus, *Epist.* 1.1.2; Ennodius, *Carm.* 1.9.3; Columella, *RR* 2.21.1.

Scholars have long focused on this fragment for two reasons: first, because it appears to echo the opening of Xenophon's *Symposium;*[42] and, second, because it is one of the earliest occurrences of the word *otium*.[43] Across the board, the fragment is understood as representing Cato's engagement with literature and as embodying a moral admonition concerning the responsibility to make a use of leisure time which stands up to scrutiny. What has gone unnoticed is that this fragment expands on the link of *discribere* with the censorial sphere through the mentioning of *rationes* and looks to the pivotal role that writing and writings played in the hierarchical organization achieved by the census.[44] Accordingly, to gauge the nuances of this further expansion we need to shift our focus to the censorial ceremony. For our purposes, it is not important to determine the exact way in which the census was taken at the time, but to identify the embodied frameworks that informed its scenario. A good way to go about it is to engage with visual enactments of it.

The elements that made up a censorial ceremony are most clearly illustrated by a highly debated archeological document known as the "altar frieze of Domitius Ahenobarbus" and located in the Louvre (Louvre inv. 975) (Fig. 5.1).[45] According to the reading of Mario Torelli, the relief needs to be read from left to right starting from the figure of a *togatus* writing on a *tabula* with another set of six lying at his feet (Ara 1). Another *togatus* stands before the first figure and holds other *tabulae* in his left hand while stretching his right hand towards the seated figure (Ara 2). A third *togatus* (Ara 3) sits on a *sella* and, while looking back at a fourth *togatus* (Ara 4), he places his left hand on the right shoulder of the fourth. The latter (Ara 4), in turn, points his forefinger to the scene following from that. For Torelli, the first two figures (Ara 1 and 2) are made to represent the first ceremony of the census, namely, the *professio*. The first figure (Ara 1) represents the *iurator* who registers the relevant informa-

---

42. Cato's dependence on Xenophon, *Symp.* 1.1 has been doubted by few (see Barwick 1948: 128 note 2; Garbarino 1973: 339). Cf. Letta 1984: 12 note 53. A close comparison between the two passages suggests that it is Cicero who embeds the citation from Cato into a structure that resembles Xenophon's passage. Accordingly, in the context of the *Pro Plancio*, Cicero may aim to cite two authorities at once.

43. Letta 1984: 24–30 (where the reference to *otium* is interpreted as literary activity in very abstract terms). In this respect, see discussion in Gruen (1992: 60–61) and Churchill (1995: 95–96). For other discussions of *otium* in Cato see Alfonsi 1954: 163–68; André 1966: 45–49.

44. The bibliography on the censorship is vast; places to start include Mommsen 1874: ii. 331–415; Greenidge 1911: 216–33; Suolahti 1963; Wiseman 1969; Nicolet 1980: 48–88; for a convenient collection of sources, see Calderini 1944.

45. Coarelli 1968; Torelli 1982: 5–25; Gruen 1992: 145–52; Kuttner 1993.

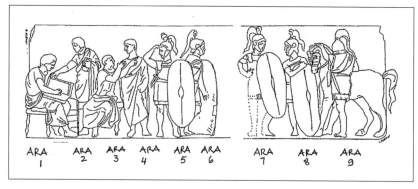

Figure 5.1. Altar of Domitius Ahenobarbus, Louvre census relief (inv. 975). Drawing by Ann Kuttner

tion on the *tabula censoria* that he holds, while the second (Ara 2) carries another *tabula* to be associated with the *codex accepti et expensi*, which contained personal data and the list of property. On one level, the scene dramatizes the shift of information from the *codex accepti et expensi* produced by the *pater familias* to the *tabula censoria* that took place during the ceremony; on another level, the stretched hand of the second figure represents the performance of the citizen's oath (*iusiurandum*). As the sources suggest, the transfer of information is generally indicated by the verbs *dedicare* or *deferre* while the acceptance of the declaration according to formalized questions arranged in a *formula census* and established by the censor is usually marked by the verbs *accipere* or *deferre*.[46] The third and fourth figures (Ara 3 and 4) are represented while performing the act of *discriptio;* seated on the *sella* is the censor in person who, by placing his right hand on the shoulder of the fourth standing figure, performs his power (*potestas*) to assign each citizen to a specific class. In turn, the fourth figure (Ara 4) points to the marshaled army to indicate the *classis* to which he has been assigned and towards which he is supposed to move. Continuing to the right, we see four infantry men in matching equipment and a horseman with his back turned towards the viewer, symbolizing the class of *equites* (Ara 5–9). The rest of the relief stages the *lustratio,* the religious purification that the censor together with his acolytes performed and that culminated in the sacrificial immolation of a bull, a sheep, and a pig, the *suovitaurilia.* In the relief the scene specifically relates to the end of the *hostiae incruentae,* the bloodless offerings and the leading of the sacrificial animals to the altar.[47]

---

46. On the *formula census* and the verbs used to indicate the transfer of information performed during the declaration, see Suolahti 1963: 37–39.

47. Some of the visual details do not match with exactitude what we learn from the

Figure 5.2. Praenestine Cist, Villa Giulia 13 133. Drawing by Ann Kuttner

Taken as a whole, the alignment of the human figures, the way they are dressed, the objects that they handle, and the actions that they perform are organized according to a scenario that promotes the inseparable relationship between the *census* and the *lustratio* together with the sociocosmological hierarchies that the entire ceremony reacknowledged and reestablished. While signaling the different places in which the *census* and the *lustratio* took place, the representation of these two ritualized moments on the relief are paratactically related and point to the effects on reality that the censorial ceremony as a whole achieved.[48] Accordingly, the "altar frieze of Domitius Ahenobarbus" does not represent the censorial ceremony with documentary exactitude; rather, it reactivates its scenario. In this scenario the *tabulae* produced by the *pater familias* at home and those on which the *iurator* writes evoke a series of patterned words and actions that identified individual male citizens and the members of their households in a hierarchical nexus of human and divine relations.

Interestingly, the crucial role played by writing and writings in the censorial scenario finds corroboration in the way Ann Kuttner has gone about interpreting a rectangular bronze cist identified as V(illa) G(iulia) 13 133 (Fig. 5.2).[49] Recovered in 1866 from a tomb in the Columbella Necropolis at Praeneste, the cist passed into the Barberini Collection until finding its final location in the Museo Etrusco di Villa Giulia in Rome. By using the census relief from the "altar of Domitius Ahenobarbus" as a guide, Kuttner finds that VG 13 133 deploys the same expository visual tradition.

---

sources, see Nicolet 1980: 97 and Torelli 1982: 11–13.
48. Torelli 1982: 13–14; Meyer 2004: 92.
49. Kuttner 1991.

Pivotal to Kuttner's interpretation of the cist is the identification of a seated *togatus* at the farthest left (VG 1) as a figure performing the *iurator*'s role. Leaning against a rise in the ground culminating with a plant growing upon it, the seated *togatus* holds a large *tabula*.[50] Next to him, another *togatus* (VG 2) stands in very close physical proximity; his body is almost frontal to the viewer and extends a hand right over the tablet. A third *togatus* (VG 3) stands frontally with his body slightly twisted towards a fourth figure (VG 4), representing an approaching *eques* with his hat or helmet off his head. This *togatus* (VG 3) looks directly at the *eques* (VG 4); at the same time, he stretches his hand over the second *togatus* (VG 2) who, in turn, "leans over VG 1 as they check and/or enter this *eques*' name in the records."[51] If Kuttner is correct, the representation on the Praenestine cist constitutes the earliest visual representation of the Latin census of military *classes* featuring a written registration of citizens lists. Moreover, it adds to the images and narratives that describe writing practices in the fourth and third century B.C.E. in Etruria and Latium.[52]

What interests us here is that the representation on the Praenestine cist does not present the *codex accepti et expensi,* the accounting-book that in the relief from the "altar of Domitius Ahenobarbus" the second *togatus* (Ara 2) holds in his hands. The scholarly discussion over this sort of writing tends to center on its legal force and its distinction from the *liber patrimonii* or *libellus familiae,* which contained the *pater familias*' inventory of his property, and the *codex rationum,* the *pater familias*' account book with receipts and expenses. Unlike these two types of financial books, the *codex accepti et expensi* was not meant merely to give evidence but affected alterations in the person's property.[53] As such, that a citizen would carry the *codex accepti et expensi* to the censorial ceremony makes absolute sense and the discrepancy that exists between the two visual repre-

---

50. The plant-motif suggests that the scene is staged outdoor in a campus, the same location in which the censorial ceremony would have taken place, see Kuttner 1991: 152–53. For census-taking at Rome in the Campus Martius starting from 435 B.C.E., see Cicero, *Pro Mil.* 73; *De Har.* 57; *Pro Cael.* 78; *Parad.* 31.

51. Kuttner 1991: 156. She also suggests that the dynamics of the censor looking at the *eques*' face matches the anecdote presented by Valerius Maximus (4.1.10) in reference to the censorship of Scipio in 143 B.C.E.

52. Colonna 1976; Cristofani 1979: 81 and fig. p. 80; Bonfante 1986: 247 fig. 8, 19 and note 37; Harris 1989: 155–59, 174 note 119; Cornell 1991. Ancient narratives focus especially on Gaius Mucius Scaevola and King Porsenna; see Livy 2.12.7; Dion. Hal. 5.28.2.

53. Malherbe 2005; Sohm 2002: 305–6; Thilo 1980; a case apart seems to be the accounting system used by the *argentarii,* see Andreau 1987 with a note of caution by Nightingale (1989: 177).

sentations may relate to the fact that in the third century B.C.E. the practice of producing financial accounts in writing was not yet fully developed or, perhaps, better still, that not every Roman citizen engaged in it.[54]

The earliest allusions to the censorial ceremony in the literary corpus are in Plautus and they all focus on the sworn declaration made by the citizen to the *iurator*. This declaration is termed *ratio* and appears in combination with *dare, reddere, referre* (with a focus on the citizen) and *accipere* (with a focus on the *iurator*).[55] Moreover, in the summoning of the citizens from the *tabulae censoriae* that Varro quotes in his *De Lingua Latina* we read in the final lines:

> Omnes Quirites pedites armatos, privatosque, curatores omnium tribuum, si quis pro se sive pro altero rationem dare volet, vocato illicium huc ad me.[56]

> Call here to me all the Roman citizen soldiers under arms (or armed) and private citizens as spokesmen of all the tribes, if anyone wishes to give an account for himself or for another person.

This latter testimony suggests that *ratio* more specifically refers to the financial account encoded in the sworn declaration; however, together with the evidence in Plautus it leaves unclear whether this declaration was based on the *codex* or the *tabulae accepti et expensi* produced at home and whether the written account was presented to the *iurator*.[57] In this respect, Cato's injunction that "no less an account (*ratio*) of leisure time than of work time of famous and great men ought to remain (*exstare*)" is noteworthy for it evokes not only the sworn declaration performed at the censorial ceremony, but also its durable and, therefore, written existence through the choice of *exstare*. Accordingly, we may say that in the Preface to the *Origines* Cato calls into play the power of the sworn declaration in effecting the standing of a Roman citizen and equates self-produced texts objectifying the social performances of *viri clari* to the act of entering economic information in the *codex* or *tabulae accepti et expensi*.[58] Finally,

---

54. Malherbe 2005: 261; Thilo 1980: 188–89.
55. Plautus, *Trin.* 876–78; *Poen.* 55–57 (cited by Calderini 1944: 3); but see also, Plautus, *Truc.* 36 (*rationes accipere*); *Aul.* 6 (*rationem reddere*); *Trin.* 114: (*rationem referre*).
56. Varro, *LL* 6.86.
57. It would seem that in Cicero the term *codex* and *tabulae* are used as synonyms, see Malherbe 2005: 263.
58. For a discussion of how the listing that typifies a censorial *ratio* informs the catalogue-like structuring of the first three books of the *Origines,* see Sciarrino 2004a: 343–47. For an

by mapping the circulation of these writings onto the ancestral convivial scenario, he constructs for them the same function and exclusivity that, according to him, the convivial songs used to fulfill.

The intersection between the convivial and the censorial scenarios that informs the opening passages of the *Origines* forces us to radically readjust the current understanding of a fragment supposedly located at the beginning of Book 4 and identified as part of the so-called Second Preface:

> Non lubet scribere quod in tabula apud pontificem maximum est, quotiens annona cara, quotiens lunae aut solis lumine caligo aut quid obstiterit.[59]

> Writing what is on the table at the public home of the *pontifex maximus* is not pleasing, namely, how often there was a crisis in grain prices, how many times we had an eclipse of the moon or the sun or something hindered it.

According to Catonian scholars, this fragment disrupts the texture of the *Origines* by adding narrative items starting from 270 B.C.E. It is generally assumed that by distancing himself from the astronomic and economic information fixed in the *tabula apud pontificem* Cato rejected the pontifical way of compiling information and, by extension, refused the aristocratic matrix underpinning the annalistic tradition in Greek (Fabius Pictor, Cincius Alimentus). While the relationship between the Roman annalistic tradition in Greek and the pontifical *tabula* is still an object of controversy, Cato is nowhere here pointing to annalistic works as such.[60] More fruitful, on the other hand, is to recognize that at this time the pontifical *tabula* offered a privileged organizational framework and constituted a source of legitimation for other forms of writing. These include the *Fasti* that Fulvius Nobilior displayed in the Aedes Herculis Musarum and Ennius' *Annales*.[61] Accordingly, Cato here discards as important the information recorded on the pontifical *tabula* while simultaneously invoking the writing activities of the *pontifex maximus* in order to construct

---

ancient description of the *Origines* that stresses this structuring, see Nepos, *Cato* 3.2–4.

59. Gellius 2.28.6 = Cato, *Orig.* 4. 81 C&Sbl.

60. Cf. discussion in Sblendorio Cugusi and Cugusi 1996: 137–39, but see also Cugusi and Sblendorio Cugusi 2001: 1.48–52. According to these two scholars, Cato changed his style after meeting Polybius. The best discussion of the *tabula* and its relation to the annalistic tradition remains Frier 1799: 69–135; however, Rüpke 1993 is a must-read for the study of the *Annales Maximi* as forgery.

61. On the use of the pontifical *tabula* as a locus of legitimation for Ennius' *Annales* and Fulvius Nobilior's fasti in the *aedes Herculis Musarum,* see Gotter 2003; for the connection between the two, see Rüpke 2006.

a privileged contrast for his own. While falling within the same elite rubric, Cato's transcribing activities expand on a series of practices that, by linking household management and sociocosmological hierarchies, were reacknowledged and reestablished by the censorial ceremony. In turn, he envisioned for his own writings a path of reception plotted on the exclusiveness of the ancestral convivial scenario. As such, what needs to be assessed next is how the intersection between the censorial and the convivial scenarios that informs Cato's prose writing is played out within its immediate sociocultural horizon.

The 'Trials' of the Scipios Reconsidered

Publius Cornelius Scipio Africanus and his brother, Lucius Cornelius Scipio Asiagenus, are famous not only for their outstanding record of victories, but also for the 'trials' that they underwent in the 180s. Although the sources offer different representations of these trials, they all agree that, at a certain point, Africanus was asked to offer an oral declaration of how, together with his brother, he had handled the money captured or extorted from Antiochus. Rather than comply with the request, Africanus had someone fetch his accounting-book. Once he had the book in his hands, he destroyed it, leaving those present at a complete loss.

Critics have long been wrestling with the legal and constitutional aspects underpinning the accusations, offering important insights into the pressures imposed by military successes in relation to the increasing number of requests made by victorious generals for triumphal honors and the procedures regulating the distribution of booty.[62] Yet, little attention has been paid to the social meaning inherent in Africanus' destruction of the accounting-book. According to Livy, Cato played a key role by standing behind the tribunes Petilii.[63] While scholars tend to use Livy to emphasize or undermine the animosity between the two, I suggest that Africanus' behavior provides us with important clues about Cato's understanding of prose writing.[64]

---

62. Fundamental in this respect are the contributions of Fraccaro [1911] 1956; Shatzmann 1972; Scullard 1973: 290–303; Gruen 1995; Churchill 1999.

63. Livy 38.54.3; 38.55.7–13.

64. For various interpretations of the animosity (alleged or not) between Cato and Africanus, see Churchill 1995: 105 and note 47; Cugusi 1994: 267–72; Gruen 1992: 73; Astin 1978: 60–64; 71–73. Sblendorio Cugusi and Cugusi (1996: 95) suggest a resolution of Cato's antagonist position in later years by reflecting on the fact that Cato became the father-in-law of Aemilius Paullus' daughter, who was also P. Cornelius Scipio Aemilianus' sister.

In Livy the episode concerning the 'trials' of the Scipios is embedded in a larger attempt to coherently narrate Africanus' life, an attempt that is constantly foiled by an excess of records and a multiplication of monuments that are flawed. As Mary Jaeger points out, the closer we get to the end of Africanus' life, the worse the situation gets. Starting from a request to render a fiscal account, the description of Africanus' last days does nothing more than underline the narrator's difficulty in rendering an historical account from the profusion and confusion of sources and monuments.[65] Accordingly, Livy points to Africanus' performance at the 'trials' as the fountainhead of his unsettled narrative; at the same time, he ends up narrating the events only in Africanus' own terms.[66] Livy introduces the moments that interest us here by way of evaluating his sources: he reports the sum of gold and silver at issue in Asiagenus' case by following the testimony of Valerius Antias. Soon enough, however, he detects a problem and excuses Antias' report by accusing the scribe (*librarius*) and shifting the focus to Africanus' actions leading up to the destruction of the accounting-book.

The other sources seem to agree with Livy about the sequence of events. The accusers ask Africanus to give an oral account (*ratio*/ λόγος. Africanus refuses to do so and destroys the accounting-book (*ratio*/ *liber*/ λογισμός/βυβλίον that he has with him or asks the brother to fetch. The book records in writing income and expenses (*acceptae et expensae summae*), according to Valerius Maximus (3.7.1d), all the money and goods derived from the booty (*omnis pecuniae omnisque praedae*), according to Aulus Gellius 4.18. The diverse ways in which each author represents the events betray the logic that stood behind Africanus' behavior. So Polybius reports:

> He said that he had the balance sheet (λογισμός) but he did not have to submit an account (λόγος) to anybody. When the senator in question pressed his demand and ordered him to bring it, Africanus asked his brother to retrieve it. Once the book (βυβλίος) was brought to him, he held it out and tore it to pieces as everyone was watching, saying to the man who had asked for it, to search for the account (λόγος) among the pieces. To the others he asked why they were asking for an account (λόγος) of how and by whom the three thousand talents had been spent, whereas they had not inquired how and by whom the fifteen thousand talents they were receiving from Antiochus were coming into the treasury

---

65. Jaeger 1997: 161.
66. Jaeger 1997: 161.

nor how they had become masters of Asia, Libya, and Spain.[67]
(trans. Paton—slightly modified)

According to Polybius, the Scipios were asked to justify the ways in which they had used the economic gains derived from their victories in the East before an audience composed of members of the ruling elite. Polybius's account suggests that for Africanus the request signifies the audience's failure to recognize the achievements of the two brothers and the benefits that both had accrued for the commonwealth. While refusing to declare the ways in which the business had been handled (λόγος), he asserts the existence of writings bearing economic transactions (λογισμός). For Africanus, however, when compared to the absolute value of their achievements, the two reports are equally faulty. Consequently, he distinguishes between oral and written accounts only to equate them by refusing to offer an oral account, first, and by destroying the written record, afterwards. Through this double move, he makes manifest that to account orally for the inner workings of his and his brother's success under the coercive conditions created by his peers is equivalent to measuring his family's excellence on a balance sheet. After destroying the written record, Africanus invites the senator interested in his declaration (λόγος) to physically kneel down and extrapolate it from the pieces of the written record scattered on the floor. Finally, he reinforces his point in words by providing the numeric figure of the brothers' contribution to the commonwealth. Moreover, he asks the members of the audience to name the authors of such a contribution and the ways in which they themselves had achieved supremacy over a large territory. Africanus' strategy of shaming turns out to be successful. Not only does he silence all, but he also leaves everybody present with the same knowledge that everybody else will always have, that is, the intangible memory of what sustained Rome's supremacy in the East and the inestimable prestige of the Scipios.

Valerius Maximus offers further grounds for interpreting the social meaning of Africanus' gesture when he reports the following:

> cum a L. Scipione ex Antiochensi pecunia sestertii quadragies ratio in curia reposceretur, prolatum ab eo librum, quo acceptae et expensae summae continebantur et refelli inimicorum accusatio poterat, discerpsit, indignatus de ea re dubitari, quae sub ipso legato administrata fuerat. Quin etiam in hunc modum egit: "non reddo, patres conscripti, aerario vestro

---

67. Polybius 23.14.7.

sestertii quadragies rationem, alieni imperii minister, quod meo ductu meisque auspiciis bis millies sestertio uberius feci."[68]

When in the Senate L. Scipio was asked for an account of four million sesterces out of the money of Antiochus, Africanus tore into pieces the book that he had brought. The book recorded income and expenses and with it he could have countered the accusation of his enemies. He felt offended that there could be doubt about the matter that he himself had managed as a legate. Moreover, he pressed forward in this manner: "Senators, I will not give the account of four million sesterces to your treasury acting as a minister to someone else's power since under my command and auspices I enriched it with two hundred million sesterces."

In Valerius Maximus' version Africanus' performance is staged in the Senate house. The declaration requested is called *ratio* and the object that contains the economic figures is called *liber*. The words that accompany Africanus' destruction of the *liber* call attention to the fact that this is not simply a balance sheet, but a valuable object as well. By comparing the accounting-book with the monetary contribution that he has made to the public treasury, Africanus underscores its sociocosmological value and the sacrifice that he has to make to save the honor of his family. Indeed, his words make clear that for Africanus to disclose the content embodied in the text or to hand the text over to the treasury under the coercive circumstances established by his peers would mean to stoop to the level of a *minister alieni imperii*. Aulus Gellius corroborates this reading.

Aulus Gellius uses the expression *rationem reddere* to describe the request made to Africanus. Afterwards, he represents Africanus responding as follows:

Illatum, ut palam recitaretur et ad aerarium deferretur, "sed enim id iam non faciam" inquit "ne me ipse afficiam contumelia" eumque librum statim coram discidit suis manibus et concerpsit.[69]

Before everybody he tore the book with his own hands and ripped it, after it had been brought forth so that it might be read publicly and turned over to the public treasury and said: "and yet I will not do it so that I may not cause an offense to myself."

---

68. Valarius Maximus 3.7.1d.
69. Gellius 4.18.11

In this passage, the written account is once again supposed to be handed over to the public treasury and its destruction is represented as a defensive ploy against a self-inflicted offense. In turn, the written record is introduced with the expectation that it will be read out. This detail suggests that Africanus' destructive gesture is also motivated by the possibility that he may be asked to justify the information read aloud. Cato in the *De Agricultura* helps us see how this would add up to a loss in *auctoritas*.

In section 2.1–10 Cato enumerates the duties of the *pater familias* at his arrival at the farm. He is supposed to check the condition of the land, what work has been completed, and what is yet to be done; moreover, he is supposed to summon the overseer and ask him about the general state of business. After that the *pater familias* must produce an account, a *ratio* (*inire rationem*) and confront the overseer. If the overseer should offer excuses that do not coincide with the master's account, the master should counter the overseer in the following manner:

Ad rationem operum operarumque vilicum revoca.[70]

Make the overseer turn back to the account of workers and works done.

In this instance of household management, to produce an account (*ratio*) is an act marking the *auctoritas* that the *pater familias* exercises over his extended household; to justify the state of business against the account produced by the *pater familias,* on the other hand, marks the lesser status of the overseer. This is what Africanus sees looming over the request of his peers for a declaration and what he averts by withholding the oral report and by destroying the written record. Interestingly, the scenario underlying our narratives has unexpected effects on Cato's construction of prose writing.

As I mentioned above, in the Preface to the *Origines* Cato asserts: "clarorum hominum atque magnorum non minus otii quam negotii rationem exstare oportet." In previous years, Catonian scholars have differentiated between the expressions *rationem exstare* and *rationem reddere:* while the first phrase would allude to the durable existence of an account, in the second, the verb *reddere* would describe the act of providing it.[71] This interpretation addresses a conceptually important differentiation but

---

70. Cato, *De Agr.* 2.2.
71. Till 1940: 170 note 28. Cf. also Schröder 1971: 53. Letta 1984: 27 note 138 acknowledges the differentiation but interprets it as a reference to the necessity of documenting the *otium* of *clari viri,* with the exclusion of Cato himself.

does not engage with the cultural and contextual meaning underpinning both expressions. In the Latin versions of the Scipios' 'trials' *reddere* is the verb used to express the request for a declaration and the act of turning over the accounting-book to the public treasury. In light of this, Cato's choice of *exstare* is rather odd but makes sense if viewed in relation to Africanus' destruction of the accounting-book.

In her book, *La raison de Rome,* Claudia Moatti identifies a relationship between Cato's fragment and Africanus' behavior at the 'trials' for what it says regarding the development of the *redditio rationis*. Performed by magistrates, this practice was meant to fight the corporate mentality of the Roman *nobiles* and their monopoly over knowledge.[72] What my analysis makes clear is that the *redditio rationis* was constructed by redeploying the sworn declaration (*ratio*) performed at the censorial ceremony and the registration of economic information on *tabulae*-like materials (*codex, liber, tabulae, rationes*) that magistrates already performed. On the other hand, the senatorial context within which the episode concerning Africanus is staged implies that the *redditio rationis* played off a privileged contrast with the census since the social agents involved belonged exclusively to the upper crust of Roman society. But read against what we find in the *De Agricultura* about the relationship of power established by a *ratio,* the episode also highlights that to be asked to provide a declaration and to justify it against a written account inevitably diminished, however temporarily, the *auctoritas* of the responding party.

In the *Origines* Cato redresses what Africanus was unwilling to bear by engaging in transcription and by displacing the coercive conditions that had triggered Africanus' response. In the mid-nineties, Paolo Cugusi argued for the inclusion of yet another fragment in its Preface:

> P. Scipionem . . . qui primus Africanus appellatus est dicere solitum scripsit Cato . . . numquam se minus otiosum, quam cum otiosus, nec minus solum, quam cum solus esset.[73]

---

72. Moatti 1997: 205–8.

73. Cicero, *De Off.* 3.1 = Cato, Orig. 1.3* C&Sbl; cf. also Cicero, *De Rep.* 1.27. Cugusi 1994: 267–68. For further references to ancient loci and discussions, see Cugusi and Sblendorio Cugusi 2001: 2. 290–93. See also Astin 1978: 221 and note 32. The passage had been already attributed to the Preface by Krause 1831: 98; Wagener 1849: 16; Bormann 1858: 29–30; Roth 1853: 268. Cf. also discussion in Sblendorio Cugusi and Cugusi 1996: 146. Standing in the way of Cugusi's intervention are two enduring arguments. The first concerns the legendary animosity between Cato and Africanus; the second relates to the suppression of names in the *Origines* as a whole. For a reassessment of this feature, see Sciarrino 2004a: 352–54

Cato wrote that P. Scipio, who was the first to be called Africanus, used to say that he was never less in leisure than when in leisure nor less lonely than when alone.

Derived from Cicero's last philosophical work, the *De Officiis,* the fragment opens up the third book and serves as a foil for a general reflection on Cicero's own writing activities in and around 44 B.C.E. In this context, Cicero explains that with this *dictum* Africanus meant that when he was not engaged in public affairs (*negotia*), he used to reflect upon them (*de negotiis cogitare*) by solitarily conversing with himself (*secum loqui*). As opposed to Africanus, Cicero represents his *otium* and *solitudo* as the outcome of his disengagement from public affairs (*inopia negotii*), a disengagement derived from the political turmoil that—he argues—had brought on the death of the Senate and the destruction of justice. As such, his *otium* is not an expression of will (*voluntas*) but what necessity demands (*necessitas*). Later on, he adds:

> Quamquam Africanus maiorem laudem meo iudicio assequabatur. Nulla enim eius ingenii monumenta mandata litteris, nullum opus otii, nullum solitudinis munus exstat; ex quo intellegi debet illum mentis agitatione investigationeque earum rerum quas cogitando consequabatur nec otiosum nec solum umquam fuisse.[74]

> And yet, in my judgment, Africanus gained a higher praise. For no memorials of his mind have been preserved in writing, no work produced in his leisure hours, no fruit of his solitude exists; from this we may infer that because of the activity of his mind and the study of those issues to which he used to direct his thought, he was never in leisure nor lonely.

The passage confirms that Africanus not only destroyed the accounting-book in question, but that he also refrained from producing any sort of writing objectifying his outstanding life performances. From Cicero's point of view, the fact that Africanus chose to do so attests to the gap that exists between his necessary *otium* and Africanus' willing *otium*. Unlike Cicero, Africanus could count on such an aristocratic pedigree and so many outstanding political and military successes that, by constituting a *monumentum* in themselves, they allowed him to dispense with writing altogether. The allusion to Africanus' *dictum* in the *Pro Plancio,* a speech

---

74. Cicero, *De Off.* 3.1.4.

performed by Cicero ten years before and a few years after his return from exile, provides further ground for interpretation:

> Nam postea quam sensi populi Romani auris hebetiores, oculos autem esse acris atque acutos, destiti quid de me audituri essent homines cogitare; feci ut postea cotidie praesentem me viderent, habitavi in oculis, pressi forum; neminem a congressu meo neque ianitor meus neque somnus absterruit. ecquid ego dicam de occupatis meis temporibus, cui fuerit ne otium quidem umquam otiosum? nam quas tu commemoras, Cassi, legere te solere orationes, cum otiosus sis, has ego scripsi ludis et feriis, ne omnino umquam essem otiosus. etenim M. Catonis illud quod in principio scripsit Originum suarum semper magnificum et praeclarum putavi, "clarorum uirorum atque magnorum non minus oti quam negoti rationem exstare oportere." itaque si quam habeo laudem, quae quanta sit nescio, parta Romae est, quaesita in foro; meaque privata consilia publici quoque casus comprobaverunt, ut etiam summa res publica mihi domi fuerit gerenda et urbs in urbe servanda. eadem igitur, Cassi, via munita Laterensi est, idem virtuti cursus ad gloriam, hoc facilior fortasse quod ego huc a me ortus et per me nixus ascendi, istius egregia virtus adiuvabitur commendatione maiorum.[75]

> For after I learned from this that the people of Rome had deaf ears, but very sharp and active eyes, I gave up listening to what men would say about me. Yet I took care that they should see me in their presence every day: I lived in their sight; I stuck to the forum; neither my porter nor even sleep was allowed to prevent anyone from having access to me. And what should I say about my time which was devoted to business, when even in my leisure time I was never at leisure? For the very orations which you say, O Cassius, that you are in the habit of reading when you are at leisure, I wrote on days of festival and on holidays, so that I never was at leisure at all. Indeed I always deemed magnificent and outstanding what Cato wrote at the beginning of his *Origines,* that "no less an account of leisure time than of work time of famous and great men ought to remain." And, therefore, if I have any praise, how great that is I don't know, but it has all been acquired at Rome and earned in the forum. And public events have sanctioned my private counsels in such a way that even at home I have had to attend to the general interests of the republic, and to preserve the city while in the city. The same road, Cassius, is open to Laterensis, the same path by virtue to glory. And it will be the easier for him perhaps on this account that I have

---

75. Cicero, *Planc.* 66–67.

reached this point without having any family backing me and relying solely on myself; but his admirable virtues will be assisted by the recommendation that the virtues of his ancestors supply him with.

Here Cicero alludes indirectly to Africanus' *dictum* to describe his politically engaged *otium* and cites Cato's words from the *Origines* to qualify his writing activities. The speeches that he textualized during his time away from business had allowed him to be visually present during his exile and, now, provide him with a means for trying to recapture the power of his consular voice. To that effect, he turns to Cassius and reminds him of his habit of reading his speeches during his time off. In turn, the comparison between his own *novitas* and the aristocratic background of Laterensis confirms that for Cicero writing represented an alternative route for fashioning his aristocratic self and for keeping at bay the upheavals of his political career. In relation to Cato's *Origines,* however, the passage acquires importance by corroborating Cugusi's philological insertion of Africanus' *dictum* into its Preface, although not in the position that he proposes.[76] Its insertion prior to Cato's injunction makes better sense by supporting the illusion that the text objectifies Cato and Africanus interacting with each other in the same setting. Indeed, as if performing in a *convivium* and following the turn-taking rule, Cato can be seen to dramatize the exchange by picking up Africanus' words concerning his *otium* and stating that this too needs to be objectified in writing. In so doing, Cato corrects the loss of *auctoritas* that Africanus feared and empowers his own writings at the same time.

Putting Cato's Prose Writing in Its Place

In his seminal article "The Model of the Text: Meaningful Action considered as a Text," Paul Ricoeur extended to the realm of live speech the primary sense of 'hermeneutics' as the set of criteria that make up a 'text.' On that occasion, Ricoeur expanded on his view of what a 'text' is and does.[77] Simply put, for Ricoeur a piece of writing can be called 'text': first,

---

76. Cugusi 1994; Cugusi and Sblendorio Cugusi 2001: 2.290. Further corroboration of the intimate relationship between the two *dicta* and their relative positioning in the Preface can be found in the "allusive dialogue" that Cicero entertains with Cato in the *Tusculan Disputations* (1.3–5). For an acute analysis of these passages, see Gildenhard 2007a: 134–43.

77. Ricoeur 1973. For a critical assessment of Ricoeur's application of the text analogy to action, see Bell 1992: 50–51,

when by objectifying a speech event, it fixes what is said by overcoming the fleeting conditions of its production; second, when it disjoins the meaning of what is said from the intentionality of the author; third, when emancipated from the situational context of its production and the intentions of the author, it develops references ushering in what he calls "new dimensions of our being-in-the-world";[78] fourth, when by drawing on its autonomy, the writing opens itself up to an infinite range of possible readers and becomes an "open work."[79]

In her book *Dionysus Writes: The Invention of Theatre in Ancient Greece,* Jennifer Wise argues against narrow ritualistic and religious interpretations of the birth of Greek drama.[80] In their stead, she contends that theater emerged as the first text-based art in Western poetic tradition whose central generic features depended on the literacy of its first practitioners. By turning to Ricoeur, Wise proposes that the dramatists of the fifth century B.C.E. were not so much innovators in their way of using writing for poetic composition. Rather, they were "revolutionary as to the degree to which they exploited the potentialities of literate modes and made use of writing as 'text' rather than as a mere reminder of a spoken performance."[81] In this sense, the decisive break made by the playwrights would have been to use writing *before* the beginning of the spoken communication. In so doing, they distanced the verbal object from their original speech act and the 'text' opened up new performative possibilities. The actors were responsible for the realization of these possibilities by returning to the 'text' and by performing it on stage. In the process, the playwright's original speech act failed to perform what he intended and the interpretative agency of the actors produced creatively different effects.[82] For my purposes, Ricoeur's notion of 'text' and Wise's redeployment of it are compelling for two seemingly contradictory reasons.

First, Ricoeur's theorization of 'text' makes explicit the tendency to valorize writing over performance by championing one form of writing, that is, when writing is used to produce a verbal objectification of speech that is divorced from its author and its initial context. On this score, what

---

78. Ricoeur 1973: 96.

79. For a critical assessment of Ricoeur's application of the text analogy to action, see Bell 1992: 50–51.

80. For a recent discussion of the relationship between ritualism and Greek drama both in historical and methodological terms, see Csapo and Miller 2007, especially pp. 1–38.

81. Wise 1998: 12.

82. Wise 1998: 148–49. Cf. Ricoeur 1973: 146: "a text is really a text when it is not restricted to transcribing an anterior speech, when instead it inscribes directly in written letters what the discourse means."

I find fascinating about Wise's work is that in retrospectively applying Ricoeur's model to the Greek world of writing she does not simply resist ritualistic readings of Greek drama; she also renders Greek dramatic texts immediately familiar and amenable to our interpretative activities. This trajectory emerges most clearly when she asserts: "the birth of text is what brings the actor as *hupokrites* into existence, for he is the first performer ever who comes *after* a writing, a writing that antedates any corporeal performance of it, and must therefore be interpreted prior to its first performance."[83]

Second, the emphasis that both Ricoeur and Wise place on the agency of the actor/reader/interpreter offers a convenient theoretical foil precisely because it obscures the possibility that authors may perceive the agency of the actor/reader/performer as a tantamount loss of agency on their part. In this respect, transcription presents important potential. For although Ricoeur situates transcription at the very fringe of hermeneutics and Wise associates it with a primeval phase of cultural development, transcription can do more than simply freeze the flux of the spoken word and make the verbal object open to interpretation. The Preface to the *Origines* provides a convenient terrain for exploring the effects of transcription and, therefore, for attempting to define transcription in theoretical terms as well. But before engaging in this exploration, let me first articulate, however simplistically, the language of performativity that Wise adopts and that will constitute our springboard for gauging the social dimension of prose's transcriptuality vis-à-vis the scriptuality of poetry in the context of second-century B.C.E. Rome.

Wise's use of "performative" draws heavily on the work of J. L. Austin and his theorization of the power of language to effect things in the world. For Austin, a performative utterance refers to cases in which "the issuing of the utterance is the performing of an action."[84] To exemplify this statement, Austin uses the framework of the marriage ceremony and the words "I do" pronounced by the groom and the bride. In his view, the conventionality and the markedness of the ceremonial procedure affect the power of the words pronounced so that, in saying "I do," the bride and the groom become an entity legally (and/or religiously) bound. In turn, uttering these words produces two different effects: *illocutionary* and *perlocutionary*. Their *illocutionary* effect can be seen in the moment of saying, and specifically in the transformation of status of two people from single to married.

---

83. Wise 1998: 149.
84. Austin [1962] 1975: 6.

Their *perlocutionary* effect, by contrast, exceeds language and relates to what follows, namely, to the fact that these two people will afterwards share a residence, children, and so on. As for the ceremonial context, this provides the conditions by which the utterance does what it says and obtains the result that it says. For this reason, the utterance can be classed as a misfire when the procedures are not accepted, presumably by persons other than the speakers.[85]

As we have seen, the surviving accounts of Africanus' performance at the 'trials' pivot around his refusal to comply with the request made by his peers. Articulated in Austin's terms, Africanus does not accept the procedures set by them; as such, their utterance can be classed as a misfire by not achieving the reality at which their request aimed. In the Preface to the *Origines* Cato counters these misfiring effects in the following ways. First, he establishes the authority of his intervention by countering poetic representations of *gesta* through a rhythmical allusion to Ennius' *Annales*. Second, he activates a convivial scenario imbued with ancestral authority by conjuring up a scene that envisions a select group of people who interact with each other by singing in turn about the achievements of the best among them. Third, Cato cites a *dictum* by Africanus in which he describes his engaged but solitary *otium;* fourth, he articulates a *dictum* of his own in turn by asserting that a *ratio* of both *negotium* and *otium* of great and outstanding men ought to exist. Whereas Africanus' *dictum* does not allude to the 'trials' in any way, Cato gestures to Africanus' destruction of the accounting-book through the verb *exstare*. Finally, Cato acts on his own *dictum* by producing an account of their interchange or, rather, by transcribing it. In so doing, Cato does not forfeit the illocutionary force of Africanus' *dictum* concerning *otium* (namely, his solitary engagement); he only diverts the perlocutionary effects of his destructive performance at the 'trials' (namely, the loss of a self-produced *ratio*). Cato is able to achieve this outcome by capitalizing on the way in which transcription extends the agency of the author and impacts on the representation of reality.

To note that Cato's exchange with Africanus may be made up is less important than to observe that, through it, Cato exemplifies how transcription empowers the author, influences the representation of reality, and affects the reception of the transcribed text. For one thing, transcription divorces the speech act from its initial communicative situation; however, it does not the break the intimate relationship between spoken and speakers. Second, transcription does not affect the objectification

---

85. Austin 1975 [1962]: 14–15; 27.

of speech alone; it also concretizes the actions that accompany it and the social environments created and qualified by both. This implies that meaning is conveyed not solely through the speech transcribed, but also through the set-ups and the actions that the author activates and objectifies in writing. Third, far from being an 'open work' addressing an undifferentiated range of readers, Cato makes perfectly clear that a transcription interpellates only a select group of social actors. This includes individuals who are in the position to perform the everyday activities that contributed to the construction of their privileged status, namely, public speaking, military command, household management, political activities, and the like. Fourth, transcription precludes the readers' appropriation of what is said; it only allows them to employ the words and actions reified in the text as benchmarks for constructing and measuring their own social performances. Following Richard Schechner, we may call these social performances "make-believe" since they created the very social reality that they enacted.[86] Accordingly, transcriptions represent social and speech acts that are constructed according to the author's own perception of reality. At the same time, they teem with impersonation or, rather, with embodiments of these acts by social actors operating in ritualized situations that are made permanent by the author's transcribing activities. When seen in this way, Cato's authorial agency is to be identified with his ability to manipulate the critical distance that stands between social roles and the patterns of speech and actions dictated by the lived prestige order in which he participated. As a practice, transcription helped Cato situate himself in this lived prestige order by allowing him to extend the power of the ritualized activities in which he engaged in such a way as to remain in control of reality and expand his *auctoritas* at the same time.

By and large, in the Preface to the *Origines* Cato presents transcription as a venue for making a text a direct and staying manifestation of the authoritative body of its author. To a certain extent, the baffling effects that the profusion of 'unauthorized' monuments have on Livy's narrative concerning Africanus and Cicero's emphasis on Africanus' unwillingness to produce *monumenta ingenii* suggest that Cato aligned his writings with the monumental constructions that Roman aristocrats were accustomed to scatter throughout the city as powerful reminders of their achievements. In a way, then, he extended the monumentalizing practices of the Roman aristocracy in a new direction by making the act of reading his transcriptions analogous to the act of viewing monumental landmarks. At the same time,

---

86. Schechner 2002: 35.

however, Cato thrust his writings into a very exclusive path of circulation and controlled their reception through the multiple frameworks that, as an author enjoying *auctoritas,* he devised for them. Accordingly, measured against the scripturality of poetry, Cato bestowed on his transcriptions a physical mobility that in no way dovetailed with the alienability that characterized poetic texts.

Praises and Textuality

Viewed from a purely methodological point of view, Cato's construction of Latin prose writing as transcription exposes the extent to which notions of textuality that dispose of the author undercut the ability to offer culturally, geographically, and chronologically specific accounts of textualities. In this sense, Cato's writings call for a major shift of approach and expectations. For a starter, they require us to think openly about the relationship between textuality and writing agents; in Cato's case, this opening implies acknowledging the aristocratic reluctance to entrust the memory of their feats to movable objects liable to be appropriated. Against this reluctance, Cato's transcribing activities constituted a venue for extending the authoritative body. The Prefaces to his major writings, the *De Agricultura* and the *Origines,* draw force and meaning from the grafting of the ancestral convivial scenario onto the censorial scenario. In the former, his strategies are less explicit and emerge only in the shift from the language of praise (*laudare*) to the language of evaluation (*existimatio*); in the second, he qualifies this shift by evoking and, more importantly, dramatizing both scenarios in very inventive ways. Taken together, these Prefaces unfold the larger scenario of exclusive reception that Cato imagined for his writings. A neglected fragment attributed to the Preface to the so-called *De Re Militari* allows us to see this fact very clearly:

> Scio ego quae scripta sunt si palam proferantur, multos fore qui vitiligent, sed ii potissimum qui verae laudis expertes sunt. Eorum ego orationes sivi praeterfluere.[87]

> I do know that if the things I have written should be divulged openly, there will be many, especially those who do not enjoy true praise, who will disparage them; I let their speeches flow past.

---

87. Pliny, *NH* praef. 30 = Cato, *de re milit.* 1 C&Sbl

Through an emphatic assertion of his selfhood, Cato anticipates the criticism that his writings may undergo once set in circulation by characterizing his detractors as "lacking true praise."[88] While helping him define the boundaries of his readership, this characterization underscores the genealogical relationship that Cato envisioned between his writings and the evaluative songs associated with the ancestral convivial scenario that we see elsewhere. In turn, the language of fluidity that he uses in this context to describe the spoken words of his detractors serves to construct a sharp contrast to the performative solidity conferred by transcription. In light of the relationship between *laudare* and *existimare* via transcription that Cato promotes, it becomes important to deal with the blind spots created by ancient constructions of poetry as loci of aristocratic praise and by modern misgivings about generic hierarchies.

Later evaluations of Ennius' activities and his poetic production all pivot around their praise-conferring qualities. Speaking on behalf of Archias' citizenship, Cicero uses the language of praise to describe the benefits that poetry bestows on individual members of the aristocracy and the community at large:

> Et eis laudibus certe non solum [i.e., Africanus] ipse qui laudatur, sed etiam populi Romani nomen ornatur. In caelum huius proavus Cato tollitur . . . omnes denique illi Maximi, Marcelli, Fulvii, non sine communi omnium nostrum laude decorantur.[89]

> And with those praises not only was he [i.e., Scipio] praised, but the name of the Roman people was adorned as well. Cato, the grandfather of this Cato, is extolled to the skies . . . indeed all of those famous Maximi, Marcelli, Fulvii, are decorated not without the consensual praise of all our ancestors.

Later in the second century C.E. Aurelius Victor uses the same language when mentioning the effect of Ennius' writings on the reputation of Marcus Fulvius Nobilior:

> Quam victoriam per se magnificam Ennius amicus eius [i.e., Nobilioris] insigni laude celebravit.[90]

---

88. See Sblendorio Cugusi 1982: 320; 42–43.
89. Cicero, *Pro Arch.* 22.
90. Aurelius Victor, *Vir. Il.* 52.2–3.

And Ennius, a friend of his (i.e., Nobilior's), celebrated with highest praise this victory (i.e., at Ambracia) already glorious in itself.

What makes these two passages compelling is the seemingly unproblematic identification of Ennius' poetry with the creation of glory and renown. In both cases, the identification draws force from the assumption that, by virtue of representing major feats, poetry automatically merges with praise. Aurelius Victor underscores that Ennius augmented the magnificence of Nobilior's already glorious victory at Ambracia; Cicero goes further by proclaiming that the *laudes* that Ennius produced for individual leaders augmented the reputation of the Roman people and expressed the consensual evaluation of all the ancient leaders.[91] In both cases, the elite debate sparked by the encroachment of alien and nonelite cultural agents on the social life of the early second century B.C.E. Roman elite is completely suppressed. Modern representations of early Roman poetry as contributing to national identity and the preoccupation with determining whether the poets were at the service of the elite's *res privata* or cared about the interests of the *res publica* bear witness to the long-term blinding effects of these narratives.[92] A closer look into the semantic field of *laus/laudare* reveals some crucial facts about the connection between textualities and sociopolitical hierarchies and the impact of Cato's invention of Latin prose on this relationship.

Besides the widespread use of *laus* to indicate praise, later grammarians indicate that this term encompassed an additional performative dimension by specifying its relationship with bringing back into being or displaying events and achievements. So, for example, Charisius asserts: *laus facti instrumentum est, laus vero est rerum gestarum relatio* ("a *laus* is an instrument of what has been done; indeed a *laus* is an exposition of things done").[93] Priscianus, on the other hand, defines *laus* as following: *laus est expositio bonorum quae alicui accidunt personae vel communiter vel priuatim* ("a *laus* is the display of the good things which happen to some person either before others or in private").[94] In both definitions a *laus* embodies (good) deeds or facts and is the means by which these deeds (*factum*) or facts (*quae accidunt*) are "brought back" (*refero*) or

---

91. The rhetorical moves adopted by Cicero in this speech by which he becomes both Archia's *laudator* and the *laudator* of himself are explored by Dugan 2001: 35–77. Most recently, Zetzel (2007) has also suggested that the representation of Ennius' relationship with his patrons that we get here is Cicero's own construction.
92. See, e.g., Gruen 1990: 106–22; Goldberg 1995: 120–23.
93. Charisius, *Gramm.* p. 403, 14 B (cited from *TLL s.v. laus*)
94. Priscianus, *Praeex.* 7

"displayed" (*exponere*). The denominative verb *laudare* expands the performative power of *laus* to the act of naming. So Gellius asserts:

> laudare significat prisca lingua nominare appellareque; sic in actionibus civilibus auctor laudari dicitur quod est nominatus.[95]

> To praise in the ancient language means to name and call upon. So in civil trials the bail-giver is said to "be called upon," that is nominated.

In this passage, Gellius highlights the ancient relationship between *laudare* and naming by using as an example its employment in the court context. This context ritualizes the act of naming by indicating that the person summoned acts as an *auctor* for someone else. Indeed, if we turn to texts more or less contemporary to Cato, the ritualized and performative power of *laudare* emerges very clearly.

In the *Captivi,* Tyndarus (a false slave) and Philocrates (a false master) discuss the report that Philocrates has to send to Tyndarus' father in order to have him pay the ransom and gain back his own freedom. Tyndarus' report is filled with praise addressed to Philocrates, to which Philocrates replies by responding in kind: *Pol istic me haud centesumam / partem laudat quam ipse meritust ut laudetur laudibus* ("For God's sake, he praises me not even an hundredth part of what he deserves to be praised with praises").[96] Later Philocrates asserts: *Iovem supremum testem laudo, me . . . infidelem non futurum Philocrati* ("I call upon Jupiter the highest as witness . . . that I won't be unfaithful to Philocrates").[97] In these passages the characters use *laudare* in a way that falls within its generalized meaning of praising, but in the latter case the act of praising enters the marked sphere of oath-giving and serves to interpellate Jupiter as the authority that validates the oath. The court setting elicited by Gellius and the oath-giving act represented by Plautus make conspicuous that *laudare* aligns the *laudatus* and the *laudator* within a series of relationships and oppositions that, by transcending the ordinary, bring into play the sociocosmological order and the divine realm, which constitutes the ultimate source of *auctoritas*.

A brief survey of the uses of *laus/laudare* in the Catonian corpus shows how Cato thrived on the performative power of *laudare* to enact an accrual

---

95. Gellius 2.6.16. Cf. Macrobius, *Sat.* 6.7.16. In addition see Nonius p.335.10 "laudare est verbis ecferre (Virgil, *Georg.* 2. 412)." For the translation of "auctor" as "bail-giver" I rely on Krostenko 2001: 36.
96. Plautus, *Capt.* 422–23.
97. Plautus, *Capt.* 426–27.

of prestige for the *laudatus* and that he sharply limited this power to *laudes* articulated by an individual or a group of individuals enjoying *auctoritas*. In turn, Cato deployed *laus*'s intimate relationship with deeds in order to sustain that these inform the performativity of the *laus* as well as the *auctoritas* of the *laudator*. Put rather simply, for Cato a *laus* engenders an accrual of *auctoritas* for the *laudatus* only if it encodes social performances that have undergone a process of evaluation by a *laudator* or group of *laudatores* who enjoy the same sort of *laus*. In addition, if a *laus* comes to be objectified, then the object is thought to embody both the *laus* and the *auctoritas* of the *laudatus*.

In a fragment of one of Cato's earliest speeches generally identified as *Dierum dictarum de consulatu suo*, *laudare* serves to introduce praises allegedly bestowed on him by an undefined group of *laudatores:*

> laudant me maximis laudibus tantum navium tantum exercitum tantum commeatum non opinatum esse quemquam hominem comparare potuisse, id tamen maturrime [me] comparavisse.[98]

> They praise me with the highest praises that, although it was thought that no man could put together such a big number of ships, such a big army, such a big levy, nevertheless I had most hastily put those things together.

In this fragment *laudare* introduces an indirect statement that encompasses a list of achievements presented in comparative terms that are absolute. Imbued with repetitive patterns typical of the *carmen* tradition, the list implies a judging audience and evokes the aristocratic practices of self-definition that characterize the more or less contemporary *elogia* located in tombs, the inscriptions placed by victorious generals in more public contexts, and the funeral orations that, once transcribed, were kept in aristocratic households.[99]

Similarities at the level of form and imagery between such disparate compositions extend to their textuality. The diverse material objects in which these compositions are embedded share the same authorial intention to permanently concretize both the achievements and the *auctoritas* acknowledged and bestowed through praise. This fact affects our under-

---

98. Charisius, *Gramm.* p. 266, 24 B = Cato, *orat.* 4.15 Sbl.
99. These include the already mentioned Scipionic *elogia* (*CIL* 1.29–30; *CIL* 1.32; *CIL* 1.33; *CIL* 1.34) and the *elogium* of Atilius Calatinus (*FPL* pgs.13–4); the *tabulae triumphales* of victorious generals (e.g. Caesius Bassius, *GL* 6.265.29; *CIL* 1.541; Livy 41.28.8–9). For the textualization of funeral orations, see Cicero, *Brut.* 61.

standing of Roman elite textualities in at least two ways. First, it suggests that the practices that defined the Roman aristocracy as such did not exist outside their material objectification; in fact, objectification was part and parcel of the very cluster of practices that informed aristocratic subjectivity. Second, Cato's transcribing activities constitute a variation on these practices in the measure that they allow him to redeploy writing materials (*tabulae*) that were integral to and integrated in ritualized activities beyond these activities. Though movable, these objects were perceived to be fundamental to the sociocosmological organization of society and final embodiments of the reality that they helped to create. What makes Cato's transcriptions distinctive, then, is the particular spin that Cato puts on them, a spin that is affected by his *novitas* and the historical juncture in which he lived. In this respect, the fragment above and the speech to which it belongs are enlightening.

Drawing on aristocratic self-defining practices, Cato unfolds praises which, attributed to unspecified *laudatores,* feature him as the *laudatus,* and inserts them into a speech most probably delivered in a senatorial context. If, as Claudia Moatti argues, the *Dierum dictarum de consulatu suo* testifies to the development of the *redditio rationis,* we can also see how he capitalized on it to lend *auctoritas* to the praises and the achievements that at the moment of his oratorical performance he had listed.[100] Once transcribed, these praises can be seen to become one and the same with his objectified oratorical performance and to stand as final judgments on his consular deeds consensually acknowledged and authorized by his peers.

In a passage from the body of the *Origines* Cato expounds on the interrelationship between praise, deeds, objectification, and *auctoritas* by featuring himself as the *laudator.* In what is the longest narrative passage that survives from this text, Cato concludes his report of exploits performed by a *tribunus militum* and identified with the name of Caedicius:

> Sed idem benefactum, quo in loco ponas, nimium interest. Leonides Laco, qui simile apud <T>hermopylas fecit, propter eius virtutes omnis Graecia gloriam atque gratiam praecipuam claritudinis inclitissimae decoravere monumentis: signis, statuis, elogiis, historiis aliisque rebus gratissimum id eius factum habuere; at tribuno militum parva laus pro factis relicta qui idem fecerat atque rem servaverat.[101]

But the same good deed changes according to the place in which you

---

100. Moatti 1997: 206.
101. Gellius 3.7.19 = Cato, *Orig.* Book IV frg. 88b.2 C&Sbl.

place it. Leonidas from Sparta did similar things at Thermopylae and for his expressions of manliness every part of Greece honored his glory and consecrated his extraordinary fame with monuments of greatest splendor. By means of portraits, statues, funerary inscriptions, narratives and other objects, Greece showed its recognition for his deed; by contrast, to the *tribunus militum* small praise remains in relation to his deeds, and yet he had done the same and saved the situation.

Here Cato enumerates the tokens of recognition (*monumenta*) that Greece bestowed on Leonidas and compares them with the small praise (*parva laus*) that the *tribunus militum* received.[102] Cato's list quantitatively differentiates the ways in which similar deeds are objectified and acknowledged; however, the differentiation also does the job of constructing a privileged contrast with his situational understanding of praise. In the case of Leonidas Cato speaks of commemorative objects (statues, paintings, eulogistic poems, narratives, etc.) produced by socially undifferentiated *auctores*.[103] In the case of the *tribunus* he interpellates his chosen reader in the second person, calling attention to the unfair treatment suffered by the *tribunus* and producing a final *laus* that finds its legitimacy in both the deeds that he assesses and his own *auctoritas*. Finally, transcription fixes the praise bestowed on the *laudatus* and his *auctoritas* as *laudator* at the same time.

The occurrence of *laudare* in the *carmen de moribus* confirms that for Cato a *laus* stood far from being a socially undifferentiated production of praise; rather, it encoded the final judgment on behaviors or actions delivered by *laudatores* enjoying *auctoritas:*

> avaritiam omnia vitia habere putabant. Sumptuosus cupidus elegans† vitiosus qui habebatur is laudatur[104]

> They [i.e., the ancestors] used to reckon that avarice contained all vice. The person who was considered wasteful, lustful, fussy, depraved was called as such (i.e., avaricious).

Similarly to what we find in the Preface to the *De Agricultura,* the verb *laudare* summons an assessment process. Located in the past (*putabant*), this process teems with *auctoritas* and leads up to a final judgment that,

---

102. Festus L123: "monimentum est ut fana, porticus, scripta et carmina."
103. Generally, the opposition emphasized is between (Greek) naming and (Roman) report of facts. Cf. Letta 1984: 23 note 117.
104. Gellius 11.2.1 = *carmen de moribus* 1 C&Sbl.

absorbed into the adjective *avarus,* is final and definitive.[105] By listing adjectives that elicit very specific behaviors and by unfolding the very process of evaluation, Cato bridges the expanse that stands between the past and the present. In so doing, he also imbues his own subjectivity with ancestral qualities and, therefore, *auctoritas.* Once transcribed, the composition and the *auctoritas* of its author is made permanent and inalienable in the measure that the reader can either acknowledge the *auctoritas* that exudes from the text in the same way as he would before a monument or use the behavioral model that it bears as a template for his own actions. Here just as in other loci, we can immediately recognize how Cato links his subjectivity to the ancestral past in a typically aristocratic manner, but suppresses any familial specificity to displace his *novitas.* Unlike other loci, the *carmen de moribus* makes particularly conspicuous the pivotal role that Cato's censorial experience played in his invention of Latin prose more generally. As Sander Goldberg has recently remarked, the underlying model for this composition is a similar *carmen* attributed to Appius Claudius Caecus, who set a rather notable and controversial censorial precedent.[106] Following this trajectory, we come to realize that Cato relied on the centrality of achievements implicit in the notion of *nobilitas* as much as he redeployed the censorial concern with *mores* beyond the limits of his censorship. Indeed, it is precisely through this latter move that Cato was able to instill his cultural inventions and the embodied frameworks that informed them with *auctoritas.*

Not surprisingly, we are returning full circle to the perception of *auctoritas* as an embodied quality and its impact on cultural forms and generic differentiations. Cato's *auctoritas* stems from his exercise of magisterial duties and, especially, from the *cura* or *regimen morum,* which the sources tend to represent as the aspect that most strongly characterized the censorship. Interestingly, nowhere do the sources formally define the phrase itself, nor is there any legal expression that embodies the powers directed to its discharge. As Alan Astin rightly points out, "although *mores regere* in broad terms undoubtedly came to be regarded as a responsibility of the censors, it was a responsibility which did not originate with a formal definition or a clear delimitation of its content."[107] By looking through the

---

105. Cf. Krostenko 2001: 36 note 51 where he rightly supports Baeheren's instinct to see "*auarus* as subsuming the following list of vices."
106. Goldberg 2005: 13 note 32. For the *carmen* in question see, Cicero, *TD* 4.4 and Valerius Maximus 7.2.1. For an exhaustive and compelling study of Appius Claudius Caecus, see now Humm 2005, especially 521–40.
107. Astin 1988: 15.

sources (in which Cato's speeches feature large), Astin points out that the *regimen morum* was given expression in the *lectio senatus,* the *recognitio equitum,* and the census itself; as a result, we should think of it as a development that stands in a direct relationship with the fulfillment of those duties. In this respect, the downgrading of an individual to a lower *classis* suggests that the *regimen morum* stemmed from judgments passed on individuals who showed themselves unfit to be members of the group or category of citizens to which they belonged. By the same token, judgments on isolated cases would have dovetailed with a larger supervision of conduct and become the prerogative of the censors.[108]

Astin dismisses on documentary grounds speculative reconstructions that trace the origins of the *regimen morum* back to "primitive practices"; however, certain cases known from later sources indicate that in the earliest time the patrician *gentes* exercised their right to watch over the morals of their members.[109] In light of this precedent, the censorship emerges as an institution that absorbed into itself an existing area of gentilician jurisdiction and extended it to the civic community even while keeping a special focus on the higher orders.[110] As such, it is perhaps not out of place to think that the *regimen morum* fell right within the area of law, without being defined anywhere in the laws themselves. This becomes especially evident if, following Aldo Schiavone, we understand that *ius* finds its roots in the network of rules that regulated the interaction between clans and covered the most important aspects of the social behavior of the *patres.*[111] Regardless of defining the *regimen morum* in legal terms, it is clear that the personal discretion that the censors exercised over the actions that merited attention makes sense only if we envision a complex system of embodied practices carrying social meaning in relation and in contrast to one another. While we can gauge this system only with a high degree of approximation, it is impossible to deny that the censorial discretion over matters of behavior expressed the enormous responsibility and, therefore, prestige that went along with the fulfillment of the censorial role. Keen as he was to displace his *novitas,* Cato was particularly effective in maximizing the possibilities that the censorship opened up

---

108. Astin 1988: 16.
109. Suolahti 1963: 48, citing Valerius Maximus 3.5.1; Livy 41.27.2 and involving the *gens Cornelia.*
110. For censorial attention to equites and senators, see Astin 1988: 17–19.
111. Schiavone 2005. The picture drawn by Schiavone is rather complex and follows a diachronic trajectory that merges with a laicization of *ius* within a continuous exclusivity. The representation of the Twelve Tables as an anti-pontifical reaction and its laicizing character is contested by M. Humbert 2005, see especially 16–23.

for him in order to remain an enduring presence in the life of the Roman elite, both during and after his own lifetime. Indeed, his most successful strategy of self-fashioning was to keep playing a censorial role beyond the limited time of his office. By doing so, he extended a specific use of writing outside the censorial sphere and granted his compositions a type of textuality that enabled him to transform their underlying scenarios into enduring *exempla* and to control his own exemplarity beyond the limits of his existence.[112]

---

112. For a recent appraisal of self-exemplarity focused on Cicero and Augustus, see Lowrie 2007.

Conclusion

In many ways the ongoing debate over the early formation of Latin literature has done much to reveal the predicaments that derive from the 'discursive' make-up of concepts like authorship, text, literature, and genre. Methodologically, 'discourse' draws its force from the feeling of groundlessness and groundedness that it triggers: on the one hand it undermines the unity of signs and the relationship between signifier (*parole*) and signified (*langue*); on the other hand it circumscribes the world within the limits of language. In the study of Latin literature the equation between 'discourse' and 'text' has helped the construction of literary histories and the theorization of intertextuality; however, this equation encounters notable limitations when the area of investigation exceeds the sphere of literary meaning and includes embodied experience.[1] This study has attempted to deal with these limitations by trying to strike a balance between how we apprehend late-third- and early-second-centuries B.C.E. Latin texts today and how their production affected and was affected by the recognition patterns of their authors and the receiving public of the time. For this purpose I relied on notions of selfhood that encompass bodily and spatial dimensions.

The notion of subjectivity that I have employed draws on the idea that in the Roman context personhood was shaped by different experiences of

---

1. On this issue from the perspective of neuroscience, see Bryson 2003.

the world and rested upon the development of a keen sense of the body's connectedness with a socio-cosmological reality in which things have meaning in themselves. This connectedness was not achieved through the *creation* of significations that were detached from the material aspect of the world; rather, it was based on the *discovery* of and *adherence* to a socio-cosmological order materially perceived.[2] Thus, I see agency as being predetermined by a person's place in this order and conceive of knowledge as being attached to this person's ability to grasp socio-cosmological relations and make them discernible through the body. In the Roman context the term that best encapsulates the power that derives from both is *auctoritas*. In this study I have argued that the degree of *auctoritas* enjoyed and achieved by an author determined his choice of forms, themes, and modalities of writing; in turn, forms, themes, and modalities of writing made manifest the author's positioning in the world and affected the reception of his texts. On this score, rather than simply summarizing the argument of the previous chapters, I thought it best in this conclusion to draw out some open-ended points.

My first point is that the coincidence between the establishment of Latin poetry and the translation activities of professional immigrants invites considerations of the histories of geographical displacement and social adaptation that informed poetic aestheticism in Rome. To take into account these histories seems *prima facie* irrelevant since the self-confident relationship that Latin poetry establishes from the outset with the Hellenistic tradition promotes the overall impression that poetry helped these immigrants to transcend effortlessly (and painlessly) barriers of language, class, status, and traditions. In her seminal work "Can the Subaltern Speak?" Gayatri Spivak asks whether it is possible for the subaltern to speak especially after intellectuals have been reporting what s/he says for generations. Rather discouragingly, she suggests that access to the 'subaltern consciousness' might be gained not through what is in the texts but through the gaps, silences, and contradictions that these texts bear.[3] To work through textual gaps, silences, and contradictions is what classicists do already on a daily basis: not only can they get their hands on a very limited number of texts, but many of the texts that have survived the shipwreck of time are shards embedded in the reports of others. Accordingly, to strip away the accretion of meanings built over time and to see antiquity as an objective reality is

---

2. I am here drawing on the typological distinction between 'meaning cultures' and 'presence cultures' outlined by Gumbrecht (2004: 78–86).

3. Spivak 1988

fraught with problems that are unsurmountable.[4] In light of this, trying to get at the consciousness of an author and passing a representation of it as a faithful reconstruction would mean to doom oneself to failure.

What I have done has been to think about the effects that the migratory experiences of the early poets may have had on their perception of the world without pretending to uncover their 'true' or even 'essential' consciousness. I have also asked whether their fictional constructs could say something about the way these poets perceived their being in the world through identification with or dissociation from them. With this in mind, I have reread some of the places in the texts where self-reference seems to emerge, following up my desire to come to a better understanding of the possibilities and constrictions that loomed over them as well as the associated costs and gains that they derived from their translating/transformational skills. I have argued that these poets manipulated Greek literary texts in order to make Rome their home and capitalized on elite desires of socio-cosmological mastery already in place. I have also raised the possibility that their crafts allowed for multiple reflections and identifications in the face of Rome's geopolitical expansion, demanding memorialization and adjustments of identificatory boundaries from the body politic.[5] My discussion includes also an account of how poetry was appropriated into elite practices through mimicry and subjection, giving, perhaps, the impression that I have worked all along with the assumption that sociopolitical power always trumps cultural power. In reality, I have operated from only four ideas: one, that immigrants do not always want or even find it easy to assimilate and conform, to seamlessly translate themselves and their knowledge into the society that hosts them just because that society offers them opportunities; two, that the immigrants' original sites of self-making are often infused with tensions and inconsistencies because they themselves include coexisting and contradictory ways of life and social organizations; three, that their multiple identification with and versatility in multiple traditions can be perceived as menacing, confusing, and irresistible. This perception triggers a wide range of responses in the receiving culture and opens up an equally wide range of possibilities. Fourth and last, the acceptance or welcoming of immigrants by the sociopolitical powerful in the hosting society does not always dovetail with a social embracing of them as equals; if so, this embracing is rather possessive and is aimed at containing and exploiting the power inherent in the expanded

---

4. For a reflection on these problems from the point of view of reception theory, see Martindale and Thomas 2006: 9–10.

5. I draw here on the comments of one of the anonymous readers of my manuscript.

knowledge of the world that immigrants inevitably carry. Translation studies and reflections on global identities may provide classicists with some useful materials for trying to make sense of Roman translation practices. In turn, classicists can offer some innovative insights in those areas of scholarly inquiry and are presented with a unique opportunity for coming to terms with classics as a multifarious and multicultural discipline, and with the translating practices that foster it.[6]

My second point is that Cato the Censor is most famous for his ambiguous relationship with both poets and Greek culture. On the one hand, he sneers at the encroachment of poetry and its practitioners on elite defining practices and resists the impact of Greek literature on the social formation of this elite; on the other, what remains of his writings make clear that he was well versed in Greek literature and adopted poetic imagery and formalities. This seemingly contradictory attitude opens up a whole set of interpretative possibilities, especially once we fully acknowledge that bilingualism, if not trilingualism, must have been a long existing reality among the Italian and Roman elites.[7] For one thing, it forces us to rethink the impact that the turns and twists of language and culture performed by the early poets had on the receiving end. In my view, Cato's ambivalent positioning explains a lot about the charm that these poets embodied and exuded; at the same time, it reveals the strategies that Cato adopted in order to compensate for his *novitas* and to valorize his *auctoritas*. As a result, Cato's choice (and invention) of Latin prose emerges as overdetermined, arising from multiple factors. Some of these are implicated in his own social and political existence.

My third point is that no discussion of early Latin prose can be fully appreciated without taking into account the *carmen* and the problems that it elicits. As challenging as it is already to work with highly fragmentary (and neglected) materials, the pervasive presence of formalities bracketed under the rubric of '*carmen* style' that these materials embed makes for more than one complication. I will only mention the two that, in my view, are most conspicuous. The first has to do with the fact that we just do not have enough material to be able to generically organize its manifestations; in fact, it would appear that there was nothing generic about it especially if by generic we mean something similar to that which Latin poetry has got us accustomed. The second complication derives from the little attention

---

6. For a recent attempt in this direction, see Lianeri and Zajko 2008. For focused work on translation practices in the ancient Mediterranean, see McElduff and Sciarrino 2011.

7. Cf. Adams (2003: 9–14) for anecdotes about elite bilingualism (Latin and Greek) and the problems associated with its interpretation.

given to the *carmen* as a cultural form manifesting a person's alignment with and mastery of a socio-cosmological reality in which humans occupy a particular space and act according to specific codes of conduct. In light of this rather unfamiliar perception of the world, any resurrection of the *carmen* seems to hit the field as a repressed memory. The psychological imagery that I am using is undoubtedly unpleasant but not inappropriate if the traditional association of the *carmen* with the primordial is given concentrated consideration. For some classicists, this resurrection may be haunted by memories of the Fascist revival of ancient Rome as an energizing myth for constructing a new national greatness. For others, it may threaten the sense of security that Latinists have been able to achieve by working hard on the reception of well-documented traditions through extended texts. For yet others, it may mean to indulge in the deluded desire to experience a past untainted by modernity. Whatever the case, this book is an invitation to use the study of archaic Latin prose as an occasion for reflecting on the assumptions that we go by.

To return to the *carmen* through the formalities and the memories that are inscribed in the texts attributed to Cato the Censor, as I have tried to do, is a way to shed its primordial connotations and to acknowledge a perception of reality that goes under as soon as we resist it. I hope to have succeeded in articulating a notion of 'literature' that better describes the textual landscape of the time and that helps account for generic distinctions in practical terms. This notion defies any disembodied sequence of literary production and consumption by foregrounding a number of variables as additional factors that affected both authors and receivers. These include the temporal relationship between the production of a text and its consumption, the modes in which a text is apprehended, and the scenarios that inform its content and form.

Finally, my decision to leave undiscussed the extensive work done on the formation of the Greek prose tradition has nothing to do with a deliberate attempt to jettison the numerous insights that they have to offer.[8] Rather, I felt that their potent explanatory power would have led me to make extensive analogies and therefore to clutter my view of the object of my inquiry. At this point, however, a few remarks are in order. It is clear that just as in other contexts, in Rome the emergence of Latin prose was chronologically secondary to versified cultural forms that enjoyed an aura of authority derived from their connection with a superordinate reality.

---

8. I am thinking especially about Hartog 1988; Louraux 1986; Farrar 1989; Wardy 1996; Goldhill 2002; Kurke 2010. But see also the last chapter in Godzich and Kittay 1987.

While these cultural forms tend to be methodologically clustered under the rubric of poetry, my study clarifies that Latin prose evolves out of and draws on the socio-cosmological power that the *carmen* (both a pre-poetic and nonpoetic cultural expression) was believed to exude. This means that the *carmen* is an additional factor that cannot be disregarded and a cultural form that helped Cato disown poetry and yet to exploit it all the same. By observing the emergence of Latin prose, the social secondariness of both poetry and its practitioners, the scriptic nature of their practices, and the metrical laws by which they abided enter our purview in ways that shed important light on Roman cultural practices in general and the Latin definition of prose as *verba soluta* (loosened words) in particular. In relation to its earliest attestations, this definition does not bring Latin prose closer to the unsophisticated and underdeveloped; rather, it expresses its sociopolitical primacy over poetry and the *auctoritas* strenuously achieved and wielded by its inventor.

Bibliography

Abel, L. 1963. *Metatheatre: A New View of Dramatic Form.* New York: Hill and Wang.

Adams, J. N. 2003. *Bilingualism and the Latin Language.* Cambridge: Cambridge University Press.

Ager, B. 2009. "Contracts and Rituals in Cato's *De Agricultura.*" Paper delivered at the American Philological Association Convention, Philadelphia.

Alfonsi, L. 1954. "Catone il Censore e l'umanesimo romano." *Parola del passato* 9: 161–76.

Anderson, B. R. 1991. *Imagined Communities: Reflections on the Origin and Spread of Nationalism.* Revised and extended edition. London: Verso.

Anderson, W. S. 1993. *Barbarian Play: Plautus' Roman Comedy.* Toronto: University of Toronto Press.

André, J.-M. 1966. *L'otium dans la vie morale et intellectuelle romaine.* Paris: Presses universitaires de France.

Andreau, J. 1987. *La vie financière dans le monde romain: Les métiers de maniers d'argent* (IVe siècle av. J.-C. IIIe siècle ap J.-C.). Rome: École Française de Rome.

Apter, E. 2006. *The Translation Zone: A New Comparative Literature.* Princeton: Princeton University Press.

Astin, A. 1967. *Scipio Aemilianus.* Oxford: Clarendon Press; New York: Oxford University Press.

———. 1978. *Cato the Censor.* Oxford: Clarendon Press; New York: Oxford University Press.

———. 1988. "Regimen Morum." *Journal of Roman Studies* 78: 14–34.

Austin, J. L. [1962] 1975. *How to Do Things with Words.* Oxford: Clarendon Press.

Badian, E. 1972. "Ennius and His Friends." *Fondation Hardt Entretiens XVII: Ennius.* Vandoeuvres-Geneva. 149–208.

———. 1985. "*Nobiles Amici:* Art and Literature in an Aristocratic Society." *Classical Philology* 18: 341–57.
Bain, D. 1979. "Plautus Vortit Barbare: Plautus, Bacchides 526–61 and Menander, Dis Exapaton, 102–12." In D. A. West and A. J. Woodman (eds.), *Creative Imitations and Latin Literature.* Cambridge: Cambridge University Press. 17–34.
Baldi, P. 1999. *The Foundations of Latin.* The Hague: Mouton de Gruyter.
Bakker, E. J. 2005. *Pointing at the Past: From Formula to Performance in Homeric Poetics.* Cambridge, MA: Harvard University Press.
Balsdon, J. P. V. D. 1979. *Romans and Aliens.* London: Duckworth.
Barchiesi, A. 1997. "Otto punti su una mappa dei naufragi." In D. Fowler and S. Hinds (eds.), *Memoria, arte allusiva, intertestualità. Materiali e Discussioni* 39: 209–26.
———. 2005. "Lane Switching and Jughandles in Contemporary Interpretations of Roman Poetry." *Transactions of the American Philological Association* 135: 135–62.
Barchiesi, M. 1962. *Nevio epico.* Padova: Cedam.
———. 1970. "Plauto e il 'metateatro' antico.'" *Verri* 4: 113–30.
Barsby, J. 2007. "Rhetoric and Comedy: Plautus and Terence." In J. W. Dominik and J. Hall, (eds.), *A Companion to Roman Rhetoric.* Oxford: Blackwell Publishing. 38–53.
Barwick, K. 1948. "Zu den Schriften des Cornelius Celsus und des alten Cato." *Würz. Jahrb. Altert.* 3: 117–32.
Bassnett, S. and Trivedi, H. (eds.), 1999. *Post-colonial Translation: Theory and Practice.* London and New York: Routledge.
Batstone, W. W. 2005. "Plautine Farce and Plautine Freedom: An Essay on the Value of Metatheatre." In W. W. Batstone and G. Tissol (eds.), *Defining Genre and Gender in Latin Literature. Essays Presented to W. S. Anderson on His Seventy-Fifth Birthday.* New York: Peter Lang. 13–46.
Beacham, R. C. 1992. *The Roman Theatre and Its Audience.* Cambridge, MA: Harvard University Press.
———. 1999. *Spectacle Entertainments of Early Imperial Rome.* New Haven: Yale University Press.
Bell, C. 1992. *Ritual Theory, Ritual Practice.* New York: Oxford University Press.
———. 1997. *Ritual: Perspectives and Dimensions.* New York: Oxford University Press.
Benjamin, W. [1936] 1969. *Illuminations: Essays and Reflections.* New York: Schocken.
Bernhardy, G. 1850. *Grundriss der Römischen Litteratur.* 2nd ed. Braunschweig: C. A. Schwetschke.
Bhabha, H. K. 1994. *The Location of Culture.* London and New York: Routledge.
Blänsford, J. 1995. *Fragmenta Poetarum Latinorum Epicorum et Lyricorum Praeter Ennium et Lucilium.* 3rd ed. Leipzig: Teubner.
Bloomer, W. M. 1997. *Latinity and Literary Society at Rome.* Philadelphia: University of Pennsylvania Press.
Blösel, W. 2000. "Die Geschichte des Begriffes *Mos Maiorum* von den Anfängen bis zu Cicero." In B. Linke and M. Stemmler (eds.), *Mos Maiorum: Untersuchungen zu den Formen der Identitätsstiftung und Stabilisierung in der römischen Republik.* Stuttgart: Franz Steiner Verlag. 25–97.

Bonfante, L. 1986. (ed.), *Etruscan Life and Afterlife. A Handbook of Etruscan Studies*. Warminster: Aris & Phillips.
Bormann, A. 1858. *M. Porcii Catonis Originum libri septem. Reliquias disposuit et de instituto operis disputauit*. A. B. Branderburgii.
Bourdieu, P. 1990. *The Logic of Practice*. Stanford: Stanford University Press.
Bowditch, P. L. 2001. *Horace and the Gift Economy of Patronage*. Berkeley: University of California Press.
Boyle, A. J. (ed.). 1993. *Roman Epic*. London and New York: Routledge.
Bradley, K. R. 1994. *Slavery and Society at Rome*. Cambridge: Cambridge University Press.
Braziel, J. E. and Mannur, A. 2003. *Theorizing Diaspora: A Reader*. Oxford: Blackwell.
Brink, C. O. 1971. *Horace on Poetry*. Cambridge: Cambridge University Press.
Brooks, R. A. [1949] 1981. *Ennius and Roman Tragedy*. New York: Arno Press.
Brown, P. G. McC. 2002. "Actors and Actor-Managers at Rome in the time of Plautus and Terence." In P. Easterling and J. Hall (eds.), *Greek and Roman Actors: Aspects of an Ancient Profession*. Cambridge and New York: Cambridge University Press. 225-37.
Brown, R. M. 1934 "A Study of the Scipionic Circle." *Iowa Studies in Classical Philology* 1: 3-84.
Brunt, P. A. 1971. *Italian Manpower, 225 B.C.–A.D. 14*. London: Oxford University Press.
Bryson, N. 2003. "Introduction: The Neural Interface." In W. Neidich, *Blow-up: Photography, Cinema and the Brain*. Riverside: D.A.P./UCR/California Museum of Photography. 11–19
Burckhardt, L. 1990. "The Political Elite of the Roman Republic: Comments on Recent Discussions of the Concepts of *Nobilitas* and *Homo Novus*." *Historia* 39: 77–99.
Butler, J. 1997. *Excitable Speech: A Politics of the Performance*. New York and London: Routledge
Butler, S. 2002. *The Hand of Cicero*. London and New York: Routledge.
Calboli, G. 2003. *Oratio pro Rhodiensibus. Catone, l'oriente greco e gli imprenditori romani*. 2nd ed. Bologna: Patron.
Calderini, A. 1944. *La Censura in Roma antica*. Milano: Università Cattolica del Sacro Cuore.
Cardinali, L. 1988. "Le *Origines* di Catone iniziavano con un esametro?" *Studi classici e orientali* 37: 205–15.
Cavarzere, A. 2000. *Oratoria a Roma. Storia di un genere pragmatico*. Roma: Carocci.
Chassignet, M. 1987. "Caton et l'impérialisme romain au IIe siècle av. J.-C. d'après les *Origines*." *Latomus* 46: 285–300.
Cheyfitz, E. 1991. *The Poetics of Imperialism: Translation and Colonization from the Tempest to Tarzan*. New York: Oxford University Press.
Churchill, Bradford J. 1995. "On the Content and the Structure of the Prologue to Cato's *Origines*." *Illinois Classical Studies* 20: 91–106.
———. 1999. "Ex qua quod vellent facerent: Roman Magistrates' Authority over Praeda and Manubiae." *Transactions of the American Philological Association* 129: 85–116.
Clackson, J. and Horrocks, G. 2007. *The Blackwell History of the Latin Language*. Oxford: Blackwell Publishing.

Clarke, M. L. 1966. *Rhetoric at Rome: A Historical Survey.* 2nd ed. London: Cohen & West.

Clover, C. 1987. "Her Body, Himself: Gender in the Slasher Film." *Representations* 20: 187–228.

Coarelli, F. 1968. "L''Ara di Domizio Enobarbo'e la cultura artistica in Roma nel II secolo a.C." *Dialoghi di Archeologia* 2: 302–68.

———. 1995. "Vino e ideologia nella Roma archaica." In O. Murray and M. Tecusan (eds.), *In Vino Veritas.* London: British School at Rome.

Colonna G. 1976. "Scriba cum rege sedens." *L'Italie préromaine et la Rome républicaine: Mélanges offerts à J. Hergon.* L'École Française de Rome. 187–95.

Connolly, J. 2005. "Border Wars: Literature, Politics, and the Public." *Transaction of the American Philological Association* 135: 103–34.

———. 2007. *The State of Speech: Rhetoric and Political Thought in Ancient Rome.* Princeton: Princeton University Press.

Connors, C. 1997. "Field and Forum: Culture and Agriculture in Roman Rhetoric." In W. J. Dominik (ed.), *Roman Eloquence: Rhetoric in Society and Literature.* New York: Routledge. 71–89.

———. 2004. "Monkey Business: Imitation, Authenticity, and Identity from Pithekoussai to Plautus." *Classical Antiquity* 23: 179–207.

Conte, G. B. 1986. *The Rhetoric of Imitation: Genre and Poetic Memory in Virgil and Other Latin Poets.* Trans. by C. Segal. Ithaca, NY: Cornell University Press.

Cooley, A. E. 2009. *Res Gestae Divi Augusti: Text, Translation, and Commentary.* Cambridge: Cambridge University Press.

Corbett, P. 1984. *The Scurra.* Edinburgh: Scottish Academic Press.

Cornell, T. J. 1991. "The Tyranny of the Evidence: A Discussion of the Possible Uses of Literacy in Etruria and Latium in the Archaic Age." In *Literacy in the Roman World, Journal of Roman Studies* Suppl. 3: 7–33.

———. 1995. *The Beginnings of Rome: Italy and Rome from the Bronze Age to the Punic Wars, c. 1000–264 B.C.* London: Routledge.

———. 1996. "Hannibal's Legacy: The Effects of the Second Punic War on Italy." In T. J. Cornell, B. Rankov, and P. Sabin (eds.), *The Second Punic War: A Reappraisal.* Bulletin of the Institute of Classical Studies, Suppl. 67. 97–117.

——— and Lomas, K. (eds.), 1997. *Gender and Ethnicity in Ancient Italy.* London: Accordia Specialist Studies on Italy.

———. 2003. "Coriolanus: Myth, History and Performance." In D. Braund and C. Gill (eds.), *Myth, History and Culture in Republican Rome: Studies in Honour of T. P. Wiseman.* Exeter: University of Exeter Press. 73–97.

Costa, G. 2000. *Sulla preistoria della tradizione poetica italica.* Firenze: Olschki Editore.

Courtney, E. 1999. *Archaic Latin Prose.* Atlanta: Scholars Press.

Crawford, M. H. 1996. *Roman Statutes. Bulletin of the Institute of Classical Studies,* Suppl. 64. London.

Cristofani, M. 1979. *The Etruscans: A New Investigation.* London: Orbis.

Crook, J. 1976. "*Sponsione Provocare:* Its Place in Roman Litigation." *Journal of Roman Studies* 64: 132–38.

Csapo, E. and Miller, M. C. 2007. *The Origins of Theater in Ancient Greece and Beyond. From Ritual to Drama.* Cambridge: Cambridge University Press.

Cugusi, P. 1994. "Il proemio delle *Origines* di Catone." *MAIA* 46: 263–72.
Cugusi, P. and Sblendorio Cugusi, M. T. 2001. *Marco Porcio Catone Censore. Opere*. 2 vols. Torino: UTET.
Dahlmann, H. 1950. "Zur Überlieferung über altrömische Tafellieder." Abhandlungen der Geistes- und Sozialwissenschaftlichen Klasse Akademie der Wissenschaften und der Literatur in Mainz: 1193–1202.
Dalby, A. 1998. *Cato, On Farming (De Agricultura)*. A modern translation with commentary. Totnes: Prospect Books.
David, J.-M. 1997. *The Roman Conquest of Italy*. Trans. by A. Nevill. Oxford: Wiley-Blackwell.
Davies, C. B. 1994. *Black Women, Writing and Identity: Migrations of the Subject*. New York and London: Routledge.
Della Corte, F. 1969. *Catone Censore. La vita e la fortuna*. 2nd ed. Firenze: La Nuova Italia.
De Meo, C. 1986. *Lingue tecniche del latino*. 2nd ed. Bologna: Patron.
Dench, E. 1995. *From Barbarians to New Men: Greek, Roman, and Modern Perceptions of Peoples of the Central Apennines*. Oxford: Clarendon Press; New York: Oxford University Press.
———. 2005. *Romulus' Asylum: Roman Identities from the Age of Alexander to the Age of Hadrian*. Oxford: Oxford University Press.
De Simone, C. 1980. "L'aspetto linguistico." In C. M. Stibbe, G. Colonna, C. de Simone, H. S. Versnel, and M. Pallottino (eds.), *Lapis Satricanus. Archaeological, Epigraphical, Linguistic and Historical Aspects of the New Inscription from Satricum*. The Hague: Staatsuitgeverij. 71–94.
Duckworth, G. E. 1994. *The Nature of Roman Comedy. A Study in Popular Entertainment*. 2nd ed. Norman: University of Oklahoma Press.
Dugan, J. 2001. "How to Make (and Break) a Cicero: Epideixis, Textuality, and Self-fashioning in the *Pro Archia* and *In Pisonem*." *Classical Antiquity* 20: 35–77.
———. 2005. *Making a New Man: Ciceronian Self-Fashioning in the Rhetorical Works*. Oxford and New York: Oxford University Press.
Dupont, F. 1985. *L'acteur-roi. Le théatre à Rome*. Paris: Belles Lettres.
———. 1999. *The Invention of Literature: From Greek Intoxication to the Latin Book*. Trans. by J. Lloyd. Baltimore and London: Johns Hopkins University Press.
———. 2000. *L'orateur sans visage. Essay sur l'acteur romain et son masque*. Paris: Presses Universitaires de France.
———. 2005. "Altérité incluse." In F. Dupont and E. Valette-Cagnac (eds.), *Façons de parler grec à Rome*. Paris: Belin. 255–77.
———. 2009. "The Corrupted Boy and the Crowned Poet." In W. A. Johnson and H. N. Parker (eds.), *Ancient Literacies: The Culture of Reading in Greece and Rome*. Oxford: Oxford University Press. 143–63.
Edmondson, J. C. 1999. "The Cultural Politics of Public Spectacle in Rome and the Greek East, 167–166 B.C.E." In B. Bergman and C. Kondoleon (eds.), *The Art of Ancient Spectacle*. Studies in the History of Art, 56. Center for Advanced Study in the Visual Arts. National Gallery of Art, Washington. 77–89.
Edmunds, L. 2001. *Intertextuality and the Reading of Roman Poetry*. Baltimore: Johns Hopkins University Press.

Edwards, C. 1993. *The Politics of Immorality in Ancient Rome.* Cambridge: Cambridge University Press.

Elliott, J. 2007. "The Voices of Ennius' *Annals.*" In W. Fitzgerald and E. Gowers (eds.), *Ennius Perennis: The Annals and Beyond.* Cambridge Classical Journal, Proceedings of the Cambridge Philological Society, Suppl. 31. Cambridge: Cambridge University Press. 38–54.

Elsner, J. (ed.). 1996. *Art and Text in Roman Culture.* Cambridge, New York and Melbourne: Cambridge University Press.

Ernout, A. [1959] 1994. *Dictionnaire etymologique de la langue latine, histoire des mots.* 4th ed. Paris: Klincksieck

Farney, G. D. 2007. *Ethnic Identity and Aristocratic Competition in Republican Rome.* Cambridge: Cambridge University Press.

Farrar, C. 1989. *The Origins of Democratic Thinking: The Invention of Politics in Classical Athens.* Cambridge: Cambridge University Press.

Farrell, J. 2007. "Sander M. Goldberg. Constructing Literature in the Roman Republic: Poetry and Its Reception" (review). *American Journal of Philology* 128.2: 283–86.

———. 2009. "The Impermanent Text in Catullus and Other Roman Poets." In W. A. Johnson and H. N. Parker (eds.), *Ancient Literacies: The Culture of Reading in Greece and Rome.* Oxford: Oxford University Press. 164–85.

Feldherr, A. 2000. *"Non inter nota sepulchra:* Catullus 101 and Roman Funerary Rituals." *Classical Antiquity,* 19.2: 209–231.

Feeney, D. 1998. *Literature and Religion at Rome: Cultures, Contexts, and Beliefs.* Cambridge and New York: Cambridge University Press.

———. 2002. "The Odiousness of Comparisons: Horace on Literary History and the Limitations of Synkrisis." In M. Paschalis (ed.), *Horace and Greek Lyric Poetry.* Rethymnon Classical Studies 1: 7–18.

———. 2005. "The Beginnings of a Literature in Latin." *Journal of Roman Studies* 95: 226–40.

Feeney, D. and Katz, J. T. 2006. "T. Habinek. *The World of Roman Song: from Ritualized Speech to Social* Order" (review). *Journal of Roman Studies* 96: 240–42.

Finley, M. I. 1980. *Ancient Slavery and Modern Ideology.* New York: Penguin Books.

Fitzgerald, W. 1995. *Catullan Provocations: Lyric Poetry and the Drama of Position.* Berkeley and Los Angeles: Berkeley University Press.

———. 2000. *Slavery and the Roman Literary Imagination.* Cambridge and New York: Cambridge University Press.

Fletcher, K. F. B. 2011. "Teaching Romans to Write Greek Myth: Parthenius, Gallus and the *Erotica Pathemata.*" In S. McElduff and E. Sciarrino (eds.), *Complicating the History of Western Translation: The Ancient Mediterranean in Perspective.* Manchester: St Jerome Publishing. 12–24.

Flintoff, E. 1988. "Naevius and Roman Satire." *Latomus* 47: 593–603.

Flores, E. 2000. *Quinto Ennio, Annali (Libri I–VIII).* Introduzione, testo critico con apparati, traduzione. Vol. I. Napoli: Liguori Editore.

———. Esposito, P., Jackson, G., and Tomasco, D. 2002. *Quinto Ennio, Annali (Libri I–VIII): Commentari.* Vol. II. Napoli: Liguori Editore.

Flower, H. I. 1995. "Fabulae Praetextae in Context: When Were Plays on Contemporary Subjects Performed in Republican Rome?" *Classical Quarterly* 45: 170–90.

———. 1996. *Ancestor Masks and Aristocratic Power in Roman Culture.* Oxford: Clarendon Press; New York: Oxford University Press.
———. 2010. *Roman Republics.* Princeton: Princeton University Press.
Fowler, D. 1995. "Modern Literary Theory and Latin Poetry: Some Anglo-American Perspectives." *Arachnion* 1.2 (http://www.cisi.unito.it/arachne/num2/fowler.html).
———. 2000. *Roman Constructions: Readings in Postmodern Latin.* Oxford and New York: Oxford University Press.
Fraccaro, P. [1911] 1956. "I processi degli Scipione." *Studi storici per l'antichità classica* 4: 217–414. Reprinted in: *Opuscula Archeologica,* 1: 263–392.
Fraenkel, E. [1922] 2007. *Plautine Elements in Plautus (Plautinisches im Plautus).* Trans. by T. Drevikovsky and F. Muecke. Oxford: Oxford University Press.
———. 1964. *Kleine Beitrage zur klassischen Philologie.* Roma: Edizioni di storia e letteratura.
———.1968. *Leseproben aus Reden Ciceros und Catos.* Roma: Edizioni di storia e letteratura.
Frier, B. W. 1979. *Liber Annales Pontificum Maximorum. The Origins of the Annalistic Tradition.* Papers and Monographs of the American Academy in Rome 27. Ann Arbor: The University of Michigan Press.
Gabba, E. 1993. *Aspetti culturali dell'imperialismo romano.* Firenze: Sansoni.
Galinsky, K. 1996. *Augustan Culture: An Interpretive Introduction.* Princeton: Princeton University Press
Gamel, M.-K. 1998. "Reading as a Man: Performance and Gender in Roman Elegy." *Helios* 25.1: 79–95.
Garbarino, G. 1973. *Roma e la filosofia greca dalle origini alla fine del II secolo a.C.* Torino: Paravia.
Gargola, D. J. 1995. *Lands, Laws, and Gods: Magistrates and Ceremony in the Regulation of Public Lands in Republican Rome.* Chapel Hill: University of North Carolina Press.
Gentili, B. 1979. *Theatrical Performances in the Ancient World: Hellenistic and Early Roman Theater.* Amsterdam: J. C. Gieben.
Gelzer, M. 1969. *The Roman Nobility.* Trans. by Robin Seager. Oxford: Blackwell.
Gildenhard, I. 2003a. "The 'Annalist' before the Annalists: Ennius and his *Annales*." In U. Eigler, U. Gotter, N. Luraghi, and U. Walter (eds.), *Formen römischer Geschichtsschreibung von den Anfängen bis Livius. Gattungen-Autoren-Kontexte.* Darmstadt: Wissenschaftliche Buchgesellschaft. 93–114.
———. 2003b. Review of Suerbaum, W. ed. 2002. *Handbuch der lateinischen Literatur der Antike. Erster Band: Die archaische Literatur. Von den Anfängen bis zu Sullas Tod. Die vorliterarische Period und die Zeit von 240 bis 78 v.Chr.* 8.1. Munich. *BMCR* 2003.09.39.
———. 2007a. *Paideia Romana. Cicero's Tusculan Disputations.* Cambridge Classical Journal, Proceedings of the Cambridge Philological Society, Suppl. 30. Cambridge: Cambridge University Press.
———. 2007b. "Virgil vs. Ennius, or: The Undoing of the Annalist." In W. Fitzgerald and E. Gowers (eds.), *Ennius Perennis: The Annals and Beyond.* Cambridge Classical Journal, Proceedings of the Cambridge Philological Society, Suppl. 31. Cambridge: Cambridge University Press. 73–102.

Giles, H. and Powesland, P. F. 1975. *Speech Style and Social Evaluation.* London: Academic Press.

Godzich, W. and Kittay, J. 1987. *The Emergence of Prose: An Essay in Prosaics.* Minneapolis: University of Minnesota Press.

Goldberg, S. M. 1986. *Understanding Terence.* Princeton: Princeton University Press.

———. 1995. *Epic in Republican Rome.* New York: Oxford University Press.

———. 2005. *Constructing Literature in the Roman Republic: Poetry and Its Reception.* Cambridge and New York: Cambridge University Press.

———. 2006. "Ennius after the Banquet." *Arethusa* 39.3: 427–48.

Goldhill, S. 2002. *The Invention of Prose.* Greece & Rome, New Surveys in Classics, 32. Oxford: Oxford University Press.

Gotter, U. 2003. "Die Vergangenheit als Kampfplatz der Gegenwart: Catos (konter) revolutionäre Konstruktion des republikanischen Erinnerungsraums." In U. Eigler, U. Gotter, N. Luraghi, and U. Walter, eds., *Formen römischer Geschichtsschreibung von den Anfängen bis Livius. Gattungen-Autoren-Kontexte.* Darmstadt: Wissenschaftliche Buchgesellschaft. 115–34.

———. 2009. "Cato's *Origines:* the Historian and His Enemies." In A. Feldherr, (ed.), *Cambridge Companion to the Roman Historians.* Cambridge: Cambridge University Press. 108–22.

Gowers, E. 2007. "The *Cor* of Ennius." In W. Fitzgerald and E. Gowers (eds.), *Ennius Perennis: The Annals and Beyond.* Cambridge Classical Journal, Proceedings of the Cambridge Philological Society, Suppl. 31. Cambridge: Cambridge University Press. 17–37.

Grandazzi, A. 1997. *The Foundation of Rome: Myth and History.* Trans. by J. M. Todd. Ithaca: Cornell University Press.

Gratwick, A. S. 2002. "A Matter of Substance: Cato's Preface to the *De Agri Cultura.*" *Mnemosyne* 55.1: 41–72

Greenberg, J. R. and Mitchell, S. A. 1983. *Object Relations in Psychoanalytic Theory.* Cambridge, MA: Harvard University Press.

Greenblatt, S. 1980. *Renaissance Self-Fashioning: From More to Shakespeare.* Chicago: University of Chicago Press.

Greenidge, A. J. 1911. *Roman Public Life.* London: McMillan.

———. [1894] 2002. *Infamia: Its Place in Roman Public and Private Law.* Buffalo, NY: W. S. Hein.

Grilli, A. 1965. *Studi Enniani.* Brescia: Paideia Editrice.

Gruen, E. S. 1990. *Studies in Greek Culture and Roman Policy.* Berkeley: University of California Press

———. 1992. *Culture and National Identity in Republican Rome.* Ithaca, NY: Cornell University Press.

———. 1995. "The 'Fall' of the Scipios." In I. Malkin and Z. W. Rubinshon (eds.), *Leaders and Masses in the Roman World. Studies in Honor of Zvi Yavetz.* Leiden, New York: Brill. 59–90.

———. 2004. "Rome and the Greek World." In I. F. Harriet (ed.), *The Cambridge Companion to the Roman Republic.* Cambridge: Cambridge University Press. 242–67.

Gumbrecht, H. U. 2004. *Production of Presence: What Meaning Cannot Convey.*

Stanford: Stanford University Press.
Gutzwiller, K. 2000. "The Tragic Mask of Comedy: Metatheatricality in Menander." *Classical Antiquity* 19.1: 102–37.
Güven, S. 1998. "Displaying the *Res Gestae* of Augustus: A Monument of Imperial Image for All." *Journal of the Society of Architectural Historians* 57.1: 30–45.
Habinek, T. N. 1985. *The Colometry of Latin Prose.* University of California Studies in Classical Philology 25. Berkeley: University of California Press.
———. 1990. "Towards a History of Friendly Advice: The Politics of *Candor* in Cicero's *De Amicitia.*" *Apeiron* 23: 165–85.
———. 1995. "Ideology for an Empire in the Prefaces to Cicero's Dialogues." In A. J. Boyle (ed.), *Roman Literature and Ideology: Ramus Essays for J. P. Sullivan.* Bendigo North: Aureal Publications. 55–67.
———. 1998a. *The Politics of Latin Literature: Writing, Identity and Empire in Ancient Rome.* Princeton: Princeton University Press.
———. 1998b. "Singing, Speaking, Making, Writing: Classical Alternatives to Literature and Literary Studies." *Stanford Humanities Review* 6: 65–75.
———. 2000. "Seneca's Renown: *Gloria, Claritudo,* and the Replication of the Roman Elite." *Classical Antiquity* 19.2: 264–303.
———. 2005a. *The World of Roman Song: From Ritualized Speech to Social Order.* Baltimore: Johns Hopkins University Press.
———. 2005b. "Latin Literature between Text and Practice." *Transactions of the American Philological Association* 135: 83–90.
———. 2006. "The Wisdom of Ennius." *Arethusa* 39: 471–88.
Hall, D. E. 2004. *Subjectivity.* London and New York: Routledge.
Halporn, J. 1993. "Roman Comedy and Greek Models." In R. Scodel (ed.), *Theatre and Society in the Classical World.* Ann Arbor: University of Michigan Press. 191–213.
Handley, E. W. 1975. "Plautus and His Public: Some Thoughts on New Comedy in Latin." *Dioniso* 46: 117–31.
Hardie, P. 1986. *Virgil's Aeneid: Cosmos and Imperium.* Oxford: Clarendon Press.
———. 2007 "Poets, Patrons, Rulers: The Ennian Traditions." In W. Fitzgerald and E. Gowers (eds.), *Ennius Perennis: The Annals and Beyond.* Cambridge Classical Journal, Proceedings of the Cambridge Philological Society, Suppl. 31. Cambridge: Cambridge University Press. 129–45.
Hardie, W. R. 1920. *Res Metrica.* Oxford: Clarendon Press.
Harris, W. V. 1989. *Ancient Literacy.* Cambridge, MA: Harvard University Press.
Hartog, F. 1988. *The Mirror of Herodotus: the Representation of the Other in the Writing of History.* Trans. by Janet Lloyd. Berkeley and Los Angeles: University of California Press.
Hartung, H.-J. 2004. "Kosmologische Aufklärung und sockratische Wende: Zwei Epochengrenzen und Paradigmenwechsel in Ciceros literarischen Entwurf der Aneignung griechischer Theorie in Rom." *Philologus* 148: 64–87.
Helm, R. 1956. *Eusebius Werke 7: Die Chronik des Hieronymus.* 2nd ed. Griechischen Christlichen Schriftsteller 47.
Helms, M. W. 1993. *Craft and the Kingly Ideal: Art, Trade, and Power.* Austin: University of Texas Press.

———. 1998. *Access to Origins: Affines, Ancestors, and Aristocrats*. Austin: University of Texas Press
Henrichs, A. 1995. "Graecia Capta: Roman Views of Greek Culture." *Harvard Studies in Classical Philology* 97: 243–61.
Herb, G. H. and Kaplan, D. H. 1999. *Nested Identities: Nationalism, Territory, and Scale*. New York: Rowman and Littlefield Publishers.
Hinds, S. 1998. *Allusion and Intertext: Dynamics of Appropriation in Roman Poetry*. New York and Cambridge: Cambridge University Press.
Hobsbawm, E. 1983. "Mass-Producing Traditions: Europe, 1870–1914." In E. Hobsbawm and T. Ranger (eds.), *The Invention of Tradition*. Cambridge: Cambridge University Press. 263–307
Hobsbawn, E. and Ranger, T. (eds.),. 1983. *The Invention of Tradition*. Cambridge: Cambridge University Press.
Hölkeskamp, K.-J. 1987. *Die Entstehung der Nobilität. Studien zur sozialen und politischen Geschichte der römischen Republik im 4. Jhdt. v. Chr.* Stuttgart: Franz Steiner Verlag.
———. 2004. *Senatus Populusque Romanus. Die politische Kultur der Republik-Dimensionen und Deutungen*. Stuttgart: Franz Steiner Verlag.
Holliday, P. J. 2002. *The Origins of Historical Commemoration in Visual Art*. Cambridge: Cambridge University Press.
Horsfall, N. 1994. "The Prehistory of Latin Poetry: Some Problems of Method." *Rivista di filologia e istruzione classica* 122: 50–75.
———. 2003. *The Culture of the Roman Plebs*. London: Duckworth.
Hose, M. 1999. "Post-Colonial Theory and Greek Literature in Rome." *Greek, Roman and Byzantine Studies* 40: 303–26.
Humbert, J. 1925. *Les pleidoyers écrits et les plaidoiries réelles de Ciceron*. Paris: Presses Universitaires de France.
Humbert, M. 2005. "La codificazione decemvirale: tentativo di interpretazione." In M. Humbert (ed.), *Le Dodici Tavole dai decemviri agli umanisti*. Pavia: IUSS Press. 3-50.
Humm, M. 2005. *Appius Claudius Caecus: La République accomplie*. Ecole Française de Rome.
Hunter, R. L. 1985. *The New Comedy of Greece and Rome*. Cambridge: Cambridge University Press.
Jaccottet, A. 2003. *Choisir Dionysos. Les associations dionysiaques ou la face cachée du dionysisme*. Vol. I: Text; II: Documents. Zürich: Akanthus.
Jaeger, M. 1997. *Livy's Written Rome*. Ann Arbor: University of Michigan Press.
Jocelyn, H. D. 1967. *The Tragedies of Ennius:* The Fragments. Cambridge: Cambridge University Press.
———. 2000. "*Accius' Aeneadae* aut *Decius:* Romans and the Gallic Other." In G. Manuwald (ed.), *Identitäten und Alteritäten in der frührömischen Tragödie*. Würzburg: Ergon. 325–61.
Johnson, M. 1990. *The Body in the Mind: the Bodily Basis of Meaning, Imagination, and Reason*. Chicago: University of Chicago Press.
Johnson, W. A. 2000. "Toward a Sociology of Reading in Classical Antiquity." *American Journal of Philology* 121: 593–627.

———, and Parker, H. 2009. *Ancient Literacies: The Culture of Reading in Greece and Rome.* Oxford: Oxford University Press.

Jongman, W. 2003 "Slavery and the Growth of Rome: The Transformation of Italy in the Second and First centuries B.C.E." In C. Edwards and G. Woolf (eds.), *Rome the Cosmopolis.* Cambridge: Cambridge University Press. 100–122.

Kaimio, J. 1979. *The Romans and the Greek Language.* Helsinki: Societas Scientiarum Fennica.

Kaster, R. A. 1995. *C. Suetonius Tranquillus: De Grammaticis et Rhetoribus.* Oxford: Clarendon Press.

———. 1998. "Becoming 'CICERO.'" In P. Knox and C. Foss (eds.), *Style and Tradition: Studies in Honor of Wendell Clausen.* Stuttgart and Leipzig: Teubner. 248–63.

Keith, A. 2007. "Women in Ennius' *Annals.*" In W. Fitzgerald and E. Gowers (eds.), *Ennius Perennis: The Annals and Beyond.* Cambridge Classical Journal, Proceedings of the Cambridge Philological Society, Suppl. 31. Cambridge: Cambridge University Press. 55–72.

Kennedy, G. A. 1994. *A New History of Classical Rhetoric.* Princeton: Princeton University Press.

Kosofsky Sedgwick, E. K. [1985] 1993. *Between Men: English Literature and Male Homosocial Desire.* New York: Columbia University Press.

Konstan, D. 1983. *Roman Comedy.* Ithaca, NY: Cornell University Press.

———. 2002. "Before Literature: A Contribution to the Colloquium on the Invention of 'Latin Literature' in Europe and Spain." Unpublished paper.

———. 2005. "Friendship and Patronage." In S. Harrison (ed.), *A Companion to Latin Literature.* Oxford: Blackwell. 345–50.

Krause, A. 1831. *Vitae et fragmenta ueterum historicorum Romanorum.* Berolini.

Krostenko, B. A. 2001. *Cicero, Catullus, and the Language of Social Performance.* Chicago: Chicago University Press.

Kuttner, A. 1993. "Some New Grounds for Narrative: Marcus Antonius's Base (The Ara Domitii Ahenobarbi) and Republican Biographies." in P. J. Holliday (ed.), *Narrative and Event in Ancient Art.* Cambridge: Cambridge University Press. 198–229.

———. 1991. "A Third Century B.C. Latin Census on a Praenestine Cist." *Romische Mitteilungen* 98: 141–61.

Kurke, L. 2006. "Plato, Aesop, and the Beginnings of Mimetic Prose." *Representations* 94: 6–52.

———. 2010. *Aesopic Conversations: Popular Tradition, Cultural Dialogue, and the Invention of Greek Prose.* Princeton: Princeton University Press.

Kytzler, B. 1989. "*Fidus Interpres:* The Theory and Practice of Translation in Classical Antiquity." *Antichthon* 23: 42–50.

Lakoff G. 2008. *The Meaning of the Body: Aesthetics of Human Understanding.* Reprint. Chicago: Chicago University Press.

———, and Johnson, M. 1999. *Philosophy in the Flesh: the Embodied Mind and Its Challenges to Western Thought.* New York: Basic Books.

Lebek, W. D. 1996. "Moneymaking on the Roman Stage." In W. J. Slater (ed.), *Roman Theater and Society: E. Togo Salmon Papers I.* Ann Arbor: University of Michigan Press.

Leeman, A. D. 1963. Orationis ratio: *The Stylistic Theories and Practice of the Roman Orators, Historians and Philosophers*. Amsterdam: A. M. Hakkert.
Lefèvre, E. 1993. "Waren horazische Gedichte zum 'öffentlichen' Vortrag bestsimmt?" In G. Vogt-Spira (ed.), *Beiträge zur mündlichen Kultur der Römer*. (ScriptOralia 47). Tübingen: GNV. 143–57.
Leigh, M. 2000. "Primitivism and Power: The Beginnings of Latin Literature." In O. Taplin (ed.), *Literature in the Greek and Roman Worlds*. Oxford: Oxford University Press. 268–310.
———. 2004. *Comedy and the Rise of Rome*. Oxford: Oxford University Press.
Lemosse, M. 1949. "L'Affranchisement per le cens." *Revue historique de droit français et étranger* 27:161–203.
Leo, F. 1913. *Geschichte der römischen Literatur* 1: *Die archaische Literatur*. Berlin: Weidmann.
———. [1912] 1966. *Plautinische Forschungen zur Kritik und Geschichte der Komödie*. 2nd ed. Darmstadt: Wissenschaftliche Buchgesellschaft.
Letta, C. 1984. "L'Italia dei mores romani nelle *Origines* di Catone." *Athenaeum* 62: 3–30, 416–39.
Lianeri, A. and Zajko, V. 2008. *Translation and the Classic: Identity as Change in the History of Culture*. Classical Presences. Oxford: Oxford University Press.
Lightfoot, J. L. (ed.), 1999. *Parthenius of Nicaea. The Poetical Fragments and the Ἐρωτικὰ παθήματα*. Oxford: Clarendon Press.
———. 2002. "Nothing to do with the *technitai* of Dionysus?" In P. Easterling and J. Hall (eds.), *Greek and Roman Actors: Aspects of an Ancient Profession*. Cambridge and New York: Cambridge University Press. 209–24.
Lintott, A. W. 1999. *The Constitution of the Roman Republic*. Oxford: Clarendon Press.
Lomas, K. 1997. "Constructing 'the Greek': Ethnic Identity in Magna Graecia." In T. Cornell and Lomas, K. (eds.), *Gender and Ethnicity in Ancient Italy*. London: Accordia Specialist Studies on Italy. 31–42.
Louraux N. 1986. *The Invention of Athens: the Funeral Oration in the Classical City*. Trans. by A. Sheridan. Cambridge, MA: Harvard University Press.
Lott, E. 1993. *Love and Theft: Blackface Minstrelsy and the American Working Class*. New York: Oxford University Press.
Lowrie, M. 1997. *Horace's Narrative Odes*. Oxford: Clarendon Press; New York: Oxford University Press.
———. 2005. "Inside Out: In Defense of Form." *Transaction of the American Philological Association* 135: 35–48.
———. 2006. "Review of T. Habinek 2005. *The World of Roman Song: From Ritualized Speech to Social Order*." *BMCR* 2006.04.34.
———. 2007. "Making an Exemplum of Yourself: Cicero and Augustus." In S. J. Heyworth, P. G. Fowler, and S. J. Harrison (eds.), *Classical Constructions: Papers in Memory of Don Fowler, Classicist and Epicurean*. New York: Oxford University Press. 91-112.
———. 2009. *Writing, Performance, and Authority in Augustan Rome*. New York: Oxford University Press.
Luiselli, B. 1967. *Il verso saturnio*. Roma: Edizioni dell'Ateneo.

———. 1969. *Il problema della più antica prosa latina.* Cagliari: Editrice sarda Fossataro.
MacCary, W. T. and Willock, M. M. 1976. *Plautus, Casina.* Cambridge: Cambridge University Press.
Malcovati, E. 1976. *Oratorum Romanorum fragmenta liberae rei publicae.* 4th ed. Torino: Paravia.
Malherbe, M. 2005. "Comptabilité privée et formation du droit romain classique." In J.-G. Degos, *L'entreprise, le chiffre et le droit: itinéraires parallèles, itineraries croises.* Actes des 11èmes journées d'histoire de la comptabilité et du management (17–18 mars 2005). Bourdeaux: Université Montesquieu. 257–72.
Mariotti, S. 1952. *Livio Andronico e la traduzione artistica.* Milano: G. de Silvestri.
Markus, D. D. 2000. "Performing the Book: The Recital of Epic in First-Century C.E. Rome." *Classical Antiquity* 19.1: 138–79
Marshall, C. W. 2006. *The Stagecraft and Performance of Roman Comedy.* Cambridge: Cambridge University Press.
Martin, R. H. [1976] 2001. Terence's *Adelphoe.* Cambridge: Cambridge University Press.
Martindale, C. 1993. *Redeeming the Text: Latin Poetry and the Hermeneutics of Reception.* Cambridge: Cambridge University Press.
———, and Thomas, R. F. 2006. *Classics and the Uses of Reception.* Oxford: Blackwell.
Massaro, M. 2001. "L'epitaffio metrico per il mimo Protogene." *Rivista di Filologia e Istruzione Classica* 129: 5–50.
Mattingly, D. 2010. *Imperialism, Power and Identity.* Princeton: Princeton University Press.
Mazzarino, A. 1952. *Introduzione al De Agri Cultura di Catone.* Roma: Atlante.
Mazzoli, G. 2004. "Riflessioni sulla semantica ciceroniana della gloria." In E. Narducci (ed.), *Cicerone tra antichi e moderni.* Atti del IV Symposium Ciceronianum Arpinas, Arpino 9 maggio 2003. Firenze. 56–81.
McCarthy, K. 1998. "Servitium amoris: Amor servitii." In S. Joshel and S. Murnaghan (eds.), *Women and Slaves in Classical Antiquity.* New York: Routledge. 174–92
———. 2000. *Slaves, Masters, and the Art of Authority in Plautine Comedy.* Princeton: Princeton University Press.
McElduff, S. 2009. "Living at the Level of the Word: Cicero's Rejection of the Interpreter as Translator." *Translation Studies* 2.2: 133–46.
———. Forthcoming. *Surpassing the Source: Roman Theories of Translation from the Beginnings of Latin Literature to the Church Fathers.*
——— and Sciarrino, E. 2011. *Complicating the History of Western Translation: The Ancient Mediterranean in Perspective.* Manchester: St Jerome Publishing.
Meyer, E. A. 2004. *Legitimacy and Law in the Roman World: Tabulae in Roman Belief and Practice.* Cambridge and New York: Cambridge University Press.
Mercado, A. O. 2006. "The Latin Saturnian and Italic Verse." PhD dissertation. Los Angeles.
Middleton, R. 1986. "In the Groove, or Blowing your Mind? The Pleasures of Musical Repetition." In T. Bennett, C. Mercer, and J. Woollacot (eds.), *Popular Culture and Social Relations.* Milton Keynes: Open University Press. 159–75.

Miller, P. A. 2006. "T. Habinek's The World of Roman Song: From Ritualized Speech to Social Order (Review)." *American Journal of Philology* 127.4: 607–11.
Moatti, C. 1997. *La Raison de Rome: Naissance de l'Esprit Critique à la fin de la République.* Paris: Seuil.
Momigliano, A. 1960. "Perizonius, Niebuhr and the Character of Early Roman Tradition." *Secondo contributo alla storia degli studi classici.* Roma: Edizioni di storia e letteratura. 69–88.
———. *Alien Wisdom: The Limits of Hellenization.* Cambridge: Cambridge University Press.
Mommsen, T. 1874. *Römische Staatsrecht.* Leipzig: S. Hirzel.
Moore, T. J. 1998. *The Theater of Plautus: Playing to the Audience.* Austin: University of Texas Press.
Morel, W. 1927. *Fragmenta Poetarum Latinorum Epicorum et Lyricorum praeter Ennium et Lucilium.* Leipzig: Teubner.
Most, G. W. 2003. "Violets in Crucibles: Translating, Traducing, and Transmuting." *Transactions of the American Philological Association* 133: 381–90.
Narducci, E. 1997. *Cicerone e l'eloquenza romana.* Roma-Bari: Laterza.
Niccolini, G. 1934. *I fasti dei tribuni della plebe.* Milano: Giuffrè.
Nicolet, C. 1980. *The World of the Citizen in Republican Rome.* Trans. by P. S. Falla. London: Batsford.
———. 1991. *Space, Geography, and Politics in the Early Roman Empire.* Ann Arbor: University of Michigan Press.
Nightingale, D. 1989. Rev. J. Andreau, *La vie financière dans le monde romain: Les métiers de manieurs d'argent* (IVe siècle av. J.-C. IIIe siècle ap J.-C.). *Journal of Roman Studies* 79: 176–77.
Niranjana, T. 1992. *Siting Translation: History, Post-structuralism, and the Colonial Context.* Berkley and Los Angeles: University of California Press.
Norden, E. 1986. *La prosa d'arte antica dal VI secolo a.C. all'età della Rinascenza.* Trans. B. Heinemann Campana. Roma (= Leipzig-Berlin 19153).
Noy, D. 2000. *Foreigners at Rome: Citizens and Strangers.* London: Classical Press of Wales.
Oakley, S. P. 1998. *A Commentary on Livy, Books VI–X.* Vol. 2. New York: Clarendon Press.
Oberhelman, S. M. 2003. *Prose Rhythm in Latin Literature of the Roman Empire. First Century B.C. to Fourth Century A.D.* Studies in Classics 27. Lewiston, NY: Edwin Mellen Press.
Oliensis, E. 1995. "Life After Publication: Horace Epistles I.20." *Arethusa* 28: 209–24.
Page, D. L. 1950. *Select Papyri.* Vol. 3. Cambridge, MA: Loeb Edition.
Pallottino, M. 1981. *Genti e culture dell'Italia preromana.* Rome: Jouvence.
Palmer, L. R. 1961. *The Latin Language.* 3rd ed. London: Faber and Faber.
Parker, H. N. 1989. "Crucially Funny, or Tranio on the Couch: The *Servus Callidus* and Jokes about Torture." *Transactions of the American Philological Association* 119: 233–46.
———. 2009. "Books and Reading Latin Poetry." In W. A. Johnson and H. Parker (eds.), *Ancient Literacies: The Culture of Reading in Greece and Rome.* Oxford: Oxford University Press. 186–232.

Parsons, J. 1999. "A New Approach to the Saturnian Verse and Its Relations to Latin Prosody." *Transactions of the American Philological Association* 129: 117–37.
Pasquali, G. 1968. *Pagine stravaganti*. Vol. 2. Firenze: Sansoni.
Peter, H. [1906] 1914. *Historicorum Romanorum Fragmenta*. 2nd ed. Leipzig: Teubner.
Petrone, G. 1983. *Teatro antico e inganno. Finzioni plautine*. Palermo: Palumbo editore.
Pierre, M. 2005. "Rome dans la balance: Le poésie augustéenne imite-t-elle la poésie grecque?" In F. Dupont and E. Valette-Cagnac (eds.), *Façons de parler grec à Rome*. Paris: Belin. 229–54.
———. 2008. "La poétique du carmen. Étude d'une énonciation romaine des Douze Tables à l'époque d'Auguste." PhD Dissertation. Paris.
Possanza, D. M. 2004. *Translating the Heavens. Aratus, Germanicus, and the Poetics of Latin Translation*. New York: Peter Lang.
Powell, J. G. P. 2005. "Cicero's Adaptation of Legal Latin." In T. Reinhardt, M. Lapidge, and J. N. Adams (eds.), *Aspects of the Language of Latin Prose*. Oxford: Oxford University Press.
Powell, J. G. F. and Paterson, J. J. (eds.), 2004. *Cicero the Advocate*. Oxford: Oxford University Press.
Pratt, M. L. 1992. *Imperial Eyes: Travel Writing and Transculturation*. New York: Routledge.
Pucci, P. 1982. "The Proem of the *Odyssey*." *Arethusa* 15: 39–62.
Pym, A. 2003. "Introduction: On the Social and Cultural in Translation Studies." In A. Pym, M. Shlesinger, and Z. Jettmarová (eds.), *Sociocultural Aspects of Translating and Interpreting*. Amsterdam: John Benjamins.
Questa, C. 1967. *Introduzione alla metrica di Plauto*. Bologna: Patron.
———. 1995. (ed.), *Titi Macci Plauti Cantica*. Ludus Philologiae 5. Urbino: Edizioni Quattro Venti.
Radice, B. 1967. *Terence. The Comedies*. London: Penguin Books.
Rafael, V. L. 1993. Rev. ed. *Contracting Colonialism: Translation and Christian Conversion in Tagalog Society under Early Spanish Rule*. Durham: Duke University Press.
Reay, B. 2005. "Agriculture, Writing, and Cato's Aristocratic Self-Fashioning." *Classical Antiquity* 24.2: 331–61.
Reggiani, R. 1979. *I proemi degli Annales: programma letterario e polemica* (Filologia e critica 28). Roma: Edizioni dell'Ateneo e Bizzarri.
Ribbeck, O. 1897. *Tragicorum Romanorum Fragmenta*. Leipzig: Teubner.
Richardson, J. 2008. *The Language of Empire: Rome and the Idea of Empire from the Third Century B.C. to the Second Century A.D.* Cambridge: Cambridge University Press.
Richlin, A. 2005. *Rome and the Mysterious Orient. Three Plays by Plautus*. Berkeley: University of California Press.
Ricoeur, P. 1973. "The Model of the Text: Meaningful Action Considered as a Text." *New Literary History* 5.1: 91–117.
Ridley, R. 2003. *The Emperor's Retrospect. Augustus' Res Gestae in Epigraphy, Historiography and Commentary*. Leuven: Peeters 2003.

Riggsby, A. M. 1999. *Crime and Community in Ciceronian Rome.* Austin: University of Texas Press.
Robinson, D. 1997. *Translation and Empire. Postcolonial Theories Explained.* Manchester: St. Jerome Publishing.
Roller, M. B. 2004. "Exemplarity in Roman Culture: the Cases of Horatius Cocles and Cloelia." *Classical Philology* 99: 1–56.
Roth, C. L. 1853. *Historicorum Veterum Romanorum Reliquiae.* In *Gai Sallusti Crispi Catilina, Iugurtha, Historiarum Reliquiae.* Basiliae: Librariae Schweighauserianae.
Rüpke, J. 1993. "Livius, Priesternamen, und die *annales maximi.*" *Klio* 75: 155–79.
———. 1995. *Kalender und Öffentlichkeit: Die Geschichte der Repräsentation und religiösen Qualifikation von Zeit in Rom.* Berlin: Walter de Gruyter.
———. 2000. "Räume literarischer Kommunication in der Formiserungs-phase römischer Literatur." In M. Braun (ed.), *Moribus antiques res stat Romana: römischer Werte und römische Literatur im 3. und 2. Jh. v. Chr.* München: Saur. 31–52.
———. 2006. "Ennius's *Fasti* in Fulvius' Temple: Greek Rationality and Roman Tradition." *Arethusa* 39: 489–512.
Saller, R. P. 1994. *Patriarchy, Property and Death in the Roman Family.* Cambridge and New York: Cambridge University Press.
Sassen, S. 1991. *The Global City.* Princeton: Princeton University Press.
Sblendorio Cugusi, M. T. 1971. "Note sullo stile dell'oratoria catoniana." *Annali della Facoltà di Lettere e Filosofia dell'Università di Cagliari* 34: 5–32.
———. 1980. "Sulla struttura dell'orazione catoniana *De Dierum Dictarum Consulatu Suo.*" *Atti dell' Accademia di Scienze di Torino* (Classe di Scienze Morali) 114: 247–58.
———. 1982. *Marci Porci Catoni Orationum Reliquiae.* Torino: Paravia.
———. 1996. "Problematica catoniana. Rassegna di studi 1978–1993 e contributi critici." *Bollettino di studi latini* 26: 82–218.
Schechner, R. 2002. *Performance Studies: An Introduction.* London and New York: Routledge.
Scheid, J. 1984. "Contraria Facere: Renversements et déplacements dans les rites funéraires." *AION* 6: 117–39.
———. 2007. *Res Gestae Divi Augusti: Hauts faits du divin Auguste.* Paris: Belles Lettres.
Schiavone, A. 2005. *Ius. L'invenzione del diritto in Occidente.* Torino: Einaudi.
Schröder, W. A. 1971. *M. Porcius Cato. Das erste Buch der Origines. Ausgabe und Erklärung der Fragmente.* Meisenheim am Glan: A. Hain.
Sciarrino, E. 2004a. "Putting Cato the Censor's *Origines* in Its Place." *Classical Antiquity* 24.2: 323–57.
———. 2004b. "A Temple for the Professional Muse: The *Aedes Herculis Musarum* and Cultural Shifts in Second-Century B.C. Rome." In A. Barchiesi, J. Rüpke, and S. Stephens (eds.), *Rituals in Ink.* Stuttgart: Franz Steiner Verlag. 45–56
———. 2007. "The Elder Cato and Gaius Gracchus: Roman Oratory before Cicero." In W. J. Dominik and J. Hall (eds.), *A Companion to Roman Rhetoric.* Oxford: Blackwell. 54–66.

Scullard, H. H. 1973. *Roman Politics 220–150 B.C.* Oxford: Oxford University Press.
Segal, E. 1987. *Roman Laughter.* 2nd ed. New York: Oxford University Press.
Sharrock, A. R. 1996. "The Art of Deceit: Pseudolus and the Nature of Reading." *Classical Quarterly* 46.1: 152–74.
———. 1996. "The Art of Deceit: *Pseudolus* and the Nature of Reading." *Classical Quarterly* 46: 105–12
Shatzmann, I. 1972. "The Roman General's Authority over Booty." *Historia* 21: 177–205.
Siméoni, D. 1998. "The Pivotal Status of the Translator's *Habitus.*" *Target* 10.1: 1–39.
Skutsch, O. 1968. *Studia Enniana.* London: Athlone.
———. (ed.), 1985. *The Annals of Q. Ennius.* Oxford: Clarendon Press.
Slater, N. W. 2000. *Plautus in Performance: The Theater of the Mind.* 2nd ed. Princeton: Princeton University Press.
Small, J. P. 1997. *Wax Tablets of the Mind: Cognitive Studies of Memory and Literacy in Classical Antiquity.* London: Routledge.
Smith, C. J. 2006. *The Roman Clan. The Gens from Ancient Ideology to Modern Anthropology.* Cambridge: Cambridge University Press.
Sohm, R. 2002. *Institutes of Roman Law.* Trans. by J. C. Ledlie. Piscataway. NJ: Gorgias Press.
Spivak, G. C. 1988. "Can the Subaltern Speak?" In G. Nelson and L. Grossberg (eds.), *Marxism and the Interpretation of Culture.* Urbana, IL: University of Illinois Press. 271–313.
Stangl, T. 1912. *Ciceronis orationum scholiastae Asconius, scholia bobiensia, scholia pseudasconii sangallensia, scholia cluniacensia et recentiora ambrosiana ac vaticana, scholia lugdunensia sive gronoviana et eorum excerpta lugdunensia.* Hildesheim: Olms.
Starr R. 1991. "Reading Aloud: *Lectores* and Roman Reading." *Classical Journal* 86: 337–43.
Steel, C. E. W. 2001. *Cicero, Rhetoric, and Empire.* Oxford: Oxford University Press.
———. 2006. *Roman Oratory.* Greece & Rome, New Surveys in the Classics, 36. Cambridge: Cambridge University Press.
Stibbe, C. M. (ed.). 1980. *Lapis Satricanus. Archaeological, Epigraphical, Linguistic and Historical Aspects of the New Inscription from Satricum.* The Hague: Staatsuitgeverij.
Stroup, S. C. 2003. "*Adulta Uirgo:* The Personification of Textual Eloquence in Cicero's *Brutus.*" *Materiali e discussioni* 50: 115–40.
———. 2007. "Greek Rhetoric Meets Rome: Expansion, Resistance, and Acculturation." In W. J. Dominik and J. Hall (eds.), *A Companion to Roman Rhetoric.* Oxford: Blackwell: 23–37.
Sturtevant, E. H. 1919. "The Coincidence of Accent and Ictus in Plautus and Terence." *Classical Philology* 14: 234–44.
Sudhaus, S. (ed.), 1892. *Philodemi Volumina Rhetorica.* Leipzig: Teubner.
Suerbaum, W. 1968. *Untersuchungen zur Selbstdarstellung älterer römischer Dichter. Livius Andronicus, Naevius, Ennius.* Spudasmata 19. Hildesheim: Olms.
Suolahti, J. 1963. *The Roman Censors: A Study on Social Structure.* Helsinki: Suomalainen Tiedeakatemia.

Taussig, M. 1993. *Mimesis and Alterity: A Particular History of the Senses.* London and New York: Routledge.
Taylor, D. 2003. *The Archive and the Repertoire: Performing Cultural Memory in the Americas.* Durham: Duke University Press
Taylor L. R. 1937. "The Opportunities for Dramatic Performances in the Time of Plautus and Terence." *Transactions of the American Philological Association* 68: 284–304.
———. 1952. "Lucretius on the Roman Theatre." In M. E. White (ed.), *Studies in Honour of G. Norwood. Phoenix* Suppl. 1: 147–55.
Terrenato, N. 1998. "Tam Firmum Municipium: The Romanization of Volaterrae and Its Cultural Implications." *Journal of Roman Studies* 88: 94–114.
———. 2000. "Le sedi del potere nel territorio di Volterra: una lunga prospettiva (secoli VII a.C.–XIII D.C." In Brogiolo, G. P. (ed.), *Secondo Congresso Nazionale di Archeologia Medievale.* Firenze: Edizioni all'insegna del giglio. 298–303.
———. 2001. "The Auditorium Site and the Origins of the Roman Villa." *Journal of Roman Archaeology* 14: 5–32.
———. 2006. "The Origins of the State par Excellence: Power and Society in Iron Age Rome." In C. Haselgrove (ed.), *Celtes et Gaulois, L' Archéologie face à l'Histoire, 4: les mutations de la fin de l'âge du Fer. Glux-en-Glenne:* Collection Bibracte 12/4. 225–34.
———. 2007. "The Clans and the Peasants: Reflections on Social Structure and Change in Hellenistic Central Italy." In P. Van Dommelen and N. Terrenato (eds.), *Articulating Local Cultures: Power and Identity under the Expanding Roman Republic.* Journal of Roman Archaeology, Suppl. 63. 13–22.
———. 2011. "The Enigma of 'Catonian' Villas. The *De Agricultura* in the Context of 2nd Century B.C. Rural Italian Architecture." In J. A. Becker and N. Terrenato (eds.), *Roman Republican Villas: Architecture, Context, and Ideology.*
Thilo, R. M. 1980. *Der Codex Accepti et Expensi im Romischen Recht: Ein Beitrag Zur Lehre Von Der Litteralobligation.* Göttingen: Muster-Schmidt.
Till, R. 1940. "Die Anerkennung literarischen Schaffens in Rom." *Neue Jarbücher* 115: 161–74.
———. 1968. *La lingua di Catone.* Trans. by C. De Meo. Roma: Edizioni dell'Ateneo.
Timpanaro, S. 1988. "Alcuni tipi di sinonimi in asindeto in latino arcaico e loro sopravvivenze in latina classico." *Rivista di Filologia e di Istruzione Classica* 116: 257–97, 385–428.
Torelli, M. 1982. *Typology and Structure of Roman Historical Reliefs.* Ann Arbor: University of Michigan Press.
———. 1999. "Religious aspects of Early Roman Colonization." In M. Torelli (ed.), *Tota Italia: Essays in the Cultural Formation of Roman Italy.* Oxford: Oxford University Press. 14–42.
Traina, A. 1970. *Vortit barbare. Le traduzioni poetiche da Livio Andronico a Cicerone.* Roma: Edizioni dell'Ateneo.
———. 1977. *Forma e suono.* Roma: Edizioni dell'Ateneo e Bizzarri.
Traglia, A. 1984. "Note su Catone scrittore." *Cultura e Scuola* 90: 55–61.
———. 1985. "Osservazioni su Catone prosatore." *Latomus* 187: 344–59.
Treggiari, S. 1969. *Roman Freedmen during the Late Republic.* Oxford: Clarendon

Press.

———. 2003. "Ancestral Virtues and Vices: Cicero on Nature, Nurture and Presentation." In D. Braund and C.Gill (eds.), *Myth, History and Culture in Republican Rome. Studies in Honour of T. P. Wiseman*. Exeter: University of Exeter Press. 139–64.

Tymoczko, M. 2007. *Enlarging Translation, Empowering Translators*. Manchester: St. Jerome Publishing.

Turner, V. 1988. *The Anthropology of Performance*. New York: PAJ Publications.

Vairel-Carron, H. 1975. *Exclamation, Ordre et Défense: Analyse de deux système syntaxiques en latin*. Paris: Belles Lettres.

Valette-Cagnac, E. 1997. *La lecture à Rome. Rites et pratiques*. Paris: Belin.

Van Sickle, J. 1987. "The Elogia of the Cornelii Scipiones and the Origin of the Epigram at Rome." *American Journal of Philology* 108: 41–55.

Venuti, L. 1995. *The Translator's Invisibility: A History of Translation*. London and New York: Routledge.

Veyne, P. 1979. "The Hellenization of Rome and the Question of Acculturation." *Diogenes* 106: 1–27.

von Albrecht, M. 1989. *Masters of Roman Prose from Cato to Apuleius: Interpretative Studies*. Trans. by N. Adkin. Leeds: Francis Cairns.

Wagener, A. 1949. "M. Porcii Catonis Originum fragmenta emendata, disposita, illustrata." PhD dissertation, Bonn.

Wardy, R. 1996. *The Birth of Rhetoric: Gorgias, Plato and Their Successors*. London: Routledge.

Watkins, C. 1995. *How to Kill a Dragon: Aspect of Indo-European Poetics*. New York: Oxford University Press.

Wiles, D. 1991. *The Masks of Menander: Signs and Meanings in Greek and Roman Performances*. Cambridge: Cambridge University Press.

Weiner, A. B. 1992. *Inalienable Possessions. The Paradox of Keeping-While-Giving*. Berkeley: University of California Press.

Wise, J. 1998. *Dionysus Writes. The Invention of Theatre in Ancient Greece*. Ithaca and London. Cornell University Press.

Wiseman, T. P. 1969. "The Census in the First Century B.C." *Journal of Roman Studies* 59: 59–75.

———. 1971. *New Men in the Roman Senate 139 B.C.–A.D. 14*. London: Oxford University Press.

———. 1994. *Historiography and Imagination: Eight Essays on Roman Culture*. Exeter: University of Exeter Press.

———. 1998. *Roman Drama and Roman History*. Exeter: University of Exeter Press.

———. 2004. *The Myths of Rome*. Exeter: University of Exeter Press.

———. 2006. "Fauns, Prophets, and Ennius' *Annales*." *Arethusa* 39: 513–30.

———. 2007a. *Unwritten Rome*. Exeter: University of Exeter Press.

———. 2007b. "The Prehistory of Roman Historiography." In Marincola, J. (ed.), *A Companion to Greek and Roman Historiography*. Oxford: Blackwell Reference Online.

Witzmann, P. 2000. "Kommunikative Leistungen von Weih-, Ehren- und Grabinschriften: Wertbegriffe und Wertvorstellungen in Inschriften vorsullanischer Zeit."

In Maximilian Braun (ed.), *Moribus antiquis res stat Romana: römischer Werte und römische Literatur im 3. und 2. Jh. v. Chr.* München: 55–86.

Wolf, M. and Fukari, A. 2007. *Constructing a Sociology of Translation.* Amsterdam and Philadelphia: John Benjamins Publishing.

Woolf, G. 1996. "Monumental Writing and the Expansion of Roman Society in the Early Empire." *Journal of Roman Studies* 86: 22–39.

———. 1998. *Becoming Roman: the Origins of Provincial Civilization in Gaul.* Cambridge and New York: Cambridge University Press.

Wright, J. 1974. *Dancing in Chains: The Stylistic Unity of the Comoedia Palliata.* Rome: Papers and Monographs of the American Academy in Rome, 25.

Zaccaria Ruggiu, A. 2003. *More Regio Vivere. Il banchetto aristocratico e la casa romana di età arcaica.* Quaderni di Eutopia 4. Roma: Quasar.

Zetzel, J. E. G. 1972. "Cicero and the Scipionic Circle." *Harvard Studies in Classical Philology* 76: 173–79.

———. 2003. "Plato with Pillows: Cicero on the Uses of Greek Culture." In D. Braund and C. Gill (eds.), *Myth, History and Culture in Republican Rome: Studies in Honour of T. P. Wiseman.* Exeter: University of Exeter Press. 119–38.

———. 2007. "The Influence of Cicero on Ennius." In W. Fitzgerald and E. Gowers (eds.), *Ennius Perennis: The Annals and Beyond.* Cambridge Classical Journal, Proceedings of the Cambridge Philological Society, Suppl. 31. Cambridge: Cambridge University Press. 1–16.

Zorzetti, N. 1980. *La pretesta e il teatro latino arcaico.* Napoli: Liguori.

———. [1984] 1990. "The *Carmina Convivalia.*" In O. Murray (ed.), *Sympotica: A Symposium on the Symposion.* Oxford: Clarendon Press; New York: Oxford University Press. 289–307.

———. 1991. "Poetry and Ancient City: The Case of Rome." *Classical Journal* 86: 310–29.

Zweerlin, O. 1990. *Zur Kritik und Exegeses des Plautus I: Poenulus und Curculio.* Stuttgart: Franz Steiner Verlag.

Index Locorum

Aulus Gellius
   Noctes Atticae 2.6.16, **195**; 4.18.11, **182**; 17.21.45, **83**
Aurelius Victor
   De Viris Illustribus 52.2–3, **193**
Cato
   Ad Filium 1 C&Sbl, 4, **159**; fr *18 C&Sbl, **158**; fr *19 C&Sbl, **158**
   Carmen de moribus 1 C&Sbl, 102, **198**; 2 C&Sbl, 6n, **100**
   De Agricultura, Preface, **143–44**; 2.2, **147–48, 183**; 2.3–4, **148**; 139–41, **150–53, 154, 156**
   De Re Militari 1 C&Sbl, **192**
   Orations 1.1 Sbl, **125–26**; 1.2 Sbl **126**; 3.4 Sbl, **139**; 4.15 Sbl, **196**; 4.17 Sbl, **138**; 6.42 Sbl, **128**; 22.81 Sbl, **136**; 22.84–85 Sbl, **136–37**; 24.93 Sbl, **143**; 32.118 Sbl, **132–33**; 51.169 Sbl, **166–67**
   Origines 1.1 C&Sbl, **171**; 1.2 C&Sbl, **172, 183**; 1.3* C&Sbl, **184–85**; 1.4 C&Sbl, **172**; 4.81 C&Sbl, **178**; 4.88b.2 C&Sbl, **197–98**
Charisius
   Ars Grammatica p. 403, 14B, **194**
Cicero
   De Officiis 3.1.4, **185**
   Pro Archia 22, **193**
   Pro Plancio 66–67, **186–87**
   Tusculan Disputations 1.3, **99**; 4.3, **100**
Corpus Inscriptionum Latinarum I2, 2832 a (Lapis Satricanus), **105**
Ennius
   Annales 1.1 Sk, **90**; 1.3 Sk, **90**; 7.206–7 Sk, **90**; 7.208–10 Sk, **93**; 7.211 Sk, **92**; 8.268–86 Sk, **96, 98**; 10.322–23 Sk, **94**; Frg. 525 Sk, **3**; Frg. 576 Sk, **91, 93**
   Opera Incerta Frg. 1 Sk, **3**
Festus
   De Verborum Significatione 82.18–22L, **156–57**; 446L, **48–49**; 861L, **100n**
Horace
   Epistles 1.20, **14, 16–17**; 2.1.71–73, **73, 94**; 2.1.156–59, **74**; 2.3.141–42, **73–74**
   Odes 3.30, **16–17**
Livius Andronicus
   Oduseia 1, **70**
Livy
   Ab Urbe Condita 1.57.6, **104**; 7.2.4–7, **44–45**
Manilius
   Astronomica 1.12–24, **18–19**

Naevius
    Com. frg. 72–74 Ribbeck, **69**
Plautus
    Captivi 422–27, **195**
    Curculio 280–98, **60–61**; 462–84, **58–59**
    Miles Gloriosus 200–13, **66–67**
    Mostellaria 1149–51, **68**
    Pseudolus 401–5, **64–65**; 544–46, **66**; 562–70, **65**
Pliny
    Natural History 7.139, **121–22**
Polybius
    Histories 6.51.1–4, **119**; 23.14.7, **180–81**; 31.23.4–5, **78**; 31.24.4–8, **79**; 31.24.9–12, **79–80**; 31.25.5, **103**; 39.1.1–9, **141**
Priscianus
    Praeexercitamina 7, **194**

Pseudo-Asconius
    215 Stangl (*ad* Cicero Verrines 1.29), **84**
Quintilian
    Institutio Oratoria 1.8.2, **107**; 1.10.31, **106–7**
Suetonius
    De Poetis
    Terence 4, **114**
Terence
    Adelphoe 9–14, **110**; 15–21, **109**
    Eunuchus 22–26, **110**
    Heauton Timorumenos 16–24, **110**
Valerius Maximus
    Facta et Dicta Memorabilia 3.7.1d, **181–82**
Varro
    De Lingua Latina 6.86, **177**

General Index

Abel, L., 57
Accius, 114
accounts. See *rationes*
acculturation, and literature, 27
Acilius, C., 140
actors, 45, 47, 51, 56–58, 62–64, 76, 97; social, in scenarios, 33, 81, 82, 84
Adams, J. N., 206n
Aedes Herculis Musarum, 87, 114, 178
aediles, and the production of poetry, 49, 110
aesthetics: in drama, 70; and interpretation of literature, 9, 13, 29; as strategy, 35
Ager, B., 155
agriculture: scale of, 145; as superior to other professions, 144. See also *De Agricultura*
alienation. See commodities
allusion, 8–10
ancestors: as actors in *convivia,* 82; as guarantee of status, 118–24; heritable qualities of, 120–23; invoked by Cato, 126; as model for elite behavior, 79–80, 118, 137; as non-familial, 124, 126, 144; obligations toward, 79–80; presence of at funerals, 120. See also elite; *gentes; nobiles*
Anderson, W., 68

Antonius, Marcus (orator), 161
anxieties, cultural, 27, 46
Appius Claudius Caecus, 199
appropriation, of texts by performers and readers, 15, 17, 36, 135, 192
archaeology, as evidence for literature, 29, 30, 38, 145
aristocracy. See ancestors; elite; *gentes; nobiles*
Astin, A., 28n, 129n, 142, 199–200
Atticus, Titus Pomponius, 161
auctoritas: of authors, 204; of Augustus, 15; and the body, 15, 164; of Cato, 20–21, 35–36, 187, 199, 206; definition of, 15; language as source of, 127; and monuments, 17; and praise, 196, 198–99; and *rationes,* 184; of Scipio Africanus, 182–83; and writing, 166, 170, 171n. See also authority
audiences: for drama, 55–58, 60, 62, 65–66, 72; for funerals, 120–22; as judges, 141; for Scipio Africanus, 181; for translations, 40
Augustus, and the *Res Gestae,* 15–17
Aulus Gellius, 63, 131, 132, 182–83, 195
Aurelius Victor, 193–94
Austin, J. L., 189–90
authority: acquired through judgment, 141;

of authors, 3, 6, 14–15, 34, 86–87, 95; and *carmina*, 148, 160; of Cato, 21; and formalized speech, 127; and mimicry, 34; of Roman elites, 24, 86–87; and the Saturnian meter, 82, 85–86; and self-control, 158; and song, 11–12, 137; in speech, 158; and *tabulae*, 169; and translation, 140; and the word *dico*, 11, 85. See also *auctoritas*

authors: agency of, 189; *auctoritas* of, 204; authority of, 6, 14–15, 34, 95; death of, 2, 192; intentions of, 8, 9, 15, 196; subjectivity of, 3

authorship, poetic: of Ennius, 5–7, 89–98; of Livius Andronicus, 71–72; of Terence, 111–12, 114–15

banquets. See *convivia*
Barchiesi, A., 10, 25–26
Barchiesi, M., 58, 67
Batstone, W., 58
Beacham, R. C., 52n
beating, of Roman citizens, 128–29
Bell, C., 150, 187n, 188n
body, the: Cato's use of, 168; as central to *De Agricultura*, 146; Cicero's use of, 162; of the citizen, 130; and hierarchical schemes, 149–50; and knowledge, 98, 146; in literary interpretation, 11–12; of the master, 145; misuse of, 136–37; and oratory, 164, 168; of poets, 113; in scenarios, 81; and selfhood, 203–4; submission of, 12–13; in texts, 35, 118. See also rituals; ritualization

Caecilius Metellus, Q., 121–22
Caecilius Statius, 48
Caesar Strabo, 114
Calboli, G., 132n, 133n
Camenae, as translation of Musae, 76, 87–89, 94
canere: definition of, 106–7; distinguished from *cantare*, 108; distinguished from *loqui*, 11. See also *carmina*; song
cantare: definition of, 11; in Horace, 106
Cardinali, L., 170–71
Carmen de moribus, 30, 100, 101, 199
carmina: and authority, 148, 160; Cato's use of, 124–25, 126–27, 133–34, 148, 153–54, 207; contrasted with poetry, 102; *convivalia*, 22; definition of, 101,

108, 124; Ennius' rejection of, 102, 125; and epic, 125; as formalized, 19; and hierarchy, 101; imitation of, 45; influence of, 206–7, 208; language of, 126–27; and the origin of prose, 149; patterns of, 196; performativity of, 20; Prayer to Mars as example of, 150; rhythm of, 130–31; and ritual, 19, 149–50; as speech acts, 102, 124, 130; style of, 19–20; and writing on *tabulae*, 169. See also poetry; prose; song; writing

Carneades, 140
Cato, M. Porcius: *Ad Filium*, 156–60; ancestors invoked by, 144; *auctoritas* of, 20, 21, 35, 36, 148, 187, 199, 206; career of, 1–2, 123–24; *carmina* used by, 124–25, 126–27, 133–34, 148, 153–54, 207; as censor, 102, 135, 154, 199, 200–1; censorial scenarios in, 173; comedy used by, 138; contrasted with Cicero, 132; on *convivia*, 6, 29, 32, 82, 100–1, 103, 105, 172, 178–79; convivial scenarios in, 105, 108–9, 172; *De Agricultura*, 27–28, 35, 141–60, 183–84, 192; *De Falsis Pugnis*, 127; Demosthenes invoked by, 139; *De Re Militari*, 192; *De Sumptu Suo*, 166–69, 170; *Dierum Dictarum de Consulatu Suo*, 138; on education, 156–58; Ennius invoked by, 171, 190; Ennius sponsored by, 34, 138; formalization used by, 149, 154; on Greek culture, 4–5, 6–7, 14–15, 27, 34, 206; and Greek rhetoric, 127, 132; as *homo novus*, 34–35, 123, 165, 197, 199, 200–1, 206; identity of, 4; migration of, 3–4; on medicine, 4–5; *Origines*, 36–37, 170–71, 172, 178–79, 183, 184, 186–87, 189–92, 197–98; on *otium*, 173, 173, 177, 186–87, 190; on poets and poetry, 21, 77, 99–100, 102, 108–9, 112, 125, 206, 208; *Pro Rhodiensibus*, 132–33; on *rationes*, 177, 190; revision of texts by, 166–68; rhythm used by, 124, 127, 132–33, 149; as Sabine, 3–4; and Scipio Africanus, 166, 179–87; self-presentation of, 35, 135, 143–44, 166, 168, 194, 197; on self-sufficiency, 53, 103, 146; *sententiae* of, 125–26, 157; *Si se M. Caelius tribunus plebis appellasset*, 135–38; subjectivity of, 18; transcription by, 7, 91, 179, 184–85, 191, 197; on writing, 161, 165, 169–72; Xenophon invoked by, 173

censors: 18–19, 36; Cato as, 102, 135, 154, 199, 200–201; ceremonies conducted by, 173–79; and elite control, 200; and *rationes,* 184. *See also* scenarios, censorial
Charisius, Flavius Sosipater, 194
Cicero, M. Tullius, 29, 87, 116, 167; *Brutus,* 161–65; on *carmina convivalia,* 29–30; contrasted with Cato, 132; on Ennius, 194; as *homo novus,* 164, 187; on music, 171n; on Naevius, 84; as orator, 165; on oratory, 134, 161–65, 168; on origins of Roman poetry, 47, 99–100; and writing, 162, 185
Cincinnatus, Lucius Quinctius, 143
cist, Praenestine (VG 13 133), 175–77
collegia, of actors and poets, 47–48, 49–51, 66, 114
comedy: appropriations of, 85–86; Cato's use of, 131, 138; meters of, 131
commentarii, 37, 163, 167. *See also* transcription; writing
commodities: cultural, 41, 117; knowledge as, 82; texts as, 5, 14–15
contact zones, 25, 41–44; defined, 39–40; in drama, 60; and sound patterns, 55
contaminatio, in Terence, 110–11
Conte, G. B., 70–71, 171n
convivia, 6, 9, 22, 28–30, 32; and the battlefield, 101, 105; Cato on, 6, 29, 32, 82, 100–1, 103, 105, 172, 178–79; Cicero on, 99–100; depictions of, 31; elites structured by, 31, 101, 105; and epic, 100, 104; in Livy, 104–5; non-elite encroachment on, 100; and poetry, 22–23, 108; and praise, 36, 101, 105; scenarios concerning, 103–4, 105, 108, 172, 178–79, 192–93; and song, 170
Cornell, T. J., 105
Costa, G., 165n
Crassus, C. Licinius, 161
Crook, J., 167n
Csapo, E., 188n
Cugusi, P., 129n, 171n, 179n, 184, 187
culture: appropriation of, 46, 135; as commodity, 41, 117; and political supremacy, 139, 141
Curius Dentatus, Manlius, 143, 147

Dahlmann, H., 24
Dalby, A., 28n, 150n
Davies, C. B., 33
De Agricultura, 27–28, 35, 37, 141–60, 183–84, 192; composition of, 142; as idealized, 145; Prayer to Mars in, 150–56. *See also* Cato
de Staël, Germaine, 115
Demosthenes, 139
Dench, E., 25, 146–47
Dentatus, Manlius Curius, 143
diaspora, Roman poets as, 42
dicere: definition of, 11–12, 85; contrasted with *loqui,* 11; contrasted with *scribere,* 163
dinners, elite. See *convivia*
discriptio (discribere), 171–72, 173–74
domini, in the *De Agricultura,* 144–45, 146, 148–49, 153, 154, 155, 156. See also *pater familias*
Domitius Ahenobarbus, altar frieze of, 173–75, 176
drama: as cultural performance, 57; festival context of, 51, 63; as mirror, 57; and naturalism, 53, 57–58; origins of, 47, 115, 188–89; performances of, 51–52; and ritual, 47, 56, 60, 188; and slavery, 53; unreal worlds in, 56–57; venues for, 51–52, 60
Dugan, J., 162, 163n, 164, 194n
Dupont, F., 7, 58n

Edmunds, L., 8–10
elite, Roman: as audience for poetry, 26–27; authority of, 24; competitions among, 39, 122; and *convivia,* 31; cultural mastery of, 117; identity crisis of, 23–24; involvement of in poetry, 50–51, 82, 97, 111–12; memorialization of, 88, 90, 95, 171; and "others," 46, 116; and professional writers, 166; as readers, 162; as rivals of poets, 64, 112,114–15, 125; self-fashioning by, 143–44. *See also* ancestors; *gentes; nobiles*
embodiment: in Cato, 146; of experience, 203; of practices, 134, 136; of schemes, 33–35, 81, 134, 149, 156–57; of texts, 162. *See also* body
Ennius, Quintus, 5, 11, 30, 33–34, 37, 77, 82, 87–99, 110, 116, 178; *Annales,* 88; *carmina* avoided by, 102, 105; Cato's sponsorship of, 34, 138; Cato's invocation of, 190; contrasted with Naevius, 93, 95, 101; and Fulvius Nobilior, 96; and Horace, 16n; as Homer reincarnated, 90, 97; as immigrant, 3, 90; as praise poet, 193–94; self-

presentation by, 90, 95; social position of, 7; strategies of substitution by, 97–98; subjectivity of, 3; as translator, 6, 72
epic: and *carmina,* 125; and *convivia,* 100, 104; Greek, 34, 89; Horace's rejection of, 106; as masculine, 107; performance of, 34; and privilege, 77; translation of, 106
ethnicity, stereotyping concerning, 76–77
Etruscans: as performers, 44–45; Roman attitudes toward, 104–5
evaluation: and *auctoritas,* 199; by audiences, 141; Cato on, 144; in *convivia,* 104; contrasted with praise, 192–93, 196; by communities, 122–24; reciprocal, 105. See also *existimare; praise*
existimare, definition and use of, 27, 35–36, 144, 170, 192. *See also* evaluation; praise
expenditure: regulation of, 102–3; as source of prestige, 52, 117
expropriation, cultural, 45–46. *See also* culture

fabulae: palliatae, 53; *praetextae,* 84
farce, in Plautine drama, 53
Farrell, J., 12n
fasces, as symbolic, 128–29
Feeney, D., 24–26, 28, 29n, 39
Fenestella, 112–13
festivals, drama's role in, 23, 42, 51, 60, 63. *See also* rituals
Festus, 48–49, 51
Fitzgerald, W., 65–66
Flores, E., 91n
Flower, H. I., 84n, 120n
formalism, in criticism, 10, 26
formalization: Cato's strategies of, 130, 149, 154–55; in oratory, 130, 134
Fowler, D., 8n, 16n
Fraenkel, E., 63
Frier, B. W., 178n
Fulvius Nobilior, M., 87–89, 178, 193–94; Cato on, 99–100; and Ennius, 90, 96
funerals: as embodiment of ancestral values, 119–22

Galba, Servius Sulpicius, 163, 164–65, 167
Galinsky, K., 15n
Gamel, M.-K., 14

Gargola, D. J., 154n
gentes, importance of, 23, 30–31, 121. *See also* ancestors; elite; *nobiles*
Gentili, B., 64n
Gildenhard, I., 88n, 89n, 94–95, 187n
Goldberg, S., 26–27, 29–30, 34, 76, 89n, 100n, 102n, 110, 171n, 199
Gotter, U., 178n
Gowers, E., 3n
Greece: Cato's attitude toward, 4–5, 6–7, 14–15, 27, 34, 206; cultural influence of, 24–29, 38–40, 74–75, 83, 88, 92–93, 103, 115; Ennius' relation to, 6–7; otherness of, 62; Plautus' attitude toward, 62; as source of plunder and prestige, 39, 112, 114
Greek: Cato's use of, 139–40; 'original' texts translated from, 25, 43, 52–54, 56, 63, 68, 70–71, 76, 86, 106, 110–11; Roman competence in, 141
Grilli, A., 92
Gruen, E., 26–27, 51, 52n, 88n, 103n
guilds. See *collegia*
Gumbrecht, H. U., 204n
Gutzwiller, K., 58n

Habinek, T., 10–13, 17, 18–19, 23–24, 27–28, 30n, 35, 41, 46, 55n, 56, 79n, 92, 101, 132n, 143, 157n, 170, 172n
Hall, D. E., 2n
Halporn, J., 63
Hardie, P., 16n, 97n
Hellenism. *See* Greece
Helms, M. W., 86n, 118
Henrichs, A., 103n
Herb, G. H., 3n
heroism, comic, 58, 64n
hexameter: Ennius' use of, 77, 88–90; Horace's use of, 13, 74; Livius' avoidance of, 82
hierarchies: and *carmina,* 101; and cultural practices, 14, 41; in the Roman elite, 20, 33; sociocultural, 28; in translation, 8; and writing, 164
Hinds, S., 8–9, 71, 73, 89n
historicism, and formalism, 9–10, 26
Hobsbawm, E., 134
Hölkeskamp, K.-J., 22n
Homer: reincarnated as Ennius, 90, 97; translations of, 41
homines novi: ambitions of, 121; Cato as, 34–35, 123–24, 165, 197, 199, 200–201, 206; Cicero as, 164, 187

Horace: didactic poetry of, 73–74; and Ennius, 16n; on epic, 73, 77, 94, 106; on Greek culture, 74; hexameter used by, 13, 74; on monuments, 16–17; on play, 12; on poetry, 14, 106; as translator, 74
Horsfall, N., 24
Hose, M., 43n
Humbert, M., 163n, 200n
Humm, M., 199n

iambic senarii, Naevius' use of, 85
identity: nested, 3; Roman national, 139–41, 194; social construction of, 12–13
illocutionary effect, of language, 189–90
imitation, 20, 135–60; and authority, 34; and cultural expropriation, 45–46; in drama, 56; of foreign performers, 45, 49
immigration, and identity: 41, 205–6; as influence on Roman literature, 1. *See also* migration; subjectivity, migratory
intertextuality, 8, 15, 203
introjection: and the clever slave, 68–69; in Livius Andronicus, 72
invocations, 93–94
Italy, as influence on Rome, 25–26, 38, 147

Jaeger, M., 180
Jocelyn, H. D., 57n
judgment. *See* evaluation; *existimare*

Kaimio, J., 62n
Kaplan, D. H., 3n
Katz, J. T., 29n
Keith, A., 89n
knowledge: embodied, 98–99; transfer of, 113
Konstan, D., 112
Krostenko, B., 199n
Kuttner, A., 174, 175–76
Kytzler, B., 71n

Laelius, Gaius, as patron of Terence, 109, 112–13, 115–16
language: and national identity, 26–27; of Plautine characters, 54–55; ritual, 11–12; and text, 11. *See also* Greek; translation
Lanuvinus, Luscius, 110

laudare: definition of, 27, 194–96; distinguished from *existimare*, 35–36, 193; as performative, 195–96. See also *existimare;* praise
Lebek, W. D., 56n
Letta, C., 183n
Lianeri, A., 206n
literature: and acculturation, 27; definition of, 17, 29–30, 207; origins of in Rome, 25, 29–30, 38; poetry as, 29; and reading, 34; and song, 11; as strategy, 35. See also *carmina;* drama; epic; oratory; poetry; prose
litterae: Cato on, 34; definition of, 29
Livius Andronicus, 30, 33, 41, 47–49, 51, 70–71, 82, 83, 93–94, 97, 125; and the Camenae, 75–76; and performance, 72–73, 76; as translator, 70–72, 74
Livy, 44, 45, 49; on Scipio Africanus, 180, 191
Lowrie, M., 13, 15, 20
ludiones, 44
Ludi Romani, 23, 47
Ludi scaenici, 23
Luiselli, B., 19
lustratio, 151–54, 157, 174–75; and the census, 175

Malherbe, M., 177n
Manilius, Marcus, 18–19; on song, 18
Mannur, A., 42n
Markus, D. D., 106n
Marshall, C. W., 29n, 60
Martindale, C., 205n
masks, ancestral, 120
Massaro, M., 138n
masters. *See domini*
maxims. *See sententiae*
Mazzarino, A., 148, 149, 156n, 159
McCarthy, K., 33n, 53–54
McElduff, S., 140n, 206n
medicine, Cato on, 4–5, 159
memorialization, of elite deeds, 36, 185–86. See also *monumenta*
Menander, 110
Mercado, A. O., 75n
metatheater, 33, 57–63; in Plautus, 65–68
Metelli, Naevius' conflict with, 83–84, 85
meter, quantitative, 54–55. *See also* hexameters; iambic senarii; rhythm; Saturnians
Meyer, E. A., 20, 75n, 168–69
Middleton, R., 55

migration: of Cato, 3–4; of Ennius, 93; forced, 47–48; of poets, 2, 47–48, 51, 99, 114–15, 205; and subjectivity, 33, 40, 42, 93, 114–15. *See also* immigration
Miller, P. A., 12, 188n
mimesis. *See* imitation
Minucius Thermus, Q., 127–30
mirroring, poetic, 62
Moatti, C., 184, 197
monumenta: of Augustus, 15–17; of famous men, 123, 185, 191; Horace on, 16–17; praise as, 198; of Scipio Africanus, 166; transcriptions as, 191–92. *See also* memorialization
Moore, T. J., 62n
Most, G. W., 41
Muses: and Camenae, 75–76, 94; Ennius' invocation of, 90. *See also* Camenae
music, Cicero on, 171n. *See also* meter; rhythm; song
mythology, Romans' adaption of Greek, 83

Naevius, 30, 33–34, 48, 67, 77, 82, 83–87, 91, 110, 125; *Bellum Poenicum,* 83–87; contrasted with Ennius, 90–92, 93, 95, 101; and the Metelli, 83–84, 85
Narducci, E., 162, 164n
naturalism, in drama, 53, 57–58
Nepos, Cornelius, 169
Niebuhr, B. G., 22, 27
nobiles, influence of, 4, 22, 121. *See also* ancestors; elites; *gentes*
Noy, D., 62n

O'Sullivan, P., 93n
Oakley, S. P., 44n
Odysseus, as translated hero, 72
orality, and literature, 24, 28, 31. *See also* oratory; performance
oratory, 124–35; as elite performance, 134; as embodied practice, 134; judicial, 163–64; origins of, 134, 161, 165, 168; Roman contrasted with Greek, 164; as song, 134; as written practice, 91, 161–63. *See also* orality; performance
others: Greeks as, 62; Roman elites' relation to, 46, 80, 116
otium: Cato on, 173, 177, 186–87, 190; of Cicero, 185; of Scipio Africanus, 185
ownership, cultural, 5, 80, 111–12. *See also* commodities

Page, D. L., 97n
Parker, H. N., 6n, 15n
Parsons, J., 85n
Pasquali, G., 55
pater familias: in *De Agricultura,* 144–46; as keeper of accounts, 183. See also *domini*
patronage, 113, 115; eroticization of, 112–13. *See also* elite; poets
Paullus, L. Aemilius, 78
performance, 14–15, 29; in the *Ad Filium* of Cato, 160; and Cato, 21; of drama, 72; of epic, 72; by foreigners, 45, 49; by Livius Andronicus, 76; oratorical, 131, 168; origins of, 44–45; and poetry, 6, 34, 50–51; professionalization of, 24; and prose, 17; of scripts, 34; and song, 13; and texts, 12, 188; and writing, 188–89. *See also* drama; orality; orations; performativity
performativity: of *auctoritas,* 15; of *carmina,* 20; definitions of, 189–90; of Saturnians, 76; of translations, 42; of the word *laudare,* 195–96. *See also* performance
perlocutionary effect, of language, 189–90
philosophy, Greek, 92–93
Pierre, M., 7n, 20n, 74
Plautus (T. Maccius Plautus), 33, 48, 53, 97, 110; aesthetics of, 70; on the census, 177; *Curculio,* 58–62; language of, 54; metatheater in, 57–63, 65–68; *Miles Gloriosus,* 66–67; prologues of, 64; *Pseudolus,* 64–66, 72; sound patterns in, 55; translation by, 63–70
play: among elites, 113; poetic, 12. *See also convivia*
Pliny the Elder, 159
Plutarch, 139–40
poetry: Augustan, 8–9; Cato on, 112, 206, 208; contrasted with *carmina,* 102; contrasted with prose, 1–2, 6–8, 17–18, 21; contrasted with song, 18, 89, 91, 94; and *convivia,* 108; elites' interest in, 82, 101, 112; and literature, 29; as non-elite practice, 101; origins of, 12–13, 47, 204; and performance, 6, 34, 50–51; and persona, 9; and ritual, 53; and slavery, 14; as translation, 63; valorization of, 13–14. *See also* drama; epic; literature; prose
poets: Cato on, 21; as citizens, 51; as cultural mediators, 40; elites' relation to, 50–51, 97, 114–15; identified with clever slaves, 68, 69–70, 76; migration of,

47–48, 51, 117, 205; as non-elite, 12, 42; as performers, 50–51; and scribes, 48–49; social agency of, 32; social integration of, 49; as translators, 51
Polybius, 78–79, 116, 119–20, 140–41; on extravagance, 30; friendship with Scipio Aemilianus, 80–81, 98, 103; as immigrant, 79; on the Roman funeral, 121; on Scipio Africanus, 180–81
pontifices, 178–79
Porcius Licinius, 112–13, 114, 116
Possanza, D. M., 76n
postcolonialism, 42, 43n
praise, 36, 192–99; of ancestors, 119–22; and *auctoritas,* 196, 198–99; by Cato, 197–98; and *convivia,* 36, 100–101, 105; by Ennius, 193–94; of famous men, 100, 172; at funerals, 119–22; *monumenta* as, 198; by Polybius, 103. See also evaluation; *existimare; laudare*
Pratt, M. L., 25, 39–40
Priscianus, 194
professionalization: and literature, 27; of performance, 24
projection, psychological, 69–70; and the clever slave, 68–69; by Ennius, 97; by Livius Andronicus, 72
prologues: of Plautus, 64; of Terence, 110–11
prose: and *auctoritas,* 17; contrasted with poetry, 1–2, 6–8, 17–18, 21; and daily speech, 20–21; emergence of, 28; formal features of, 17; and song, 12, 149; as *verba soluta,* 18, 149. See also oratory; poetry; writing
psychoanalysis, 68–69
Pythagoreans, 92–93

Quintilian, 106–7; on comedy, 63

Radice, B., 115
rationes: as accounting, 176; and *auctoritas,* 184; Cato's use of, 177, 183–84, 186–87, 190; and the census, 173, 184; as declarations, 184; definitions of, 36, 176–77; and magistrates, 184; and the *pater familias,* 183; and praise, 177–78; of Scipio Africanus, 179–81
readers: appropriations of texts by, 15, 17, 191; construction of meaning by, 15
reading: and aesthetics, 9; and literature, 34; subjectivity structured by, 10

Reay, B. 143, 144–45
responsa, juridical, 157–58
rhetoric, Greek, 127, 132
rhythm: Cato's use of, 124, 127, 130–33, 135, 149, 171; comic, 131
Richlin, A., 62n
Ricoeur, P., 187–88
ritualization: and song 12, 19; process of, 149–50
rituals: agricultural, 150–54; and *carmina,* 3, 19, 149–50; and contracts, 155–56; and drama, 56, 60, 188; mastery of, 150; and poetry, 53; and privileging, 150; and prose, 18; and song, 18–19; of speech and practice, 11, 20; and speech acts, 191; and *tabulae,* 169. See also festivals
Robinson, D., 42
rusticity, of Rome, 74–75, 88–89, 90–91
Rüpke, J., 30, 178n

sapientia, 22–23; definition of, 92
Sassen, S., 41
Saturnians: as authoritative, 75, 82, 85–86, 95; cultural prestige of, 77; Ennius' avoidance of, 88, 90–92, 95; Naevius' failure at, 85; as performative, 76
Sblendorio Cugusi, M. T., 99n, 139n, 133n, 135n, 136n, 171n, 179n
scenarios: of agriculture and politics, 146; and the body, 81; censorial, 175, 192; convivial, 103–4, 105, 108, 172, 178–79, 192–93; defined, 31–32, 81; and embodiment, 84; epic, 89; as formulaic, 32; and historical reality, 104; of the intellectual circle, 115–16; transmission of, 82; use of, 86
Schechner, R., 191
Schiavone, A., 157, 165n, 200
Scipio Aemilianus, P. Cornelius: as friend of Polybius, 78–81, 98, 103; as patron of Terence, 109, 112–13, 115–16
Scipio Africanus, P. Cornelius, 36, 166; Cato on, 184–86; *otium* of, 184–86; and performative language, 190; "trial" of, 179–87
Scipionic circle, 115–16
scribere, contrasted with *dicere,* 163. See also writing
scribes: and oratory, 163; and poets, 48–49
scripts: dramatic, 51; and oratory, 163–64; performance of, 34; production of, 51; writing of, 165, 167–68

self-presentation: by Cato, 35, 135, 143–44, 166, 168, 194, 197; by Cicero, 162, 164; by elites, 34, 197; by Ennius, 90, 93, 95, 98; by poets, 50, 86
self-sufficiency: Cato on, 53, 103, 146; of the Roman elite, 53
sententiae: Cato's use of, 125–26, 133, 157–59; and the *vates,* 22
Skutsch, O., 88, 93, 97n
Slater, N., 58, 70
slaves: in drama, 53, 58, 62n, 64–68; as objects, 69; and poetry, 12, 14; Roman attitudes toward, 69; as scribes, 168; subjectivity of, 69; as tools, 145
Smith, C. J., 31n
sodalitates, 22, 23, 105–6
song: and authority, 11–12, 137; and *convivia,* 170; as independent, 140; and literature, 11; limits of, 14; Manilius on, 18; non-poetic, 94; oratory as, 134; and performance, 13; and poetry, 18; pre-poetic, 89, 91, 93, 102; prose as, 17–18; in Quintilian, 107–8; and ritual, 18–19; and writing, 36. See also *carmina;* poetry; prose; speech
speech: formalized, 127; and ritual, 11; and song, 17. See also *carmina;* oratory; poetry; prose; song
speech acts: *carmina* as, 19, 102, 124, 130; in Cato, 7; de-contextualization of, 20; *dicta* as, 85; effects of, 191; and ritual, 191. See also performance; performativity; ritual
speeches. See oratory
Spivak, G., 204
Steel, C., 163–64
subjectivity: of authors, 3, 76; of Cato, 18; competing types of, 35; construction of, 98–99; definitions of, 2, 203–4; of Ennius, 3, 90, 98; as mediated, 2; migratory, 33, 40, 42, 93, 114–15; and slavery, 69; as structured by reading, 10; writing as expression of, 6
Suetonius, 72–73
Suolahti, J., 174n
sympotic culture, 29. See also *convivia*

tabulae: and authority, 169; and *carmina,* 20, 169; pontifical, 178–79; production of, 20; and ritual, 169; uses of, 36, 168–69, 173–75, 176, 177–78. See also writing
Taussig, M., 25

Taylor, D., 31–32, 81, 104n
Terence (P. Terentius Afer): contested authorship of, 71–72, 111–12, 114–15; elite connections of, 109–10; life of, 109, 114–16; prologues of, 110–11; and the Scipionic circle, 115–16; translation by, 110–11
Terrenato, N., 31n, 145
texts: alienation of, 14–15; and the body, 118, 162; Cato's revision of, 166–68; circulation of, 24; and cultural mastery, 118; definitions of, 187–88; and language, 11; as monumental, 16–17; and performance, 12, 188; and practices, 81; unity of, 8
Thomas, R. F., 205n
Tiro, 132–33
Tomasco, D., 93n
Torelli, M., 173
Traglia, A., 127
Traina, A., 54, 55, 131n
transcription: and appropriation, 191; and *auctoritas,* 170; by Cato, 7, 36, 179, 184–85, 191, 197; definition of, 7; effects of, 189; as *monumentum,* 191–92; of speeches, 164–65, 168, 170. See also scripts; writing
translation: and authority, 140; and colonialism, 43; and cultural mastery, 140–41; demarginalization of, 42–43; as empowering, 42; by Ennius, 6; of epic, 70–77, 106; from Greek 'originals,' 2, 43, 52–54, 56, 63, 68, 70–71, 76, 86, 106, 110–11; by Livius Andronicus, 83; as performative, 42; by Plautus, 63–70; poetry as, 63; and poets' social position, 51; practices of, 206; social context of, 39, 204; of speeches, 140; by Terence, 110–11, 115; terminology of, 71
Turner, V., 57

Vairel-Carron, H., 153n
Valerius Maximus, 114; on Scipio Africanus, 181–82
value: ambiguities of, 27; concerns about, 35–36. See also commodities
Van Sickle, J., 75n
Varro, M. Terentius, 29, 177
vates, 5, 90–91, 95, 106; Cato as, 159; definition of, 91n; and *sententiae,* 22
verba soluta, prose as, 18, 149–50
vilici, 145, 147–49; speech of, 154–55, 147–49; role of, 183. See also *domini*

Wiles, D., 62n
Wise, J., 188–89
Wiseman, T. P., 84n
Woolf, G., 16
writing: and accounting, 176–77; and *auctoritas,* 166, 171–72; Cato on, 165, 171–72; and the census, 176; Cicero's use of, 162; and commodification, 116; dependence on, 24; and hierarchies, 164; and *ingenium,* 163; as medium for scenarios, 82; of oratory, 91, 161–63, 169–70; and performance, 188–89; and prose, 6, 17–18; and Scipio Africanus, 183, 185; and song, 36; and *tabulae,* 169; as text, 188. *See also* scripts; *tabulae;* transcription

Xenophon, invoked by Cato, 173

Zaccaria Ruggiu, A., 30n, 104
Zajko, V., 206n
Zetzel, J. E. G., 194n
Zorzetti, N., 21–23, 84n